Praise for *The Elem*

"[An] inspiring, well-researched, interesting, and deeply personal book...It masterfully weaves together the history of the human-horse relationship, the mystical influence of horse energy, our physical connection with horses, and the relational benefits and healing qualities of being with our equine friends...[this book] is a multi-dimensional manual for personal growth, interpersonal relationships, and healing on all levels."

—Lokita Carter, cofounder of the Ecstatic Living Institute

"The gift of self-realization and the higher octave of life lies within the essence of the horse—sacred, powerful, beautiful, wild, joyful, intelligent, and adventurous...Informative and delightful, a tale of one woman's incredible journey into healing. A true shamanic inspiration. The prose glitters. An excellent story of 'Yes, you can!'"

—Silver RavenWolf, author of *Poppet Magick*

"An epic, yet intensely personal and practical book...Debra's perspective on the role of horses in our lives is deeply meaningful and incredibly thorough."

—Sunny Schlenger, author of *Organizing for the Spirit*

The ELEMENTS *of* HORSE SPIRIT

About the Author

Debra DeAngelo is a garden-variety Pagan with many eclectic spiritual interests and pursuits, in particular, endlessly studying tarot and facilitating small tarot workshops. After twenty-six years as a managing editor in the field of print journalism, she decided to forge out onto a new path, turning her focus to books and freelance writing. An award-winning formerly syndicated columnist, she now writes feature stories and book reviews for *SageWoman* and *Witches & Pagans* magazines. She is additionally a lifelong horse lover, mama to a spectacular old Hanoverian gelding, and one hell of a massage therapist. She lives in Northern California with The Cutest Man In The World, where they parent two neurotic cats. Find her at www.debradeangelo.com, Facebook, Instagram, and Twitter.

The ELEMENTS *of* HORSE SPIRIT

The Magical Bond Between Humans *and* Horses

Debra DeAngelo

Llewellyn Publications
Woodbury, Minnesota

FIRST EDITION
First Printing, 2020

Cover design by Shira Atakpu
Editing by Marjorie Otto
Interior art by the Llewellyn Art Department
Chakra figure © Mary Ann Zapalac

Llewellyn Publications is a registered trademark of Llewellyn Worldwide Ltd.

Library of Congress Cataloging-in-Publication Data (Pending)
ISBN: 978-0-7387-6380-4

Llewellyn Worldwide Ltd. does not participate in, endorse, or have any authority or responsibility concerning private business transactions between our authors and the public.

All mail addressed to the author is forwarded but the publisher cannot, unless specifically instructed by the author, give out an address or phone number.

Any internet references contained in this work are current at publication time, but the publisher cannot guarantee that a specific location will continue to be maintained. Please refer to the publisher's website for links to authors' websites and other sources.

Llewellyn Publications
A Division of Llewellyn Worldwide Ltd.
2143 Wooddale Drive
Woodbury, MN 55125-2989
www.llewellyn.com

Printed in the United States of America

Forthcoming Books by Debra DeAngelo

Garden-Variety Pagan: The Art of Going Feral

Dedication

This book is dedicated to my four-legged soul mate, Pendragon, who quietly and patiently showed me how to heal and changed the course of my life. You are my clarity, my partner, my friend. You are proof that magic exists.

Contents

Acknowledgments

So many planets had to align for this book to materialize. If just *one* of the following people had not played a part, there would be no book. My sincere thanks to each one:

- To Sarah, who practically dragged me back to the world of horses by the scruff of my neck and brought Penn and me together, and for the hours upon hours of time, insight, and guidance she provided me. She is the best pal a Horsey Girl could ever have. Thank you!

- To Debbie, who loved her horse so much that she selflessly gave him to someone who could take care of him when she no longer could. She saved Penn's life and changed the trajectory of mine. Thank you!

- To Joe, who encouraged me and had my back when I wanted to get a horse. Thank you!

- To Jason, who told me to try again, just one more time. Thank you!

- To Heather, who gave me a chance when I doubted I'd ever get one. Thank you!

I also wish to thank my children—Jimmy, for endless enthusiasm over my new venture in life, and Janine, for believing in me more than I believe in myself. You two are my heart.

FOREWORD
BY SARAH DICKINSON

I never understood all the clichés: "Live in the moment." "Seize the day." "Live your best life." It seemed to me, while rocketing my way through life, that the day was seizing me.

When I returned to horses after college and children, I learned the meaning of those clichés. They became truisms in my life. Spending time with horses and cultivating a life that includes horsemanship gave me a deep understanding of what it means to live your best life.

For me, horsemanship is a passion, not a hobby. It's a never-ending quest for excellence that leaks into the rest of my life. Education, empathy and compassion, inner and outer strength and fitness, letting go of ego, kindness, softness, and deep knowledge of myself comes from my passion for horses.

Being educated, aware, and striving for excellence in every aspect of the horse is true horsemanship, from feet to feed, or biomechanics to proper equitation. If you're intensely interested in every aspect of the horse, you can spend a lifetime in the pursuit of horsemanship excellence.

Letting go of ego is one of the most rewarding aspects not only in my horsemanship journey, but also in my personal and professional life. Letting go of ego means putting the horse's, and others', wellbeing first. As my partner, my horse should enjoy our time together as much as I do.

Learning to accept feedback with regards to my horsemanship is part of my journey. It took me some time to find the value in paying someone to give me feedback about my horsemanship. My ego had to take a step down and be willing to accept the feedback. One of the best life lessons is learning to accept feedback—any feedback, good or bad—especially if you're paying for it.

Horses bring abundant compassion and empathy into my life. Seeing the horse as a living, breathing, feeling creature with a heartbeat, desires, and emotions inspires a level of empathy and compassion in my soul that no other being has been able to awaken. Looking into a horse's soft eyes and seeing a soul so deep and pure, a healer, a friend, a partner, gives me compassion not only for horses, but for all animals and people.

Spending time with horses shows me what it really means to be a partner and communicate with an animal. We've all seen dude ranches where people ride single file on a horse trained to dully follow the horse in front of it, nose to tail. The folks enjoying this ride are passengers. However, riding a horse requires full participation and communication between both parties.

Harmonious riding is a conversation between the horse and rider. The rider uses their entire body to communicate to the horse, and the horse is listening and returning the communication. The hours I spent learning to speak the language of riding became a beautiful conversation, a dance, barely perceivable to the observer. Harmony between horse and rider is difficult to describe, but you know it when you see it.

A large part of horsemanship is "feel," meaning the ability to feel the horse's movement and intention, and being able to react immediately. When a horse and rider move together with imperceptible cues, the rider is "feeling" where the horse will go, what the horse is communicating back, and adjusting. "Feel" is a cultivated skill, Some people are better at it than others, but everyone can have "feel," not just for horses, but for everything in their life.

Horses are a driving factor in my life. I'm driven to excel in my career so I can continue to provide for my horses and to be independent so nobody can take my horses away. Horses also drive me to be healthy and fit so I can enjoy what I love to do.

Because I strive to be a partner with my horse, I work hard at fitness for both of us. Just like any high-performing athlete, his needs—like nutrition, bodywork, foot care, vitamins, and dietary supplements—must be met. Horsemanship is physically demanding work, and for my own safety, and the benefit of my horse, I make sure that I'm fit enough to ride and work around my horse to keep us both safe.

For much of my life, a passion for horses was considered "girlish"— something to be abandoned for womanly pursuits. Although I followed the expected path of college, marriage, and children, the love and longing for horses never left me. When I returned to horses later in life and fell in love with a horse again, I felt like a part of me was awakened.

Lesson learned: Know yourself, forge your own path, and be brave enough to follow that path no matter what others say. With a grand passion, something so encompassing and beautiful, there is really nothing that can stop you.

Ultimately, what do horses mean to me? Happiness, partnership, beauty, passion, friendship, love, learning, adventure, curiosity, personal excellence, grounding, challenge … I could go on and on. For me, life without horses would be shallow and empty. I wouldn't have my deep meaningful friendships, empathy, calmness, or softness. I have inner and outer strength as a result of hours spent outdoors with my horses, doing what I love. Some of my best days are horse days, filled with sun and dirt, horse smells, wide-open spaces, and adventure.

This book takes horsemanship into the spiritual realm of horse-related energy and insight. It gives both horse lovers and horse owners a glimpse into the colorful, symbolic, and spiritual realm of horses. You'll never look at horses the same way again!

About Sarah

Sarah Dickinson is a lifelong horse lover and equestrian, and enjoys going out on adventures with her horse. Softness, kindness, keeping harmony, and partnership are the driving principles of her horsemanship journey. She is an information systems manager working remotely from her home in California.

PROLOGUE

I don't know what I'm doing with a horse. This is absolutely nuts."

That's what I told my darling, effervescent, fluffy-haired friend Lyndsay over chicken salad one afternoon at a local diner.

"I'm fifty-eight years old, I haven't ridden a horse in thirty-five years, the meniscus on my right knee is shredded, I'll be in this leg brace for at least two months, I need to lose fifty pounds, *and* I'm a newspaper editor with crap wages. I can't afford a horse!"

Well, that wasn't timely or useful insight, given that as of the week prior, that horse was already mine. There's that old cliché about closing the barn door after the horses have escaped. Well, the door was closed, all right, but the horse was still inside, snug as a bug, and his boarding fee would soon be due.

"This is insanity! Why do I have a horse!?"

Lyndsay purposefully set down her fork, set her dancing blue eyes right on mine, and replied intently, "Because you were meant to write a book!"

I laughed out loud, and quickly apologized, lest she perceive my cynicism as ridicule.

"Oh, Lyndsay, I'm sorry! I didn't mean to piss on your suggestion. It's just that every horse book imaginable has already been written, ten times over. There's just nothing else to say about horses. It's all been done already."

She cocked one skeptical eyebrow, skewered some lettuce, and tipped her loaded fork at me for emphasis.

"No, I'm certain of it. You were meant to write a book about horses. It's perfectly clear to me."

Oh my! Write a horse book! How precious is that!

That lunch date was three years ago. Now, here I am, with a prologue to my horse book.

You were right, Lyndsay! Thanks for planting that seed. It wouldn't have occurred to me on my own over the weeks, months, and years that followed. I'd have been so preoccupied with the joy of having a horse again, I'd never have connected those dots. I'd never have shared my experience with anyone—just kept it all to my newly joyful, blissful self.

Thanks, babe! Next time, lunch is on me!

Goodbye to Horses

At the other end of my colorful spectrum of friends is my rock-solid buddy Sarah, an expert horsewoman. Different as night and day, and yet, just like Lyndsay, Sarah's blue eyes are also ever-dancing, and squint up into happy little sunrises, as if she knows the punch line to the joke and you don't.

Just like me, Sarah was a born "Horsey Girl." It's in our DNA. As kids, we preferred Breyer horse models to Barbie dolls. We read every Marguerite Henry or Walter Farley book ever written, drew horses, dreamed about horses, and talked about horses until everybody told us to shut up about horses.

The difference between Sarah and me was that she'd kept horses in her life, whereas I'd shut them out. I'd concluded years prior that I couldn't have them anymore, and I'd just rather not think about them. That chapter of my life was over. Why dig in that wound?

Sarah would tell me about her horsey adventures, and I'd respond that that's just wonderful, but inside, I was quietly and sourly jealous. How can she still be riding? Aren't we too old for this? If I fell off now, I won't bounce the way I used to. I'll just break. Besides, I used to do show jumping, and doing that again was clearly insanity. If I couldn't jump anymore, what was the point in riding? If I wasn't going to ride anymore, what was the point of having a horse? There was also the time and expense, adding to my familiar safety blanket of excuses.

Why did I abandon horses? First off, I was in a marriage where I was alone in my love of horses, and second, children. The ongoing marital friction about the expense and bother of having horses was emotionally draining. The tipping point was my first baby. There just wasn't the time, energy, money, or emotional bandwidth to do it all, and so, I surrendered. No more horses.

Given those challenges, I gave my sweet old Thoroughbred mare, Rosie, to someone who promised to give her a comfortable retirement, and her yearling colt was purchased by someone who planned to turn him into a show horse. I didn't cry when I said goodbye, because my new baby son had become the center of my world, and it didn't seem so bad to let the horses go. I got rid of all my tack and equipment, but stalled over selling my beautiful tooled Western saddle, for which I'd scrimped and saved. When someone bought it and carried it away, the tears finally fell. It was symbolic, like the end of the final chapter: Horses were out of my life forever.

Oooh, That Smell

The years peeled away, another baby arrived, and my life became a whirl of Little League games, teacher conferences, and proms. There was a divorce and a remarriage in there too. I was working full-time as a local newspaper editor and doing massage in my home office in the evenings. There wasn't any time to think about horses.

During that span of time, I'd become great friends with Sarah. We met while we were both in a community play, which had a skit about singing vegetables. I was the tomato and she was the asparagus. We've been pals ever since. We'd often talk about horses, until it pinched too much and I'd divert the topic to something else, but Sarah sensed my longing. She'd invite me to come see her horses, but I always declined because the thought of being around horses seemed like torture. However, Sarah didn't give up so easily.

One innocent night, we were going get some dinner. When she picked me up, she said, "I need to swing by the barn first and feed my horse. Do you mind?"

"Sure, no problem."

We drove a couple miles through the lush green hills just outside of town, and pulled onto a nearby horse ranch, hopped out of the car, and strolled into a big, wooden barn.

And then it hit me.

A wonderful, familiar but long-forgotten scent. I inhaled deeply like someone sucking in oxygen after being underwater a moment too long. It was like emerging from a cloud of amnesia and suddenly remembering who I was.

It was the smell of Farnam fly spray that we used to keep all the nasty biting beasties off our horses back in the day. That scent got right in under my defenses and grabbed me. *Oh, that smell … I remember … horses … oh my God, I love horses so much … where have they been … where have I been … what happened …*

Standing there in the barn, huffing the air with my eyes closed in delight, I said to Sarah, "Oh my God … the smell of fly spray … it's heaven!"

She chuckled and said it wasn't the first time she'd heard someone squee over fly spray. That scent is to Horsey Girls what Grandma's cookies baking are to everyone else.

High on fly spray, I followed Sarah to her horse's stall and held my hand out to her handsome palomino gelding. Chills tickled up my arm when his whiskers grazed my palm, and my heart ached.

"Horses used to be my world," I sighed. "But, that's all over now. I'll never have horses again. It's impossible."

"Uh-huh," Sarah replied thoughtfully. She wasn't brushing me off; she just didn't believe me.

Just Come Look

As a couple more years passed, Sarah invited me to the barn over and over—*come out and ride, or just visit with my horses*—but I always had an excuse. Why torture yourself by going to a smorgasbord when your jaws are permanently wired shut? Literally, just don't *go* there. Stay far, far away. One day, however, Sarah was entirely more insistent than usual.

"There's this horse up at the barn that you need to see."

Before I could start reciting my familiar list of protests and excuses, she cut me off.

"Just come see him. You don't have to do anything or make any commitments. Just come see him."

"Ooookaaaaaaay, fine. But I don't see the point."

We rumbled up to the barn in her old white Suburban, strewn with hay, horse tack, and lots and lots of dust. Sarah led me over to one of the paddocks where a big, dirty, unkempt old chestnut horse hung his head listlessly in the far corner as if he'd just mentally checked out from life. The fly mask covering his face was so filthy, it was nearly opaque.

"Hey, Penn," she called to him.

One weary ear tipped in our direction at the sound of his name, and very slowly, as if mere existence was too burdensome, he plodded toward us, stopped, and reached out his nose, hoping these visitors might have a treat. Sarah pulled a horse cookie from her pocket and held it out to him, and he gobbled it up. Under all that dirt, he had a bright copper colored coat. But what a mess. His hooves were overgrown and ragged as broken potato chips, his mane and tail hung in tangles, and most concerning of all, the tendon on his left front leg was quite visibly bowed (a potentially handicapping injury for a horse). On his fetlock was a weird, bony growth the size of a large walnut. His leg looked kind of Z-shaped.

I pointed out his weird leg to Sarah, and she agreed that it was ugly, but said he was functionally sound because his owner, Debbie, used to ride him all the time. Sarah told me he was a purebred Hanoverian, an extremely well-trained former show jumper and dressage horse. At nineteen years old with a funky front leg, his useful days as a show horse were over. Debbie saw him at a show stable, fell in love with him, and bought him as a pleasure horse. Had she not, he'd have ended up where all unwanted horses go: "to auction" (read: slaughterhouse).

Although Debbie was crazy about Penn and had taken great care of him, her husband had become very ill, potentially terminally so, and required twenty-four-hour care. Debbie could scarcely leave his side and was forced to pick between her horse and her husband. That left Penn just standing there in his dusty paddock waiting for the stable hand to throw him hay, and that had become his whole life.

"He just stands there in the corner, day after day, with his head hanging," Sarah said, suggesting that since Debbie couldn't spend time with him, maybe she'd let me take care of him and get my horsey fix while she paid the board.

"Well, okay. Maybe," I said. "Let's have a look at him."

Sarah pulled the fly mask off, and I gasped. The heavens split open and the sighs of angels beamed down in showers of sparkling golden light all over that face—the color of a bright copper penny, with a big white star on his forehead between huge, curious brown eyes. He looked at me, and I looked at him, and all those angels had a collective heavenly orgasm. I was completely, instantly smitten.

Sarah buckled his halter on, led him around a bit, and then handed me the lead rope. My shimmering excitement gave way to apprehension. I hadn't handled a horse in over thirty years, but I took the rope anyway. Penn walked quietly alongside me, a little bored, a little disengaged, just going along with it for lack of anything better to do. He'd been passed along like a tool in the horse show world, his current owner had disappeared, and he wasn't investing anything in a new human other than basic cooperation. He'd given up on ever having a human of his own again, just as I'd given up on ever having a horse again. What irony.

As we walked, I slowly leaned into his neck and inhaled. There it was, Horsey Girl opium: the scent of a horse. Some people like misters that spritz lavender or vanilla into the air. The scent of a horse is all the aromatherapy Horsey Girls need—for us, a rose by any other name would smell as sweet, but not as sweet as a horse.

That moment sealed it.

"How do we make this happen?"

Sarah said she'd contact Debbie and see if she was okay with me taking care of Penn. Not to ride, just to hang out with him, lead him around, brush him. I was four years old again, wishing and wishing and wishing that this Christmas, I might get a pony. *This* pony. I was lovestruck.

But that name. What was up with that?

"Penn is sort of a strange name," I commented, because there are way sexier actors to name a horse after … Clooney, for example. Now, that would be a kickass sexy movie star name.

"Penn's his nickname. His name is Pendragon," Sarah replied.

I gasped so hard I nearly choked on myself.

"Pendragon? As in Uther Pendragon from *The Mists of Avalon?*"

Sarah shrugged. "I guess so?"

Pendragon! From *The Mists of Avalon*, one of my favorite books of all time! It was a huge, flashing neon sign from the universe! This was meant to be!

The Love Story Begins

Penn's owner was relieved to have someone take care of him, so I immediately started spending all the time with him I could. My life swerved in a completely different direction—straight to the barn. I was there every day, brushing Penn, cleaning his hooves, scratching his neck, sharing my secrets, and gazing at him like a lovesick teenager. He quickly started recognizing my car pulling in and he'd trot to his gate, ears pricked toward me, eyes bright in anticipation. Then came the day when he whinnied at me for the first time as I arrived—a big old rumbly "Hello, Mama!" My heart melted into my boots.

Soon after, I turned Penn out in the arena to let him run. He had a long, luxurious roll in the sand, lurched back to his feet, grunting in satisfaction, shook himself like a wet dog, and then exploded into a rollicking gallop, all around the arena, bucking and snorting. He cavorted around as I stood there just inside the gate, and then he came thundering around the curve and spotted me. He arched his big neck, locked his eyes right on me, and suddenly came barreling straight at me, the ground thundering under his hooves.

Part of me panicked. I was still getting to know this horse. Would he stop or plow right over me? Something inside of me said *just stay,* so I did, completely still, and held my hand out. He was nearly on top of me when he skidded to a stop at the last possible moment, dirt flying, and then reached out his nose to touch my hand. It felt like a velvety kiss. At that moment I knew: This is my horse.

Except he wasn't.

Penn still belonged to someone else. Our time together was borrowed. At any moment, Debbie could say, "Sorry, I changed my mind. I decided to keep him." I kept batting that reality away, and clung to each wonderful moment like a string of miracles.

The following month, I got a terse, unexpected text message from Debbie: "I want to give Penn to you." I nearly burst from joy and disbelief. I immediately shared the news with Sarah, who told me that Debbie had heard how well Penn was doing with all my attention. She saw an opportunity for him to have a life again and the love he deserved, and decided to feel the heartbreak and let go anyway. To love more than to want; that's true love.

Then the other foot fell: What was I thinking? I can't have a horse. My joy deflated like a sad, spent birthday balloon.

"Haha, isn't that nuts, give me a horse," I told my husband later. "Ridiculous! I can't afford it. I'll tell her to forget it."

He reached over, took my hand, looked into my eyes, and replied, "You need to do this. You must do this. If not now, when?"

He added the clincher, "Don't worry about the money. I have your back."

I didn't see that coming. I was still subconsciously harboring a belief from my first marriage: *You can't have a horse. They're too expensive and they're a waste of money.* Nobody was oppressing me anymore but me. I hadn't updated my belief system to Husband 2.0. I assumed he'd veto any mention of getting a horse. This was the first of many self-defeating beliefs and behaviors that unraveled when I reconnected to horses and Horse Spirit, learning to let go of that which no longer served me, but held me back.

Let's Take a Walk

Just after I got Penn, I was leaning over my bed to close the window, as I had done ten thousand times before, and on that particular morning, I felt a pop in my left knee and then what felt like a knife stabbing into the soft spot below the kneecap. Suddenly, I could barely walk. What followed was a trip to the doctor, a MRI scan, and within days, I was sporting a bulky bendable leg brace, extending from mid-thigh to mid-calf. I was told to just deal with it, because I'd shredded my meniscus, and I'd be sporting this bulky contraption for at least eight weeks.

Fabulous.

Just when I got a horse, I was unable to ride him. However, with the brace on, I could at least still walk him. Walk we did, for weeks and weeks, in slow circles around the hay barn and back and forth down between the long row of paddocks, over and over and over.

Tearing my meniscus was the best thing that could have happened. Had I just started riding again, I'd never have discovered that just spending time with a horse was therapy. It was my gateway to groundwork—all the things you can do with a horse besides ride it.

Look, Ma—No Ropes

Time rolled on and one day, Sarah suggested we try some groundwork in the round pen. She wanted to start with longeing, an exercise in which a horse is on a long rope and given commands as it travels in a circle. I told her I already knew how to do that, but she told me we'd be doing it without a rope.

"Whaaaat?" I asked incredulously.

"I'll move him with my energy."

"Uhhh ... Sarah ... what *are* you smoking?"

She stood in the middle of the ring, and leaned toward Penn a little, clucked to him and pointed in the direction she wanted him to go. There was no way this was going to work. Suddenly, Penn started walking around the ring, one ear tipped toward Sarah, apparently unfamiliar with this rope-less thing. He went around a couple times and then she communicated to him with her body language and energy to stop, turn, and go the other way. He did, slowly and hesitantly. After a circle around the other way, the lesson was over. Sarah praised him and offered treats. Penn seemed pleased with himself.

"It's all about energy," she said.

My mouth was actually hanging open. I couldn't believe what I'd just witnessed. Longe without a rope? Communicate with energy? Crazy talk! I grew up learning that you command a horse until it fears you, respects you, and obeys! Too slow? Wear spurs. Acting up? Jerk his head around in the halter, and maybe run a stud chain under his chin, and jerk harder. Won't get in the trailer? Whip him until he's more afraid of you than the trailer. If all else fails, tranquilize him until he's too doped up to resist. But use energy to control a horse? That's just nuts!

I grew up in a world where horses were treated like dirt bikes: take it out, get on, go. You wouldn't worry about the dirt bike's feelings, it was irrelevant. Clearly, in the thirty-five-year gap since I'd left the horse world, horsemanship had undergone a metamorphosis. It wasn't about bullying and brutality anymore. It was all about "natural horsemanship" and communicating with a horse in its own language; being firm, but kind and patient, and treating it like a sentient, intelligent, intuitive creature.

Everything I knew and believed about horses took a tectonic shift watching Sarah that day. I wasn't returning to something—I was starting all over again.

Sarah demonstrated more groundwork lessons over the next few weeks with her own horses, who quickly obeyed her, spinning, backing up, sidling up to the mounting block—whatever she wanted, without a harsh word or smack of a whip, just very subtle movements and cues.

It's like magic, I was thinking one day while watching her—and then it hit me: It *is* magic: Sarah sets an intention, plans an outcome, and then carries out that plan in a particular way to get the desired result, manifesting her intention. I was witnessing a high priestess perform an elegant, effective ritual!

We've Come a Long Way

When I sat down to write this book in 2019, three years had rolled by since horses and Horse Spirit reappeared in my life, seeing me through sadness and loss, death and destruction. But, I had my four-legged therapist to lean on and remind me that even bad days can have beautiful moments. I had plenty of physical challenges too. Just healing my leg was a challenge, and even after the brace came off, it was weeks before it felt stable and strong, and even longer before I tried getting in the saddle. Penn is very tall, and even more so wearing a Western saddle and thick pads. I could barely swing my leg over the back of the saddle to get on. Getting off was almost as difficult. The best I could do was to drag my boot over Penn's rump. He would cock his head a bit and look back at me as if to say, "You're such a dork," but he tolerated my clumsiness. Carrots mitigate everything.

The barn where Penn is boarded was a constant thrum of equestrian activity in the early days of our relationship. We were surrounded by fancy dressage riders, continually working in pursuit of that blue ribbon. If I rode, Penn and I just walked slowly around the arena, maybe trotted a little, and called it a day. Most of our time was spent walking out into the hills, side by side, talking and grazing, in sweet, quiet bliss.

To the other equestrians, I'm that weird old lady who shows up every day, fawns over her old horse, and then just leads him around like a big puppy dog—kind of a joke. Meanwhile, the other riders canter around the arena, jump fences, and obsess with perfecting their skills, even in bitter cold, pouring rain, or scorching, triple-digit heat. They ride the way I used to: get on that dirt bike and *go*. I imagine that they felt quite superior when they saw Penn and me ambling around, but that's okay. I didn't have anything to prove to anyone but myself anymore.

They saw a weird old lady and her has-been old horse. They didn't see a refreshed, revived, rejuvenated woman who, through the magic of horses and Horse Spirit, completely rewired her life. My "riding" happens on a different plane, and there, I'm a champion.

INTRODUCTION

This book isn't just a collection of cool horse information; it's my own personal experience and outlook on life. What horses have done historically for humankind, they can do for individuals as well: change the topography of lives, carry people to where they need to go physically *and* emotionally, and help individuals achieve their goals.

While I've found having a horse is transformative for learning to settle into yourself and decide what you really want from your life, it's not actually necessary. Harnessing the power of Horse Spirit doesn't require owning a horse. It's available for anyone, regardless of age, physical challenges, or financial limitations. If you believe you'll never get what you want from your life, let Horse Spirit take you there and manifest it. You don't think I got this book done all by myself, do you?

The Ground We'll Cover

In addition to exploring horses—both physical and metaphysical—we'll cover basic horsemanship, with a focus on equine companionship. We'll journey through evolution, history, culture, language, mythology, and spirituality, and come to a deeper appreciation of horses and their emotional and spiritual lives. You'll discover that when you look at a horse, you're looking at much more than a large, strong, beautiful animal; you're looking at time and evolution and mystery, all rolled into one amazing, spiritual creature—and it's looking right back at you!

Hopefully, this book will inspire new ways of thinking and perceiving people, situations, and most important of all, yourself. You may be inspired to define new goals, make new choices, and call upon Horse Spirit to assist you.

If you're dealing with an obstacle or challenge, whether psychological, emotional, financial, or physical, or if you just feel lost and drifting through life, hop onto Horse Spirit's back, and let it take you where you need to go.

Getting to Know My Friends

You'll be hearing more about Penn and Sarah as we go along. Penn is my equine soul mate. We are a reflection of each other, in both good and not so good ways. To some, we're both over the hill, but we've redefined the hill: It's not about getting to the top and coasting down to the bottom—it's about the climb. It's about experiencing the steps, not the finish line.

As for Sarah—my pal, mentor, and personal horsemanship guru—her insight has been invaluable to me in returning to horses and starting over from scratch to learn a new approach. There's not quite enough Sarah to go around, so I'll share her tips and insight right here on these pages, so she can be your guru too.

What I Bring to the Table

Besides a lifelong love and obsession with horses, in my younger days I was a pretty respectable English rider and show jumper. I had a wall of colorful ribbons for my efforts and dreamed of one day having an amazing horse farm. My parents were horse racing addicts and brought me along with them to the races whenever possible. I learned to read from a racing program before reading from a kindergarten book. My first job was mucking stalls at the racetrack at 5 o'clock in the morning during the state fair when I was twelve. I reeked of horse manure every day, but it was *heaven*.

Horses, horse showing, horse racing, and horse breeding shaped our family and my own development. Sadly, alcoholism and dysfunction also shaped our family and me—and many of the choices I made for the first forty years of my life. Slowly teasing out the tangled threads of my childhood trauma was a decades-long process. If they offered degrees in "Adult Children of Alcoholics," I'd have a PhD. I read just about every book on codependency there was, attended—and sometimes ran—support groups, meetings, and workshops on family alcoholism, and worshipped at the feet of self-help authors John Bradshaw and Melody Beattie.

My own troubled past initially drew me toward the social services field. I majored in psychology at the University of California at Davis, planning to get a PhD in clinical psychology, but then I got married, and had a baby.

Hard stop.

Hard right turn.

My early employment years were in the social services and counseling field: crisis intervention, working with "at risk" and pregnant teens, and later on, working for the county social services department, specializing in employment and training, helping people assess their needs, temperaments, strengths, and weaknesses to create an achievable and fulfilling career path. That was the job where I discovered temperament assessments and how they could be used as a structure for understanding and interacting with people, which I continued to use long after I left the social services field for journalism. I spent twenty-six years as a community newspaper editor and columnist, during which time I also became a massage therapist to supplement my income after my divorce. Massage therapy expanded my knowledge of relaxation, breathing, stress reduction, and connecting mind and body.

I also call myself a perpetual student of the Pagan arts—in particular, tarot—and hold monthly workshops where participants gain personal insight using tarot. It's deeply gratifying to me to observe people identify their own issues and recognize new angles and new solutions. I love seeing people succeed!

Also, as we go along, you'll discover that I'm an incorrigible cheerleader, insisting that you *can* change, and you *can* succeed. I was a cheerleading coach when my daughter was a youngster, and we even won a divisional state championship once, so I know my way around a pom-pom, and I'm going to be shaking them at you!

Of all the information and skills I've gathered up over the years, the psychological metamorphosis I experienced after returning to horses midlife has been the most transformative experience of all. My life is a quantum leap away from where it was only a few years ago, when I felt stagnant, hopeless, and trapped.

My story is not an anomaly. Over and over and over, I hear stories from people whose lives changed after they started working with horses; however, *none* from people who worked with Horse Spirit. I discovered a missing link between the physical world of horses and the metaphysical world of Horse Spirit, and that's what this book is: the bridge. I will share all the methods and mental twists I took to tap into Horse Spirit energy, as well as my own stories with Penn. Some will be stories of huge successes and others, well, sort of the "fashion don'ts" of horsemanship, much of which I learned from Sarah.

If you don't know a thing about horses, don't despair. In the first two sections, we'll focus on the contributions horses have made to human history and culture, and meet the metaphysical horses. In the third and fourth sections, we'll learn about real horses, how to understand and handle them, and how to find a horse of your own. Don't fret about what you think you don't know, just believe that anything is possible. That's the only skill you need to start your journey with horses and Horse Spirit. Also, if you're already stacking up the reasons why you think you'll never have a horse, I'll give you the same response Sarah gave me: "Uh-huh."

To Saddle Up...or Not?

While riding a horse is deeply exhilarating and satisfying, it's not the focus of this book. Riding isn't required to experience the emotional transformation that a relationship with a horse brings, and it's not necessary for connecting with Horse Spirit. We'll touch on riding a bit, but in working with real horses, the aim is equine companionship.

Besides riding not being our focus, you can't learn to ride a horse from reading a book. You can get fantastic insight and great tips from books, but riding is a kinesthetic learning process. It's like learning to ski. You could read every book there is on skiing, but when you get up on those skis for the first time, you'll look like Bambi scrambling and sliding around on a frozen pond, and discover that your brain has no clue what to tell your legs to do.

Like skiing, riding is about balance and muscle memory, reflex and skill, and hours and hours of having your butt actually in the saddle. Your brain must learn new messages to send to your muscles, and your muscles have to learn how to respond. If you really want to learn to ride, you'll have to take lessons. There's no other way to do it except to *do* it.

Another reason why riding isn't our focus is that there are about a million other riding experts out there who are infinitely more qualified than I to offer commentary, let alone instruction. I don't intend to guide you toward your first dressage event. I am spectacularly unqualified for that. That said, I'm exquisitely qualified to show you how much deeper, richer, and more fulfilling your relationship with a horse can be if you stay on the ground. I'll offer some tips and ideas for handling a horse, but like riding, you really can't learn that from a book either. It won't happen until you snap that lead rope to the halter and set out on foot together.

A relationship with a horse heals your soul more than years in therapy ever could. Horses teach you to live in your own body, right there in that moment, breathing, feeling grounded, releasing tension, and actually noticing what goes on around you, and inside you. It's a spiritual "coming home."

So, we aren't striving for blue ribbons in the show ring here. Our goal is simply wholeness, genuineness, and serenity—simply *be*-ing, comfortable in our own skin. My "disposable" old horse changed the entire trajectory of my life. Because of Penn, I began connecting all the dots. He's the only reason this book exists. He's a gift from the universe, an equine miracle worker, and would be so if I'd never gotten on his back at all.

Horse vs. horse

Just a little housekeeping before we proceed. You've already noticed that sometimes I'm talking about real horses, and other times, that more ethereal, mystical "Horse Spirit" or simply "Horse." When I'm discussing real live physical horses, the word will always be lowercase. When I'm talking about Horse Spirit—Horse as a power animal, totem, spirit guide, or spiritual energy—the word is always capitalized.

I use the word in the same spirit as Native Americans in their teaching stories about moral character or lessons for living in tune with the earth and nature. There are Native American stories about Eagle or Bear or Coyote, who often have the gift of human language, and are associated with particular qualities, talents, wisdom, or energies. These simple stories are brilliantly enlightening and inspiring. Just as Native American stories refer to animal spirit guides as the capitalized name of a particular animal, I will do so with Horse Spirit or, more simply, Horse, from now on.

This is where you have to really pay attention: In chapter 4: Elemental Horses, we will learn about Spirit Horse. This is not the same thing as Horse or Horse Spirit. Spirit Horse is a specific energy—the domain of our own internal, pure, divine selves, and works in concert with the four other Elemental Horses. To help keep this straight, going forward, I will refer only to stand-alone Horse—not Horse Spirit—when I'm talking about that spirit animal, as opposed to Spirit Horse, which is about that central Elemental Horse *specifically*. To help keep it clear, here's a little cheat sheet:

- Real, live horses: a horse, the horse(s), horses.
- Horse as power animal, totem, spirit guide: Horse.
- The specific central, divine Elemental Horse energy: Spirit Horse.

Got it? Great! Let's get going! As the old West cowhands used to say, "We're burnin' daylight!"

— I —

HORSES & HUMANS,
HISTORY & CULTURE

Chapter 1
HORSES CHANGED EVERYTHING

Aside from humans, no other creature has changed the face and nature of the planet more than horses—and, humans could not have made those changes without them. Without the power and speed of horses, human culture, countries, and kingdoms would not look the way they do today. The world as we know it would not look the way it does today.

As horses and humans evolved alongside each other, a symbiotic relationship formed. Each early species discovered that cooperation made survival easier. At some point over the shared evolution, humans would switch sides and view horses as food. Generally, though, humans found that horses were far more valuable alive than roasted over a fire. Horses, to their credit, seemed to forgive humans for their egregious transgression.

The contribution of horses to human culture is documented in artwork, song, literature, mythology, fiction, history, poetry, religion, and language. Not even our beloved dogs and cats can claim the status and influence on humanity that belongs solely to the preeminent equine.

Horses and humans have quite literally always been together: lived, evolved, and survived right alongside each other. Whether our survival was because of or in spite of each other is debatable. I suppose it depends on whether you ask the horses or the humans. Initially, however, our distant ancestors likely co-existed peacefully, to each other's mutual benefit.

Our earliest ancestors bore little resemblance to today's *Homo sapiens* and *Equus caballus*. The common ancestor to both humans and apes, *Prosimian*, was a small omnivore about the size and shape of a tree shrew and resembling a modern lemur. It was arboreal and lived on whatever it could reach from the treetops—insects, grubs, berries, and even smaller animals.

9

The earliest ancestor of the horse, *Hyracotherium*—also called *Eohippus* or *Dawn Horse*—had four toes on the front feet and three on the back, helping it to navigate swampy ground under the tree canopy where it dwelled—right underneath *Prosimian*! An herbivore, *Hyracotherium* mostly ate leaves and berries. It was less than twenty inches tall, and roughly resembled a small, tiny-eared fawn with a bony tail.

Prosimian and *Hyracotherium* appeared during the Eocene epoch, with fossil evidence dating back fifty-five million years for both species. Mammals thrived in this period, following the extinction of dinosaurs sixty-five million years earlier when global temperatures suddenly plummeted, wiping the dinosaurs out. The planet later warmed at the end of the Cretaceous period in the Mesozoic era, which suited early mammals just fine.

Making its appearance alongside the earliest horse and human ancestors was the earliest ancestor of many of today's carnivores, from lions and tigers to the family dog and cat: *Dormaalocyon latouri*. In a *National Geographic* article, writer Brian Handwerk describes the creature as a "cross between a squirrel and a small cougar."[1] Somewhere along the distant evolutionary line, the descendants of that squirrel cougar started eating the descendants of the little tree shrew and the tiny-eared fawn. One could imagine that the shrew and fawn had a common goal: Stay away from the squirrel cougar! It could also be further imagined that they actually helped each other by learning to run if they heard an alert from the other species.

All these animals existed and evolved millions of years before the earliest human cave art appeared in the Paleolithic period of the Pleistocene epoch —2.58 million years ago and extending to about twelve thousand years ago. In fact, they existed before genus *Homo* even appeared, about when the Paleolithic period began. At this point in evolution, whatever eons-ago mutually beneficial relationship existed between *Prosimian* and *Hyracotherium*, it was likely destroyed by *Homo's* appetite for meat. By the Paleolithic period, *Homo habilis* was using tools, and by 1.8 to 1.5 million years ago, *Homo erectus* had become an alpha predator, and *Equus* was most likely on its menu.

During that time, horses also evolved, adapting to their new appetite for grass, with elongated heads, necks, and legs, as well as speed and vigilance to avoid predators. Genus *Equus* evolved from *Pliohippus*—which walked on a single "toe" rather than three or four—toward the end of the Pliocene era.

---

1. Handwerk, "Ancient Arboreal Mammal Discovered at Root of Carnivore Family Tree."

By the Pleistocene epoch, *Equus* was thriving and dispersed across Europe and Asia, and also into North America, where it disappeared between eight thousand to ten thousand years ago, for reasons still unknown. *Equus* did not appear again in North or South America until transported there by Spanish explorers in the 1500s, seeking to establish themselves in the "New World." By the time humans began depicting their world in the form of Paleolithic cave art, the predator-prey relationship between humans and horses was already well established. However, there may be more to that story.

The "Writing" Is on the Wall

In Wendy Williams's exquisitely detailed and well-researched book *The Horse: The Epic History of Our Noble Companion*, she recounts her visits to many cave sites adorned with Paleolithic human art from Spain to Asia, and everywhere in between. Horses were clearly on the radar of those earliest artists, depicting horses not only as part of that period's abundant wildlife, but also showing a shift in how horses were depicted as compared to other species. In particular, Williams compares the horses painted on the Chauvet and Lascaux caves in France, which depicted horses differently than other common prey animals such as reindeer.

Williams says the Chauvet Cave shows a panorama of animals, amongst them, lions, reindeer, bison, bears, ibexes, and owls, and "in this raucous panoply, the horses are essential. They are watchers. Many of the Chauvet animals are shown interacting with each other, walking in groups along ridgelines that run along the walls or fighting with each other or even preparing to mate—but not the horses. They stand quietly, some in small groups, some solitary."[2]

Watchers. Most curious. Amongst species that live in the wild together today, many have symbiotic, mutually beneficial relationships. Cattle egrets pick bugs off the backs of, you guessed it, cattle. Sharks do not eat the pilot fish that snack on the parasites that bother them. In Africa and South America, the alarm calls of birds and monkeys alert each other of predators, and other species have learned to recognize those calls and benefit from their vigilance.

In the article "Impalas are the Wimps of the Animal Kingdom and Other Species Know It," writer Kate Baggaley says, "There are plenty of animals that listen in on other species' chatter, including birds, primates, and rodents. Scrubwrens and fairy wrens flee when they hear each other's alarm calls, while nuthatches

2. Williams, *The Horse: The Epic History of Our Noble Companion*.

eavesdrop on chickadees, and vervet monkeys heed superb starling warnings. Eavesdropping lets an animal stay in the know without much effort."

She adds, "It's common for wildebeests, zebras, and impalas to group together while grazing, and all three have distinctive alarm calls. Startled impalas let out a series of short barks, while wildebeests make sneeze-like snorts and zebras bray, whinny, and snort."[3]

Since these species live side by side, they've learned to distinguish a greeting from a warning, and flee accordingly. Given that our human and equine Eocene ancestors also evolved together, it's not hard to imagine that the herbivorous *Hyracotherium* and omnivorous *Prosimian* learned to identify each other's vocalizations and behaviors while still forest dwellers and warn of any *Dormaalocyon latouri* lurking in the neighborhood. Even later down the evolutionary path, it's possible that although humans and horses had a predator-prey relationship, humans observed that horses were ever-vigilant for approaching predators and may have been humanity's first watchdogs. Those humans may have decided that overall, it served them more to let the horses watch for predators than to treat them as prey. Even now, horses are hypervigilant, often ridiculously so (from a human perspective, anyway), as evidenced by the snorting panic caused by something as simple as a plastic bag blowing by. From a horse's perspective, anything could be a predator until proven otherwise. Those who snort and run away live to graze another day!

While it's not hard to imagine those Paleolithic horses serving as predator alarm systems for their human counterparts, what did the horses gain from being in the proximity of humans? Maybe they learned that fewer predators would approach a group of creatures armed with clubs, rocks, spears, and skilled coordinated hunting tactics, and therefore hung a little closer to human dwellings? If those horse herds stayed at a safe distance but close enough to be observed, might this be what gave those early cave artists access to them and inspired the artwork? We can't know for sure, but if you consider all the known factors, this is the picture that seems to emerge—and is indicated by the changing cave art.

According to Williams, the Chauvet Cave artwork dates back more than thirty thousand years ago, while the Lascaux Cave dates back to about seventeen thousand years ago. Unlike the Chauvet "watchers" who kept an alert distance, the Lascaux horses are "merry little things, delightfully capricious."

---

3. Baggaley, "Impalas are the Wimps of the Animal Kingdom and Other Species Know It."

"In Lascaux," she notes, "the horses' motto seems to be 'Don't worry. Be happy' ... They are positively prancing in their excitement." With good reason, because the climate was warming, grasslands were expanding, and there was food and wildlife aplenty.

"It was a great time to be alive," Williams writes, "and so Lascaux is filled with joyfulness, a bit of craziness, and plenty of variety."[4]

It appears that the cave artists observed horses frolicking in their little bands, squealing, kicking, and nuzzling each other, and translated that observation to their "canvasses." This means that not only did Paleolithic humans spend time watching horses graze and frolic, they enjoyed it—just as people do now.

We Still Love to Watch

A herd of horses is amazingly entertaining to watch if you have the patience to simply observe. Just walk up to a pasture where horses are grazing sometime, lean your chin on your hands on the fence, and get lost in the quiet pleasure of just observing horses. It seems to trigger a relaxation response. Maybe somewhere in our DNA we know that if the horses are calm, the area is free of predators, and everyone can relax and enjoy the moment? I find it to be similar to the relaxation response experienced while listening to ocean waves, or crickets chirping while gazing up at the stars in the dark night sky. We don't *learn* to relax to these sounds, it's in our cellular memory. It occurs naturally, as does joy and laughter while watching animals frolic and cavort. The sight of playful horses still brings joy, and the sight of peaceful horses still brings calm—just as it did seventeen thousand years ago, and maybe even longer.

Where Horses Run Free

The ultimate destination for experiencing the joy and wonder of observing horses is where wild horses still roam free, such as Gardnerville, Nevada, where a few herds roam the Fish Springs Range in the Pine Nut Mountains.

These horses are commonly called Mustangs; however, purists prefer to call them "wild horses," because they have mixed bloodlines from domesticated horses joining their herds.

It's best to see wild horses with a guide. For one thing, you won't know where to find them, and for another, it's usually a bad plan to drive out into the high desert where there's no road, cell phone coverage is sketchy, and you

---

4. Williams, *The Horse: The Epic History of Our Noble Companion.*

have no idea of what you're doing or where you're going. Also, the last thing the wild horses need are hordes of humans in cars and trucks invading their territory, trashing it, tearing it up, and getting too close. The most enchanting reason to go with an escort is because they will know the horses and their histories. Without a guide like that, even if you do find the horses, you'll miss out on ninety-five percent of the subtle and detailed equine interactions that are taking place before your eyes.

Seeing Mustangs in the wild was a huge bucket list experience for me. My husband and I, along with my Horsey Girl friend Karen, drove to Carson City, Nevada, and got up before sunrise to meet our guide, Mary, in Gardnerville. Mary was already there waiting for us, and we hopped into her big four-wheel drive SUV, lurching off-road onto dusty trails and through jarring, rocky gullies, and into the rolling brown hills, covered mostly with sparse pale green sagebrush. In the distance, the deep blue Sierra Mountains were still capped with snow, even in June, creating a gorgeous hazy blue, green, and gold panoramic backdrop under a bright azure dome.

As we topped a hill, I gasped as a large herd of horses—bays and palominos, blue and red roans, coal black and dark brown—was suddenly right before us. Amid the adult mares, there were even a few whimsical, tiny foal faces peeking out. Much to my amazement and delight, binoculars weren't even necessary to see the horses—although they were nice to have to really zoom in. We pulled up to about one hundred yards from the herd, which seemed unconcerned with our presence. Mary explained that these horses recognized her truck and her, and had grown accustomed to occasional visits from small, quiet groups of onlookers, as long as we kept a respectful distance.

I was nearly giddy. I'd dreamed all my life of seeing wild horses and never imagined it would be this easy or this close. I couldn't help but creep nearer and nearer until Mary cautioned me, "That's close enough." The stallion that owned that band of mares and foals—a stunning dark palomino with a full, flowing flaxen mane and unruly forelock that spilled over his eyes and face— had turned toward me, calmly watching. This muscled, massive, battle-scarred stallion's message was crystal clear: *Stop, or else.* He didn't pin his ears or shake his head at me, nor stomp or threaten me in any way. He didn't have to. He was the king of this empire, and he knew it.

His name was Blondie, and Mary said he had sired many of the horses both in this herd and others we'd be seeing. She pointed out many individuals, telling us their names, lineage, and what they were doing at that particular moment.

Just then, a stunning dark bay stallion with white socks and a much smaller band of mares approached. Rather than fight, Blondie and this stallion squealed and pawed at each other a bit in what almost seemed like a greeting. Blondie reinforced his alpha status, and that was that. The stallion, named Mystique, exhibited no intention of challenging Blondie, apparently just passing through toward the common watering hole a few hundred yards away. Mary explained that the watering hole has strict rules, down to which band drinks first, and which horses within the band drink first. Wild horses have an organized pecking order and social system, both within and between herds.

Off in the distance, a small band of horses galloped and cavorted, bucking, kicking, and play-biting each other. This was a "bachelor band," young males that are forced out of the herds when the ruling stallion decides that they're old enough to challenge him. Because horses are herd animals and fear being alone, the outcast bachelors form little herds of their own like teenage hooligans wandering the neighborhood, creating a ruckus, until they're big enough and bold enough to challenge a stallion for his mares.

As we watched in delight, Mary told us about the threats wild horses face, not the least of which was the U.S. government's Bureau of Land Management, with its ongoing efforts to round up wild horses all over the country and contain them in large, crowded holding pens where they languish unless they're lucky enough to be adopted. Most aren't, and their futures are dim (read: slaughterhouse).[5]

Of all the behaviors and interactions we witnessed that day, the one that impressed me most was when a small bachelor band galloped up and stopped near Blondie's herd. He observed them calmly, went over for a greeting, and with carefully controlled teeth and hooves, reminded them who was boss. Although most of it was for show, the bachelors paid attention and got right out of his way. But then, Blondie left them alone to mill about, and walked back to his band. He nosed up to a young colt—maybe a two-year-old or so—that was

5. Wild Horse Education, "Reality of Wild Horse Slaughter—Caught in a Tangled Web, the Reality of Wild Horse Slaughter."

his spitting image, just smaller and more delicate, and with none of Blondie's badass sexy stallion mojo—not yet anyway.

"That's Cree, his colt," Mary said, and we watched as Blondie patiently and skillfully cut the youngster away from the herd and gently guided him toward the bachelor group. Mary explained that Blondie had decided it would soon be time for Cree to move on. Dad was introducing him to the bachelors for a play date.

Cree and the bachelors snuffled at each other's noses and squealed, and there was some dusty excitement and frolicking as Blondie stood by and observed. The bachelors seemed to like this new pal. Then a dark bay mare, Star, stepped away from Blondie's band, her head held high and her eyes and ears fixed on Blondie. He returned her gaze.

"Mama has decided 'not yet,'" said Mary. Star had "told" Blondie that it wasn't time for Cree to start running with the bachelors. It was time to bring him home.

Blondie "heard" Star's request, gathered up Cree, and escorted him back to the band without objection, as if to say, "Well, okay then." Mary explained that it's not the stallion, but the mares—particularly the lead mare—that make the decisions and decide what's what. The stallion's job is to protect the band from predators and other dangers, drive away interlopers, and sire as many foals as possible. But in the world of wild horses, Mom's the boss—to a point. When Cree becomes bigger and beefier, all full of his big, bad testosterone-soaked self and actually challenges Blondie for the herd, that will be the day Blondie puts his hoof down: "Adios, Junior." It won't matter what Mama thinks. Sometimes Papa exercises his veto power.

I was simply in awe of the entire scenario I'd just witnessed, right there in real time. Had we ventured out on our own, I'd never have understood what I'd just witnessed. All I would have seen were groups of horses milling about, coming and going.

It's been years since we saw those wild horses, and even now, I get a rush of joy just thinking about them.

I keep up with them on the Pine Nut Wild Horse Advocates' Facebook page, and had a photo that I took of Blondie sparring with Mystique enlarged to a wall-sized framed photo. While I would recommend making your own visit to the herd, the Bureau of Land Management captured some of the Pine Nut wild horses in 2019, leaving fewer than one hundred horses out in the wild. Activists for the Pine Nut horses fear more will be rounded up, making it uncertain if any will remain wild in the near future. If you want to see those horses, don't delay.

My photo of Blondie brings us back to our Paleolithic ancestors who painted horses on the walls of the Chauvet and Lascaux caves—weren't the cave painters and I essentially doing the same thing? Observing a group of fascinating, entertaining, beautiful creatures, and then capturing their images? The only difference is that I used a camera rather than ochre dust to put an image of a horse on my own cave wall.

I imagine those early artists also watched bands of wild horses, had names for each, and knew their families and stories, just like Mary. I like to think they enjoyed observing the horses' antics and squabbles, new foals being born, and new alliances being made. Those horses were their Netflix, and they enjoyed watching.

Paleolithic men and women likely felt the same wonder and amusement while watching horses that we do now and captured those moments on cave walls. How purely awesome is that? We can have a Paleolithic experience watching horses just as we can by looking up at the moon and stars in the night sky, and realizing that early humans did—and saw—the same thing, tens of thousands of years ago. Horses connect us to our own very distant ancestors. We still love horses, and we still express ourselves through art. That much hasn't changed. Maybe we aren't as different from our ancient ancestors as we like to fancy ourselves.

Touching Time

Those horses our Paleolithic ancestors watched are long gone. However, there is one place in the world where their descendants still exist. They're called Przewalski's horses and are described by *National Geographic* as the last surviving subspecies of wild horse. Nineteenth-century Russian explorer N. M. Przewalski, after whom the horses were named, is given credit for first scientifically describing the horses that roamed the steppe on the Mongolian-China border.

These small, stocky horses have a uniformly reddish coat, light-colored nose and underbelly, and black lower legs, tail and short mane—which sticks up like a zebra's. In Wendy Williams's book, she notes that local breeding efforts to reestablish pure herds of this horse—called *Takhi* by Mongolians—have been successful, as the horse was teetering on the brink of extinction. The notoriously recalcitrant animals are not only making a comeback, but are the pride and joy of the local people, despite the fact that the love is unrequited: these horses simply don't care for humans.

Could it be that their ancestors weren't interested in staying near Paleolithic humans, recognized them as predators exclusively, and got as far away from humans as their hooves would carry them? Why do they seem completely different in their tolerance for humans? Well, here's an interesting tidbit to consider: domestic horses have sixty-four chromosomes, while Przewalski's horses have sixty-six.[6] Maybe the "humans are enemies" gene rests upon one of those two extra chromosomes, and the equines that didn't have those extra genes had more trusting dispositions, and ended up being more easily domesticated (and eaten).

The early Pleistocene equines living on the Mongolian-China border are the likely ancestors of not only Przewalski's horses, but also the horses domesticated by Genghis Khan, enabling him to conquer most anyone and anything that stood in his path of wrath. This hunch is confirmed by a 1994 Columbia University paper, "All the Khan's Horses," written by Morris Rossabi: "Genghis Khan and his descendents [sic] could not have conquered and ruled the largest land empire in world history without their diminutive but extremely hardy steeds. In some respects, these Mongolian ponies resembled what is now known as Przewalski's horse."

These Mongolian horses changed the game of war and the shape of nations. Khan's ability to exploit the horses' abilities propelled him to widespread domination of much of the Eurasian continent. Notes Rossabi, "Horses could, without exaggeration, be referred to as the intercontinental ballistic missiles of the thirteenth century."[7] Countries and kingdoms balanced upon their ability to amass horses and use them as weapons. Before the invention of tanks and airplanes, bombs and battleships, it was horses that determined victory on the battlefield. Although humans drastically changed the size and appearance of horses over time through selective breeding to suit their needs and whims, from shaggy ponies to mighty draft horses and everything in between, the evidence thus far indicates that the lines of all those horses trace back to those watchful, frolicking images on those caves in France.

---

6. Smithsonian's National Zoo & Conservation Biology Institute, "Przewalski's Horse."
7. Rossabi, "All the Khan's Horses."

The particular significance of Przewalski's horse is that we can see something very much like those Paleolithic images in real time. That's as close as we can get to peering back through the eons and seeing what our Paleolithic ancestors saw. Put a photo of a Przewalski's horse next to a photo of a Chauvet Cave painting and see if doesn't give you chill—they look nearly identical. A horse very much like this one, and certainly related to it, now wanders free in Mongolia. You are seeing a slice of ancient time, a horse that looks just like the ones drawn by your Paleolithic ancestors. How cool is *that*?

Saddling Up

As for evidence of domesticating and riding horses in Williams's *The Horse: The Epic History of Our Noble Companion*, she notes that the earliest proof of domesticated horses was discovered at an archaeological site in Kazakhstan called Botai. The site has small corrals that were likely used to hold mares, which were milked for human consumption. Broken pottery from the site had evidence of animal fat that is unique to horse milk. The site dates back to fifty-five hundred years ago and although there is no evidence that horses were ridden at Botai, Williams emphasizes that "absence of evidence, though, is not evidence of absence."[8]

An article from the University of Exeter says that archaeologists at Botai found bit damage on the teeth of fossilized horse remains, indicating that the horses had been harnessed or bridled. The article quotes Dr. Alan Outram of the University of Exeter as having said, "The domestication of horses is known to have had immense social and economic significance, advancing communications, transport, food production, and warfare. Our findings indicate that horses were being domesticated about 1,000 years earlier than previously thought. This is significant because it changes our understanding of how these early societies developed."[9]

The first evidence of humans on horseback that Williams cites in her book is through post-Pleistocene art, and is depicted on rock and cliff carvings spread throughout Europe. Williams cites the Holocene (current) epoch artwork in Galicia, Spain, depicting a quite different image than the watchful, playful horses of cave art past.

8. Williams, *The Horse: The Epic History of Our Noble Companion*.
9. University of Exeter, "Archaeologists Find Earliest Known Domestic Horses: Harnessed and Milked."

"Holocene Galician art shows the horse as a tool of humans. People are now at the center of the action; horses are now animals to be subdued and used. They are objects of manipulation," writes Williams.[10] Galician art shows the use of horses in full swing, rather than at its beginnings. An internet search on the topic of "earliest images of humans on horses" mostly reveals artwork and sculpture from well-established ancient cultures like Rome, Persia, and Egypt. It seems that there's a huge gap between the horse artwork of the Pleistocene epoch and the days of antiquity.

Writer Jesslyn Shields in her article "If Those Aren't Human Hands in Ancient Cave Art—What Are They?" reveals that stencils of human hands are amongst the artwork on the walls of "The Cave of Beasts"—also known as Cave Wadi Sura II—located in the Gilf Kebir Mountains in Egypt, as well as human figures. The humans seem to be very busy, and intermingled with a variety of animals, including what appear to be horses. However, they aren't riding the horses. Shields says these paintings are about eight thousand years old.[11]

The bottom line is, a lot of time passed between the Paleolithic cave paintings of horses in France and the Galician artwork, and even more passed from then until the detailed artwork of antiquity showing horses across cultures, already pulling chariots and carts, and eventually shown being ridden. Finding artwork that pins down the exact point in time when some adventurous ancient human first got the bright idea to climb onto some ancient horse's back—and lived to tell—is elusive, but clearly that moment happened. When it did, ancient humans discovered that atop horses, they could cover a lot of ground quickly, and that being carried on an animal that could keep up with prey made it easier to hunt. This made horses valuable. From that point on, humans started capturing and domesticating horses, and further discovered that mare's milk was a satisfying source of nutrition. The human-horse partnership was *on*. Sadly, this is probably when humans began viewing horses as tools, rather than lovely creatures to watch and enjoy. Because we're in search of that simple pleasure, our journey to discover Horse now dials us back to the time when horses were simply joyful and we enjoyed watching them—we loved horses long before we rode them.

10. Williams, *The Horse: The Epic History of Our Noble Companion*.
11. Shields, "If Those Aren't Human Hands in Ancient Cave Art—What Are They?"

Meditation to Meet Horse

A leap of faith is what you take when being asked to accept something that can't be proven. We can take a "leap of imagination," and try to get inside the heads of our Paleolithic ancestors. Let's reach back and touch that place in time when horses and humans, in whatever form they were in, coexisted in a pure, clean, peaceful, green environment, and simply watch. Our spiritual journey to meet Horse begins there.

Getting Ready for Meditation

Set aside fifteen to twenty minutes when you won't be interrupted, and find a quiet place as free as possible of human-made noise like people talking, cell phones, televisions, and traffic. A nature soundtrack set at low volume can help induce relaxation, but sweet, simple quiet works just fine too.

Before you begin, read through the entire meditation so you know what imagery to create in your mind. You can also read it out loud, record it, and play it back as you meditate. If you make your own recording, make sure you are calm, breathing peacefully, and unbothered by any external interruptions. Don't race through it. Pause after each sentence, inhale and exhale peacefully, and then proceed.

Before beginning, get a notebook and something to write with, and place it by your side so that you can jot down images, thoughts, feelings, or insight you experience during your meditation.

Let's begin.

A Meditative Meeting with Horse

Get in a comfortable position that you can maintain for a while without effort, sitting or lying down. Close your eyes … and just breathe. If words or thoughts pop into your head, imagine them being captured by a bubble and floating away into the atmosphere. Acknowledge the bubbles and just let them go. Focus on your breathing, and settle into a slow, deep, relaxed rhythm. Try to breathe from deep in your belly, just above your belly button, keeping your stomach soft and relaxed.

Stay there for a moment and just experience the peace.

Look around … what surroundings has your mind's eye created? Forest? Beach? Plains? Morning? Sunset? Nighttime? Observe your surroundings for a bit, and when you feel calm and comfortable, invite Horse to come into that place. Be patient. Horse may appear to you in any form, from a shaggy Paleolithic pony to a shiny Thoroughbred or a pawing wild Mustang. Go with it. Don't shape it, don't judge it, just watch.

How does Horse look to you? What is it doing? Is it moving around or still? Does it step toward you or seem aloof or timid? What color is it? Does it have white markings? Is it male or female? Look into its eyes… is it sending you a message?

How does Horse make you feel? What word or words come to mind that capture your feelings as you look at it?

Reach in your pocket… there's a piece of carrot there. Take it out and offer it to Horse in the palm of your hand. How does it respond? How does its response make you feel? Now, just observe it… be with it.

When you feel ready, thank Horse for spending time with you, bid it farewell, and watch it depart. As it disappears to go back from whence it came, return your attention to your breathing, inhaling and exhaling from just above your belly button. If you're enjoying this internal peace, stay with it for as long as you like.

When you feel refreshed and ready to return from your meditation, move your awareness from your breathing back to the room or area around you, slowly open your eyes, and breathe normally until you feel fully present.

Jot down anything you felt or experienced that seems interesting, enlightening, or just curious. Even if it's nonsensical, record that too. Sometimes things that seem ridiculous one day make sense later on. Don't worry about grammar, spelling, or penmanship—your notes only need to make sense to you and to be legible to you. If you'd rather draw images than jot down words, that's perfectly fine too. Or maybe you want to do both. Whatever feels right to you is the right way to do it.

When you feel stressed or are lying awake unable to sleep, close your eyes and return to that place you created in your mind anytime you like. Horse will be waiting for you.

En-joy Yourself

In our Paleolithic past and also in our meditation, enjoying the present moment is central to the experience. Let's consider the word "enjoy." We know that to "enliven" means to liven things up. To "enact" means to act something out. But we typically only use the word "enjoy" as to passively experience pleasure and not as an active verb.

Consider what it means to actively "en-joy" yourself, to purposefully infuse yourself with joy; to make it happen rather than sit there passively, hoping it happens. In your meditation, and afterward, as you see horses around you or watch internet videos, "en-joy" yourself with the wonder of watching them. Infuse yourself with that experience. En-joy yourself by inviting horses, and Horse, into your life.

Chapter 2

HORSES IN CULTURE AND LANGUAGE

Horses are interwoven in language and lore across many cultures, religions, and spirituality. While horses literally carried humans from one place to another, the mythologies associated with horses carried our imaginations through time. In this chapter, we'll explore some of the ways horses changed the course of human life, and how their contribution is represented in both culture and language.

In the gap between the Paleolithic cave paintings and recorded history, the symbiotic relationship between horses and humans expanded exponentially. However, with not much evidence to rely upon in that nine-thousand-year gap, we are catapulted from watching whimsical "horse as art" and even "horse as meal" evolve into "horse as tool" and "horse as weapon." However, once horses do appear in written and relatively modern artwork and sculpture, they are ubiquitous.

According to the "horse" entry on the Ancient History Encyclopedia website, horses don't appear in written material until after the point when they become useful. The invention of the wheel in 3100 BCE in the Middle East preceded the invention of the chariot around 2000 BCE in the area known as the Eurasian steppe, a strip of grassland stretching from Hungary to China—the same area where Przewalski's horse still exist and the Mongolian ponies of Genghis Khan were first domesticated.

The word for "horse" appears for the first time in Mesopotamia (where written language emerged there about one thousand years earlier, around 3500 to 3000 BCE) at about the same time as the invention of the chariot—surely not a coincidence. Horses were the engines for chariots. Chariots were pretty much useless without horses to pull them. Stories and myths older than this were apparently either recorded in hieroglyphs, as in ancient Egypt, or passed through the generations orally.

The Multicultural Horse

It would be an exhaustive effort to catalog each appearance and mention of horses across human culture and time, but following are some of the horse's cultural "greatest hits," both ancient and modern:

- *Black Jack:* One of the most striking features of President John F. Kennedy's funeral procession was Black Jack, a rider-less black horse with the empty boots backward in the stirrups, signifying a fallen hero. The tradition of the rider-less or "caparisoned horse" extends back to the reign of Genghis Khan; however, those horses were sacrificed so their spirits could travel to meet with their deceased riders. Today's caparisoned horses are spared from that gruesome fate.

  Black Jack had twenty-nine years of military service to his credit, serving as the caparisoned horse in the funerals of presidents Herbert Hoover, Lyndon B. Johnson, and General Douglas MacArthur, in addition to JFK. Black Jack was the second horse in U.S. history, after Comanche, to receive full military honors upon his death. He was buried at Fort Myer in Virginia.

- *Clever Hans:* In 1891, in Berlin, Germany, a big brown horse named Hans and his trainer, Wilhelm von Osten, convinced both the scientific community and the public that he was capable of extraordinary feats: math, reading, spelling, and identifying colors and musical tones. The horse's skills were so astounding, they made the front page of the *New York Times.* However, Oskar Pfungst, a student at the psychological department at the University of Berlin, examined the case more deeply and published a report in 1907 debunking the notion of a genius horse, revealing that Hans was being subtly—likely involuntarily—cued by his handler. This phenomenon was dubbed the "Clever Hans effect," meaning the unintentional cueing of desired behavior in a scientific experiment.

- *Comanche:* A stocky warhorse named Comanche has been portrayed as the lone survivor of the Battle of Little Big Horn in 1876, standing by his fallen owner's body amongst a sea of dead bodies, after being shot seven times in the battle. Comanche belonged to Captain Myles Keogh of the Seventh Cavalry, fighting under General George Custer, and was not Custer's horse, as is sometimes claimed.

The true part of Comanche's story is that he continued to carry his rider in battle, even when wounded. His preserved body is on display in the University of Kansas Natural History Museum; however, the brass plaque declaring him the "Sole survivor of the Battle of Little Big Horn" was removed at the request of local Native American tribes, which rightfully pointed out that many Native Americans survived the battle—which they won—as did many uninjured horses that were taken by the victorious warriors. Ironically, Keogh named the horse Comanche as a nod to the Comanche warriors, whom he admired for their fierce fighting abilities. When Comanche died at age twenty-nine, he was recognized with the highest of military honors.

- *Dude ranches:* In the late 1800s, East Coast city slickers, or "dudes" as the cowboys called them, visited western cattle ranches to get their cowboy groove on. These "dudes" learned to ride horses, spent time with real cowboys, and even participated on real cattle drives astride real cattle horses. The dude ranch industry blossomed over the last century into an Old West vacation and to this day visitors can still get a taste of the ranch hand life.

- *Ehwaz:* This Viking rune is translated as "horse," signifying speed, strength, momentum, and making progress toward a goal. Runes are an ancient divination system, composed of symbols on stones or small flat pieces of wood, each inscribed with an ancient form of the Germanic or Norse alphabets. They are associated with Norse and Viking lore and mythology. Ehwaz is nearly identical to the rune Mannaz, meaning "mankind" or "humankind." You can't draw Mannaz without drawing Ehwaz, which in my mind translates to "Without Horse, mankind is nothing."

- *Eohomo and Eohippus:* This whimsical 1876 drawing by Thomas Henry Huxley shows a happy little pre-human, Eohomo, astride a happy little *Eohippus* (Dawn Horse, *Hyracotherium*). Although not factually accurate (*Eohippus* and genus *Homo* do not appear at the same time in evolutionary history), the famous drawing is a nod to Huxley's belief in evolution.

- *Foxhunting:* The English sport of foxhunting involves a group of horses and riders led by a pack of hounds, chasing down a live fox. The sound of a horn and the cry "tally-ho" comes from this sport, now viewed by many as cruel, as the fox is caught and killed by the frantic hounds, and parts of its body given away to the riders as trophies. The traditional red riding coat comes from the sport of foxhunting. Foxhunting was banned in Scotland in 2002 and in England in 2005.

  A horse riding in a foxhunt must stay under control amid frantic circumstances and clear hurdles and obstacles, which is where the horseshow term "hunter" comes from. A "hunter" shows style, control, and finesse in addition to being able to clear the jumps. A "jumper," by contrast, must clear the jumps, but equitation, horsemanship, and style don't count. The rider merely needs to manage to stay in the saddle for the entire course.

- *Gauchos:* Gauchos are the South American counterparts of the American cowboy and Mexican vaquero. These nomadic horsemen of Argentina, Brazil, and Uruguay were hired by mid-eighteenth-century landowners to work horses and cattle, and helped develop the elegant four-gaited Peruvian Pasos and Paso Finos.

- *Hobbyhorse competition:* Riding a stick horse or "hobbyhorse" through a series of jumps or in dressage competition has become all the rage for girls and young women in Finland, where it is considered a legitimate organized sport.

- *Horse racing:* Racing horses is such an ancient sport that an Encyclopedia Britannica entry notes that its origins are "lost in prehistory." Horse racing was a key feature of the original Olympic games in Greece, going back as far as 700 BCE. Horse racing has a history in Europe, China, Persia (now Iran), and other countries in the Middle East and North Africa. In medieval England, horses were raced to display speed to potential buyers. King Charles II popularized horse racing in the mid-seventeenth century and it became a gambling sport in the late eighteenth century.

  Horse racing arrived in the U.S. in the mid-1600s while America was still a British-occupied territory. It has since evolved into sport, entertainment, and a multi-million-dollar industry. Amongst the biggest American races are the Triple Crown events: the Kentucky Derby, the Preakness Stakes, and the Belmont Stakes.

- *Horsing:* Described as the consensual possession of a human by a spirit, god, or deity, "horsing" gets its name from allowing the possessing spirit to "ride" along in a human body. It is believed that when a person allows themself to be "horsed," they run the risk that the spirit may harm that body or may not want to give it back, even if that was the agreed-upon arrangement. Horsing falls under the "do not try this at home" umbrella.

- *Jousting:* Jousting was Europe's "extreme sport" in the Middle Ages, featuring warriors and horses in battle armor, facing off in pairs at opposite ends of a field, and galloping toward each other with lances down in an attempt to unseat each other. What began as military training on massive, sturdy "heavy horses" evolved into sports and entertainment, particularly for nobility, royalty, and courtiers. Less deadly versions of jousting competitions are a staple of Renaissance fairs in the U.S. and medieval reenactment events.

- *Lady Godiva (Godgifu):* This eleventh-century noblewoman appealed to her husband, Leofric, Lord of Coventry and Earl of Mercia, to lower taxes on his citizens. He agreed, if she would ride naked on horseback through town. She called his bluff but ordered the people to stay inside and not peek at her. Leofric honored his dare and lowered the taxes. Although Lady Godiva was a real person, some scholars believe her famed naked ride is an embellished or purely fictional. Her story is inexorably linked to her horse, without which she'd be just another long-haired naked protester walking down the middle of a medieval cobblestone street.

- *Mari Lwyd:* This Welsh wintertime ritual seems like part Halloween trick-or-treating and part nightmare. Celebrated during the Christmas season on Twelfth Night, a group of men—one operating a horse-like creature while hiding under a white sheet—goes from house to house, singing songs until invited inside. The fearsome horse they carry is created from a real decorated horse skull on a sheet-draped stick. The Mari Lwyd is thought to have originated in pre-Christian Wales and is still practiced today. In Welsh Celtic mythology, horses could cross between this world and the otherworld. Crossing the threshold of a home symbolizes crossing the threshold into the otherworld. The Mari Lwyd horse is white, a nod to the horse ridden by Welsh goddess Rhiannon.

- *Pony Play:* In the kinky BDSM world of "pony play," adults dress up as horses, wearing any combination of bridles, blinders, horse masks, manes, tails, and hooves, and usually tight, sexy, sometimes skimpy outfits, often made of studded black leather. Along with their masters, participants attend pony fetish events and competitions, complete with dressage and jumping. "Ponies" also pull their masters/mistresses in carts and chariots. A pony may only communicate like a real horse—whinnying, tossing the head, stamping the foot—and must obey its master, or suffer the consequences. Pony play is related to the larger animal-play fetish scene, wherein participants are called "furries."

- *Rodeos:* Rodeos give cowboys and cowgirls a chance to show off their roping and riding skills, with competitions including team roping, cutting cattle, and bronco riding. The iconic bucking bronco comes from the rodeo world; however, most aren't bucking naturally. A bucking strap is pulled tightly around a horse's very sensitive flanks, and the horse bucks to relieve the discomfort. When the cowboy has stayed on for the allotted time, another rider comes up alongside, releases the strap, and the bucking stops. The horses are additionally agitated into bucking by constant raking of spurs over their sides and shoulders, which earns extra points for the cowboy, but only causes pain for the horse.

- *Sergeant Reckless:* This little chestnut mare with Mongolian bloodlines served with the Fifth Marine Regiment during the Korean War and was promoted to the title of staff sergeant. Purchased for $250 in Korea from a young boy who needed money for a leg prostheses for his sister after she was injured by a landmine, Reckless was trained to haul ammunition from the supply point to firing sites, almost always on her own. During the five-day Battle of Outpost Vegas in March 1953, she made fifty-one trips through rice paddies and up steep mountains, amid heavy enemy fire. After delivering her load, she then carried wounded soldiers back down to safety.

  Her military decorations include two Purple Hearts, a Good Conduct Medal, Presidential Unit Citation with star, National Defense Service Medal, Korean Service Medal, United Nations Service Medal, Navy Unit Commendation, and Republic of Korea Presidential Unit Citation.

A statue honoring Reckless was unveiled at Camp Pendleton in October 2016.

- *Stanwick Horse Mask:* This piece of Celtic art discovered in the 1840s near Stanwick Camp in North Yorkshire, England, was created in the Bronze Age, and was amongst a cache of more than a hundred horse-related items, such as harnesses and fittings for chariots and carts, illustrating the importance of horses to the people of that time and place. Likely made in the first century CE, this smooth, simple, almost abstract representation of a horse head has been featured in many books on Celtic art and is available in reproductions. It is on display in the British Museum in London. It is nearly four inches long, about two and a half inches wide, and weighs less than a pound.

- *Steeplechasing:* Steeplechasing is a horse race, but with a series of jumps that often look like long, tall hedges. The sport is most popular in Great Britain. The name comes from eighteenth-century Ireland, where church steeples served as landmarks for foxhunters. The races can be as long as four miles, with as many as thirty fences, all taken at full gallop.

  Steeplechasing, along with foxhunting, are the likely roots of cross-country jumping and three-day "eventing," which includes a cross-country segment. Like horse racing, steeplechasers routinely face injury, sometimes lethally so. Thoroughbreds are commonly used in steeplechasing. Amongst the most famous steeplechase events is the Queen's Cup in Great Britain, held every April.

- *Trevi Fountain horses:* Horses are amongst the creatures carved into this fountain in Rome created by Nicola Salvi in 1732. The fountain stands about eighty-five feet high and one hundred and sixty feet wide. The central figure is the Greek titan Oceanus, standing in a chariot pulled by winged sea horses, also known as hippocampi. Legend has it that if you throw a coin with your right hand over your left shoulder into the fountain, you will return to Rome someday.

- *Trojan Horse:* This massive wooden horse was constructed by the Greeks (Spartans) in their efforts to penetrate into the city of Troy. The Trojans accepted the horse as a gift, not realizing that Greek warriors were hiding inside. While the Trojans were asleep, the Greeks climbed out and sacked Troy. The story is told in Homer's *The Odyssey*.

- *Uffington Horse:* The three-thousand-year-old chalk outline of a horse on a hillside near the village of Uffington in Oxfordshire, England, has been there for centuries, tended by locals, keeping it clean and replenishing the chalk. As large as a football field, the symbology of this horse is debated. Some believe it honors the Celtic goddesses Epona or Rhiannon, while others claim it isn't a horse at all, but rather, a mythical dragon slain by St. George while riding a white horse.

- *Vaqueros:* The iconic American cowboy owes most of its lore and reputation to the excellent Mexican horsemen—vaqueros—who brought their knowledge of cattle, cattle driving, and horsemanship to the Texas area in the mid-1800s to teach American cattlemen a thing or two. Most of the familiar trappings of the cowboy, from the ten-gallon hat to the lariat, have vaquero roots. When their work was done, vaqueros would hold friendly competitions to show off their roping and riding skills, which is how rodeos began.

- *White horses:* The white horse appears over and over in historical and mythological lore, across cultures and through generations. It is an archetype for strength, nobility, and purity, which is likely why they were often singled out for ritual sacrifice. For white horses, it's been both a good thing and a bad thing to be lacking melanocytes.

  Henry VIII, Napoleon, and George Washington all rode white horses into battle and had iconic portraits made of them on their brilliant steeds. Christian saints James and George were also depicted riding white horses. Even life itself, according to the Celtic *Origin of the Universe* mythology of Eiocha, began with a white horse.

  The iconic black horse, by contrast, is very large and sexy, sexy, sexy. If a maiden is out walking and spots a black horse near a cherry tree, it may propose to her.

The Horse in Native American Culture

The spiritual relationship between Native Americans and their horses is so similar to the perspective and approach we'll explore later on when working with real horses that it deserves its own spotlight.

The average horse owner views their horse like a car. It's a *thing* from which the owner gains pride and pleasure, particularly when it's new and shiny. Drive it when you want, leave it when you don't. When it starts to sputter a little with age and shows some wear and tear, just junk it or trade it in for a new one.

Contrast this to how Native Americans view the horse: as a brother, a partner, and a spiritual creature with special gifts and teaching. Horses were invaluable to Native Americans as war ponies and required extensive and nuanced training to teach them to become one with their riders. Horses also allowed nomadic Native American tribes more mobility, and vastly improved their success in hunting swift prey like buffalo and deer.

Horses are cherished to this day in Native American culture, and gifting a horse to someone is considered a huge honor, for both the giver and the receiver. Horses are the embodiment of Horse, one of the many Native American spirit animal teachers that offer "medicine." Medicine in Native American culture isn't something you get at the drug store or study in college to become a doctor. Medicine in Native American terms is a powerful energy that heals, transforms, and is used and spoken of in a similar way to the Pagan usage of "magick."

The first New Age-y book I ever read, *Medicine Cards* by Jamie Sams and David Carson, came with a pack of corresponding cards, each featuring a specific spirit animal with its own story to inspire reflection and insight, and also to bring healing. Like all divination cards, the particular message can be reinforcing, or it can be challenging. The stories in *Medicine Cards* were an amalgamation of teachings passed down by elders from many tribes, including Choctaw, Lakota, Seneca, Aztec, Yaqui, Cheyenne, Cherokee, Iroquois, and Maya.

Horse is included on those medicine cards and honored as a creature so powerful and transformative, its contribution to human life is akin to the use of fire. Horse is also viewed in various aspects that are linked to positions on the Medicine Wheel, which has a correlation to the four elements ("directions" on the Medicine Wheel) and a resemblance to the solar cross, which we'll discuss in chapter 4. Horse's aspects are Black Stallion, Yellow Stallion, Red Stallion, and White Stallion, each linked to the same color on the Medicine Wheel.

Horses Arrive in the "New World"

Spanish explorer Hernando Cortés is credited for reintroducing horses to North and South America when he arrived in Mexico in 1519. Cortés, and the

Spanish explorers who came after him, discovered that horses were effective tools for frightening and subduing indigenous people because they had never seen horses before, let alone carrying a rider. They viewed this new "beast" as one creature This overwhelming new "creature" also introduced indigenous people to guns, which the riders carried.

As the Spaniards set out to conquer the indigenous people, they enslaved many, and in doing so, introduced horses and horsemanship to them. The indigenous people were entranced with this new creature and realized it could assist them in hunting and in pulling much larger loads than the dogs they used for these purposes. The translation of one of the first Native American words for "horse" was "elk-dog" the only frame of reference they had for an animal that performed these difficult tasks.

The Apache are credited as the first Native American tribe to take horses from Spanish ranches near Santa Fe, New Mexico, and therein, a partnership was formed, particularly amongst the Plateau and Plains tribes. The Comanche were also amongst the first tribes to acquire horses, and became known as fearsome, highly skilled opponents.[12] As horses became part of the indigenous culture, stealing them from enemies—and each other—became a regular endeavor. A seasoned war pony was so valuable, warriors often kept them inside their tipis to keep them from being stolen.

Like nearly every human culture on the planet, the introduction of horses to Native American life was a quantum leap in their advancement. Horses made indigenous Americans stronger, faster, and entirely more mobile. Native Americans amassed huge herds of horses through theft (considered a noble skill) and breeding. They also did some selective breeding to produce the best war ponies. The Nez Perce tribe, for example, is credited with developing the spotted Appaloosa breed.

Crushing a People

As the brand-new country called the United States of America began forming and settlers and pioneers pushed westward into Native American territories, conflicts arose. Native American warriors became feared opponents, and the U.S. government ultimately set out to annihilate all indigenous people via the mass slaughtering of buffalo, upon which these people depended for their very

12. Patent, *The Horse and the Plains Indians: A Powerful Partnership.*

existence. The U.S. government also slaughtered their horses, shooting them en masse before their eyes—soul-crushing to a people who so prized their horses.

After many bloody battles, the American government succeeded in crushing indigenous populations, herding them onto unfarmable reservations and an impoverished existence, but it didn't succeed in crushing their relationship with horses. Little by little, horses made it onto the reservations and their numbers grew.

Horses are still cherished and revered by Native Americans, and are a central figure in celebrations or "powwows," which are social gatherings and celebrations between tribes, such as the four-day Crow Fair Celebration Powwow and Rodeo, held in Montana.

To get a little taste of the Native American way of honoring horses through song, dance, and attire, look up "Native American Horse Dance" to see some current celebrations of horses in various indigenous cultures. The dances are simply mesmerizing.

Native Americans are amongst the most skillful of all equestrians, able to mount and dismount running horses, slide down a running horse's side to use bows and arrows or guns, and ride with only the simplest of saddles or often bareback, using only a rope looped and tied through a horse's mouth as a bridle. Native Americans learned to guide and control their horses using only their legs, seat, and intention, so that their hands were free for hunting or battle. These skills are often demonstrated at Native American riding competitions.

The Markings Have Meaning

The iconic Native American war pony is often pictured with a variety of painted markings that have specific meanings, often relating to battle. In his book *Horse, Follow Closely: Native American Horsemanship,* expert horseman GaWaNi Pony Boy explains that the markings were drawn with "special symbolic medicine paints to intimidate the enemy, give their horses strength and courage in battle, and advertise the achievements of both horse and rider."[13] The paints were made from natural pigments and berries, mixed with water or animal fat.

13. Pony Boy, *Horse, Follow Closely—Native American Horsemanship,* 16–19.

A horse bearing this "war paint" signified prowess in battle, and these symbols were recognized by all Native American horse culture tribes:

- *Circle around the eye:* better vision for the horse.
- *Hail marks:* made famous by Crazy Horse, these gave the horse and rider the "strength and fury of a great hailstorm."
- *Handprints:* one for each enemy killed by the rider in hand-to-hand combat.
- *Keyhole-shaped design:* a blessing and sign of protection when drawn by a Medicine Man or spiritual leader.
- *Lightning bolts (zigzags) on the legs:* superior speed for that horse.
- *Stacked horizontal lines:* a way to "count coup," which dishonored an enemy by touching him and humiliating him rather than killing him. It was believed that touching an opponent siphoned off some of his soul, as well as strength, energy, and courage, motivating warriors to count coup rather than kill an enemy whenever possible.
- *Upside-down horseshoe:* the number of raids in which the rider participated.

Pony Boy says Native Americans also placed other symbols on their horses to communicate a variety of things, such as weaving a lock of the rider's hair into the mane of his horse so that their spirits could become one, or feathers from hawks, eagles, or falcons to give the horse the speed and agility of that bird.

Horses in Toys and Games

Children have an entire world of horses all their own, with which they can indulge their horsey dreams and wishes through toys and play, and are particularly treasured by those who don't have access to real horses. Here are some Horsey Girl toy staples:

- *Breyer horse models:* These plastic horses, which come in every color, breed, shape, and pose imaginable, are to Horsey Girls what Barbie dolls are to everyone else. Today they also come in fantasy creatures, like unicorns and Pegasus, as well as blank models that can be custom painted. My Barbies are long gone, but I still have all my Breyer horses.

- *Drugstore ponies:* These coin-operated kiddie rides were invented in the 1930s and were often stationed outside drugstores and grocery stores. The kiddie rides slowly disappeared in the 1980s, and it's rare to see a drugstore pony anymore. Vintage drugstore ponies are now collectors' items.

- *Hobbyhorse:* Also known as a stick horse, this is basically a broomstick with a horse or pony head on it and usually a little bridle and reins. Hobbyhorses go back as far as the Middle Ages and lasted through the centuries as a popular children's toy until the 1960s, when the toy industry exploded to cater to the young baby boomers who preferred Slinkies and Lawn Darts to silly horse heads on sticks.

- *HORSE basketball:* In this basketball court game, spelling out the word "H-O-R-S-E" is the goal. Players take turns shooting for the basket from various locations, with various added challenges, like shooting with one hand. When a player misses a shot, they get a letter from the word "HORSE," and when the whole word is spelled out, that player must sit down. The last one standing wins the game.

- *My Horse:* Similar to the Farmville craze of years past, "My Horse," is a smartphone and tablet app. In the game, you design a horse for yourself, which you care for, feed, and train. You can ride your virtual horse in competitions and interact with other horse owners. As is the case with many apps, you can only do so much before having to whip out the credit card and purchase food and necessities for your horse, which isn't so different from real life.

- *Rocking horse:* Rocking horses started appearing in the 1600s. The earliest were carved wooden horses on curved wooden rockers. Over the years, rocking horse designs became more elaborate and found their niche amongst collectors. Carved horses on wheels preceded rocking horses, going back as far as 500 BCE, keeping company with other toy horses of ancient Egypt, Greece, and Rome, made of terra cotta clay.

- *Star Stable:* This online video game and smartphone app allows players to go on treks and tackle a variety of challenges. Players care for and train their virtual horses, solve quests and mysteries, and ride into various fantastical worlds. The horses are mythical Jorvik Wild Horses that have

"Pandoric magic," which creates beautiful, magical coat colors that lose their color when the horses are captured and stabled near humans.

- *Thunderbolt:* In the late 1960s, the twelve-inch action figure known as Johnny West appeared on the toy scene, going toe to toe with G.I. Joe. Unlike the classic unbendable and rather easily breakable Breyer horse models, Johnny's horse Thunderbolt had bendable legs just like his plastic partner. Johnny's equally bendable girlfriend, Jane West, had one advantage over Barbie dolls: I didn't have to crack her legs at the hip to let her ride my Breyer horses.

- *Wonder Horse:* This early 1960s fiberglass horse was the next level of rocking horse, and a staple of baby boomer childhoods. If you ever had blood blisters from your fingers getting pinched in the tight springs that held the horse to its frame, you're probably a boomer. Vintage Wonder Horses can still be found on eBay, allowing today's children to experience vintage injuries from the decidedly unsafe but extremely fun vintage toys of the 1960s.

Horses in Literature and Entertainment

Horses have long been a favorite topic of writers and screenwriters alike, and have captivated our imaginations in countless books and novels, entertained us in their brave and sometimes whimsical movie and television roles, and served as key entertainment attractions at circuses, fairs, and amusement parks. Here are a few:

- *Black Beauty:* This classic novel by Anna Sewell is told entirely from the perspective of a beautiful black horse that changes hands many times, suffering mightily at the hands of humans, and offering commentary and insight on how a horse might like to be treated. One of the best-selling books of all time, *Black Beauty* teaches the importance of treating animals with gentleness, kindness, and dignity.

- *The Black Stallion:* The series of books by Walter Farley feature a black Arabian stallion known simply as "The Black," and his loyal owner, Alec Ramsey. The two get into all sorts of situations and adventures. I was so obsessed with these books in the third grade that I snuck every one from the school library and hid them under my bed. Don't worry, my mother found them and made me return them.

- *Boxer:* In George Orwell's allegory *Animal Farm*, Boxer was the workhorse who obeyed the ruling pigs, and through his brute strength, loyalty, and tenacity, did the bulk of the hard work on the farm. When he fell short, his response was always, "I will work harder." Although the main muscle behind the farm, Boxer is portrayed as an obedient but stupid animal, and when injured, the pigs quickly turn him over to the rendering plant. Horses don't fare well in Orwell's book. The other horse, Mollie, is vain and pleasure-seeking, and ditches Animal Farm for humans who will put ribbons in her hair and give her sugar cubes.

- *Carousel (Merry-Go-Round) horses:* Colorful, musical carousels got their start in Europe in the late eighteenth century and appeared in America in 1799 in Salem, Massachusetts. The original horses were made of wood, but are now made mostly of fiberglass. The modern ones are also brightly painted, have various decorations and postures, and are mounted on a spinning circular platform, with bright, cheerful calliope-style music.

- *Charlie Horse:* Puppeteer Shari Lewis introduced the rather obnoxious little Charlie Horse along with his puppet friends Lamb Chop and Hush Puppy on her 1960s television program *The Shari Lewis Show*. Charlie Horse is best known for singing *The Song That Doesn't End* at the end of each segment of *Lamb Chop's Play-Along*, to the extreme frustration of Shari and anyone else who has ever heard it. If you've never heard this song, do *not* go listen to it. You have been warned.

- *Circus horses:* In many traveling circuses, trained horses were a central feature, particularly teams of white horses with tall, colorful feathers on their heads, performing synchronized routines. Other circus horses were wide-backed draft horse breeds, like Percherons, upon which beautiful, lithe women performed gymnastic tricks while the horse trotted or cantered around the circus ring. Some circus horses even jumped from platforms into pools.

- *Direhorse (Pa'li):* These six-legged elephant-sized horse-creatures were created by master film producer James Cameron and appear in the 2009 film *Avatar*. Called "pa'li" by the Na'vi, the indigenous people of the mythical planet Pandora, a rider would mingle the fibers at the end of their very long ponytails with similar fibers on the long antennae of the pa'li to instantly bond and ride together as one.

- *Equestria Girls:* An offshoot of the *My Little Pony* toys and cartoons, these "ponies" take on human form and pass through a mirror into a parallel world, where they attend Canterlot High School, dealing with a variety of teen drama and lots of mean girls. Just like the *My Little Pony* toys and TV series, *Equestria Girls* also targets preteens.

- *Flicka:* The 1950s television series *My Friend Flicka* was based upon a series of books by Mary O'Hara, featuring the adventures of young Ken McLaughlin and his horse, Flicka, on the Goose Bar Ranch in Montana in the early 1900s.

- *Hollywood horses:* From starring roles to equine extras, horses have been a Hollywood staple. In scores of mounted battle scenes and westerns churned out over the decades, humans always got top billing, but horses did the real grunt work, and it was often deadly. In the filming of the chariot race in the 1920s movie *Ben-Hur*, more than a hundred horses died.

  To make it look like a running horse was felled by gunshot, a wire was strung to one of the horse's front fetlocks as it galloped away in a battle scene. When the horse hit the end of the wire, its forelegs were jerked out from under it, smashing the horse to the ground. The horse was usually severely injured or required euthanasia due to the injuries. Horses jumping from tall cliffs or platforms often met the same fate. In 1988, the American Humane Association created a list of guidelines on the treatment of animals used in film and television production, raising awareness about this issue and prompting the familiar disclaimer in the credits noting that, "no animals were harmed in the making of this film."

- *Horse of a Different Color:* When Dorothy and her pals get into a carriage as they enter Emerald City in *The Wizard of Oz*, the white horse drawing that carriage turns green, blue, orange, red, yellow, and purple as it prances along. A different horse was used for each color change, each covered in non-toxic, flavored powdered gelatin, like lemon, cherry, and grape.

- *Mister Ed:* The loquacious palomino, Mister Ed, was a 1960s television star on a show of the same name who created all sorts of hijinks with his rather doofy owner, Wilber Post. Wilber was the only one who could hear Mister Ed speak, with the exceptions of those at the other end of his many prank phone calls—he dialed the phone with his lips. Mister Ed was played by an American Saddlebred-Arabian gelding named Bamboo Harvester, and voiced by Western film star Allan Lane.

- *Misty of Chincoteague*: This iconic children's novel by Marguerite Henry features the story of brother and sister Paul and Maurine Beebe, who save their money to buy a wild Chincoteague pony named Misty. The story was based on a real Chincoteague pony named Misty, that lived on the real Beebe Ranch on Chincoteague Island, Virginia. Sadly, the Beebe ranch burned down in 2019.

- *My Little Pony:* First introduced in the 1980s as "My Pretty Pony," this colorful plastic pony had a mane and tail that could be brushed. It morphed into the *My Little Pony* franchise of toys, cartoons, and movies. All of the ponies had different names and different magical powers. The sparkly ponies were blatantly aimed at little girls; however, some boys—Bronies, who are male teens and young adults who embrace *My Little Pony's* innocence and sparkle—love them too.

- *Pendragon:* Also known as Penn, after this old Hanoverian gelding's glory days in the show ring were over, he was adopted by a loving woman, who ultimately gave him to another woman, whose life he transformed. His story is told in her book *The Elements of Horse Spirit: The Magical Bond Between Humans and Horses.* The name comes the character Uther Pendragon, the powerful warrior king and father of King Arthur, from the book *The Mists of Avalon* by Marion Zimmer Bradley.

- *Pokey:* This bendable little red clay horse was the sidekick of the equally bendable and rather bizarrely shaped green clay Gumby. The characters on the 1960s claymation children's program *The Gumby Show* became a series of beloved classic bendable rubber toys, which are still produced today.

- *The Red Pony:* This John Steinbeck novel is a four-part story about a young boy, Jody, whose father gives him a pony that soon falls ill. His breathing becomes so strained, Jody's father punches a hole in its windpipe so it won't suffocate. Jody stays by the pony to keep the wound clear; however, when he falls asleep, the pony escapes. Jody sets out to find him and follows some buzzards, discovering his dead pony as a buzzard eats its eye. He reacts with fury and beats the buzzard to death. (Holes in windpipes and eye-eating buzzards totally traumatized *this* little Horsey Girl.)

- *Silver:* "Hi ho, Silver, and away we go!" was the familiar cry of the Lone Ranger, astride his trusty iconic white steed, Silver, in the 1930s radio series and movies, and on the television series of the same name in the 1940s and 1950s.

- *Trigger:* This golden palomino was the favored iconic horse of kindly cowboy Roy Rogers of the 1940s and 1950s, and inspired an array of toy entertainment palominos of the era. He was played by a crossbred palomino, who was named Golden Cloud in real life. Rogers was so attached to Golden Cloud that when the horse died at age 33, Rogers had Golden Cloud's body preserved and put on display in the Roy Rogers Museum, located in Branson, Missouri.

Horses in Language

Horses were central to humanity across time and cultures because they were the key to survival. Life without them meant hardship. Horses were our cars, pickup trucks, vans, tractors, and trains, and were the standard by which power was measured—a standard still used today. Engines in everything from cars to chainsaws are still measured in horsepower today—even though they run on gas instead of grass.

Horses were our only frame of reference when new forms of transportation appeared. When the steam locomotive rolled out in the early 1800s, it was called the "iron horse." When the car debuted in the late 1800s, it was the "horseless carriage." The invention of train and car, along with the Industrial Revolution in the late 1880s to 1890s in both Europe and the United States, marked the beginning of the end for our horse-centric world. The ascent of the combustion engine, as well as the increasing popularity of travel and transportation of goods by train in the beginning of the twentieth century marked the decline of horses being used for transportation and practical purposes.

Although machines edged out horses to do our most laborious work, horses are so etched in human culture that horse-related sayings and terms are sprinkled throughout our language. The horse has inspired many of our most familiar sayings:

- *Back in the saddle:* getting back to something after a long absence.
- *Bunching up in the halter:* about to pull away because of something frightening or unpleasant.
- *Charley horse:* a muscle cramp, usually in the calf or thigh.
- *Chomping at the bit:* can't wait to get going.
- *Closing the barn door after the horses have escaped:* attempting to solve a problem when it's too late.
- *Clotheshorse:* someone who looks great in a variety of clothing styles.
- *Dark horse:* an unlikely choice.
- *Don't change horses in midstream:* changing plans or strategies in the middle of a task will make everything more difficult.
- *Don't look a gift horse in the mouth:* don't question or criticize something given to you for free; if you do, you might not like what you find.
- *Get off your high horse:* quit being so uppity.
- *Hold your horses:* stop right there.
- *Horse feathers:* nonsense.
- *Horse laugh:* a huge belly laugh.
- *Horse of a different color:* something completely unusual or novel.
- *Horse sense:* common sense.
- *Horse trader:* a shifty person, often in sales, whose word can't be trusted.
- *Horsing around:* playing or roughhousing a little too vigorously.
- *Hungry as a horse:* starving.
- *I could eat a horse:* really famished.
- *In the home stretch:* in the final phase of a long, difficult project or effort.
- *Long shot:* someone or something unlikely to win or prevail.
- *Nightmare:* a terrifying bad dream.
- *No horse in the race:* not having an issue pertinent to the argument or situation.
- *One horse town:* small, podunk town with few businesses or residents.

- *Piss like a racehorse:* really, really, really gotta go.
- *Put out to pasture:* retired.
- *Putting the horse before the cart:* doing things backwards.
- *Rode hard and put away wet:* overly exhausted, aching, and unkempt.
- *Straight from the horse's mouth:* information from the genuine source.
- *Trojan horse:* something snuck in to destroy everything around it once inside; also, a computer virus.
- *Wild horses couldn't drag me away:* nothing could make me leave.
- *Work like a horse:* work to the point of exhaustion.
- *You can lead a horse to water but you can't make it drink:* you can offer something to someone, but they aren't obliged to accept it.

Come to think of it, all these sayings have a huge streak of Horse Sense!

Chapter 3

HORSES IN
MYTHOLOGY AND RELIGION

I n this chapter, we'll explore some of the gods, goddesses, and deities associated with horses over the centuries and across cultures, as well as the mythical, magical horses and horse-like creatures that have occupied our fantasies
ever since the stories of their amazing feats and abilities were told around the
campfires of our ancient ancestors.

Is It Accurate?

By the time the oral myths and stories were actually written down, there was
plenty of opportunity for human massaging of the details. In Juliette Wood's
contribution to the anthology *The Horse in Celtic Culture—Medieval Welsh Perspectives*, she notes that people are really attached to their own versions of stories: "Myth has become misunderstood through time, although no satisfactory
mechanism for this has been proposed. Rather, it is assumed that the elements
which match expectations of Celtic myths are genuine survivals and anything
else is a corruption or later intrusion."[14] So, we shouldn't invest too much energy in the purity of any story from antiquity, regardless of the topic. Most mythology, arguably all of it, first existed in the form of oral storytelling, passed
through generations until recorded in writing, often not even in the same culture from whence the story began.

If you've ever played the game "Telephone," whispering a message down a
line of children and howling at the final result, you know how mangled a story
can become when passed along orally. Our myths have not only been passed

---

14. Davies and Jones, *The Horse in Celtic Culture: Medieval Welsh Perspectives*.

between people, they've also been translated into different languages, across centuries. Playing "Telephone" would seem highly accurate by comparison. It's impossible to know the absolute pure version of any mythology that begins from an oral story predating the written word, in a different culture, and a different language. But we can draw inspiration and insight from these stories and mythologies, regardless of their rank on the validity or purity scale.

Wood also notes that people will believe their own version of a story rather than any other. We're very attached to our own version of the myths and stories we love, sometimes to the exclusion of all variations. Complicating the matter further is that there may be several versions of stories or mythology for the same character. For our purposes, we'll focus upon the versions that enhance our appreciation and understanding of Horse.

The Horse Goddesses

If you do a search of the term "horse goddess," three names always pop up: Epona, Rhiannon, and Macha. All are classically associated with horses, and each with her own mythology.

Eiocha and Epona

Our exploration of horse goddesses begins with Epona, whose name was translated from Gaulish into Latin by the Romans as the "Great Mare" or the "Divine Mare." Epona makes her first appearance—in fact, before pretty much everything else—in the Celtic *Origin of the Universe* creation story, which begins when time itself doesn't exist, nor do gods or humans. There is only land and sea.

A white mare made of sea foam emerges where the sea meets the land. Her name is Eiocha. (Hit pause right there: In this mythos, human life begins with a horse!) Eiocha rises from the sea to walk on land and eats some seeds from an oak tree, which impregnate her. In this Celtic creation myth, Eiocha then gives birth to the first Celtic god, Cernunnos.

Having no other options, Cernunnos mates with Eiocha, and from their union came the gods Maponos, Tauranis, Teutates, and Epona. Eiocha eventually tires of being a land creature and returns to the sea, whereupon she transforms into the goddess of the deep water, Tethra. Meanwhile, Cernunnos and his offspring with Eiocha set about to create trees, animals, birds, thunderbolts, and weapons. But Epona "made only the horse, mare and stallion alike, in remembrance of Eiocha, who was no more." The story introduces some of the original Celtic gods and goddesses, including the Dagda and his daughter with the Morrigan, Brigid.[15]

An article on the Order of Bards, Ovates and Druids website attributes Epona's birth to an entirely different set of circumstances (attributed, however, to a much later Greek writer, Agesilaos). In this version of Epona's creation, she was birthed by a mare, but fathered by a man, Phoulonios Stellos, who disliked women so intensely, he preferred to mate instead with a mare. After he did, the mare gave birth to a human girl and named her Epona.

The article notes, "The naming of Epona by her mother implies that the mare may have had a divine nature herself, and that Epona followed on in some way from an earlier Horse Goddess." It also notes that the lore of Epona was venerated amongst Gaulic Celts, whose original stories were lost entirely, while the myths of the British Celts passed through the lens of early Christian monks, opening up the possibility that there may have been some tinkering with the details. [16]

The two versions contradict each other, but they agree on this point: Epona's mother was a horse. We'll stick to the Celtic version because the imagery of white horses, and white horses rising from the sea, is a theme that comes up again and again in various mythologies—there seems to be something significant about the white horse in our collective unconscious.

Respected by Rome

In *Epona: Hidden Goddess of the Celts*, author MacKenzie Cook says that Epona predates the mythology of Rhiannon and Macha, and that not only was she venerated by the Gauls, but also by the Romans, who employed horses as a key weapon in their quest to expand their empire.

Epona is depicted in relief sculpture as early as the first century CE in various European locations, riding side-saddle, semi-clad and sometimes nude, on the back of a mare, often with foals nearby, and sometimes feeding them, signifying fertile and well-fed horses. She is also shown seated or standing between two or more horses, and in each case, she and the horses seem quite peaceful and content. A feistier image of her appears on coins exchanged by the Celts,

---

15. The Celtic Religion, "Origins of the Universe."
16. The Order of the Bards and Druids, "Epona."

spanning the early second to late fourth century, possibly symbolizing the Gauls' efforts to survive the crush of Roman dominance. Cook suggests that on these coins, Epona symbolized a "divine female 'warrior' astride her horse, and the indomitability of the Celtic Spirit symbolized by a raised fist."

The Roman-Gaul clash was epic. When the Roman empire pushed up against the Gauls, the Gauls pushed back, sacking Rome in 390 BCE. Rome ultimately defeated the Gauls under Julius Caesar in the Gallic Wars beginning in 58 BCE. Caesar then pushed onward into Britain, rolling through many Celtic territories. The Romans also rolled over many Celtic gods and goddesses, changing them to Roman versions, but not Epona. Although Epona was a Celtic goddess, the Romans viewed her as a skilled equestrian and protector of mounted warriors and cavalry, and embraced her. Rome declared an annual festival in her honor every December 18. Depictions of Epona can be found alongside those of classic Roman gods and goddesses.

Cook additionally asserts that Epona was a sovereignty and fertility goddess: "Symbolically, images of Epona astride her horse carry a rich array of meaning—from intimacy and exhilaration, exultation or ecstasy to freedom. The earlier coin-imagery hints not only at victory in battle but at a deeper pagan eroticism grounded in the natural power and flowing rhythm of the horse's movement, and in the intimacy of the physical connection between horse and rider—freely and unashamedly expressed in the rider's spontaneous exultation."

For women, riding astride a horse was considered indecent in many ancient and medieval cultures, where proper etiquette dictated that women should ride sidesaddle so as not to rupture their hymens, thereby protecting their virginity—and their value as potential wives. Some women, such as Joan of Arc and Catherine the Great, refused to cooperate with this patriarchal oppression, and proudly rode astride. The pressure to keep women riding sidesaddle to protect their virtue continued on up into the nineteenth century.

So connected with horses was Epona that Cook says they are "absolutely fundamental to Epona's identity and nature, and it was the only symbol invariably used in all her artwork. She was so strongly associated with horses in fact, that even the image of a mare and foal on their own could represent her."[17]

---

17. Cook, *Epona: Hidden Goddess of the Celts*, 625–823, 1119.

Epona inspires a deep love of horses first and foremost, horsemanship, horse breeding and care, a sense of oneness with a horse, and even fertility, courage, and sovereignty. And, she didn't need no stinkin' sidesaddle. Surely, Epona's spirit lives on in every Horsey Girl who thinks about, talks about, and lusts after horses.

Rhiannon

The Welsh queen Rhiannon seems to be the goddess most widely declared a "horse goddess." Her connection to horses is drawn from the mysterious white mare upon which she rode and the humiliating horse-like punishment she suffered for a crime she didn't commit. Her story was written in a medieval Welsh manuscript from around 1350, *The Four Branches of the Mabinogi*. The authorship of the epic prose is unclear, but stands in company with the epic work *Beowulf* (also of unknown authorship), as well as *The Iliad* and *The Odyssey*, attributed to the epic Greek poet Homer (authorship now disputed).

Wood, in *The Horse in Celtic Culture—Medieval Welsh Perspectives*, makes the case that Rhiannon's story may have some roots in the Gaulish accounts of Epona, prior to their appearance in *The Four Branches of the Mabinogi*. Wood notes that the story of Rhiannon may have originated from the story of another great Celtic queen, Rigantona, also associated with horses and with some similarities to Epona, and from whose name "Rhiannon" may actually have been derived.

In her book *Pagan Portals—Rhiannon: Divine Queen of the Celtic Britons*, author Jhenah Telyndru retells Rhiannon's story. She appears as a beautiful, golden-haired, strong-willed, mysterious woman dressed in silk, and emerges from a magical mound of earth, riding on a stunning white horse in the countryside. She is spotted by Pwyll, the prince of the Welsh kingdom of Dyfed, who is smitten with her and sends his men after her, but they're unable to catch up with her even though the horse appears only to be walking. Pwyll returns the next day with his own horse and manages to get close enough to call out to Rhiannon. She stops, introduces herself, and explains that she is betrothed to another, but would much prefer Pwyll.

Rhiannon, through her own magical workings, escapes the betrothal and marries Pwyll, becoming queen of Dyfed. After three years of marriage, she finally gives birth, but her newborn son disappears the same night he is born.

While Rhiannon is sleeping, the six nursemaids charged with watching over the baby fall asleep and discover him missing when they wake. To keep from being blamed, they kill the puppies of the house's hunting dogs, smear their blood on sleeping Rhiannon's face, and spread their bones around her. This "evidence" results in Rhiannon being accused of both infanticide and cannibalism. Her penance is to sit at the mounting block at the castle gate for seven years, confessing this story to passersby, and offering to carry them to court on her back—like a horse.

The missing infant, meanwhile, mysteriously turns up at the house of Teyrnon Twrf Lliant, lord of a nearby town. He is vexed because every time his fine white mare births a foal, it disappears without a trace on the same night. The night that Rhiannon gives birth, Teyrnon's mare is about to foal, and he brings the mare into his house to keep watch. When a monster's arm reaches in to grab the newborn foal in the middle of the night, Teyrnon slashes its arm off and bolts out the door to chase it, but realizing that he left his front door wide open, he turns back. Upon returning, he finds an infant. Teyrnon and his wife name the child Gwri Wallt Euryn (Blooming Golden Hair), who matures very quickly and is intensely drawn to horses.

When Gwri is still a toddler, Teyrnon learns of Rhiannon's story. He and his wife decide to make things right and return Gwri to his rightful mother and father. They travel to the castle in Dyfed, finding Rhiannon still stationed at the mounting block, offering to carry passersby to the courthouse. She is relieved to discover that her child is alive and renames him Pryderi. Exonerated, Rhiannon regains her status as Divine Queen.

After Pryderi is grown, Rhiannon suffers further horse-related punishment after going to rescue him after he accidentally gets stuck in the otherworld, and must wear a horse's yoke until she and Pryderi are rescued of this fate. Eventually, they are, and Rhiannon is finally restored to honor, a queen of faerie blood and magical abilities, able to travel back and forth between this world and the otherworld upon a mystical threshold-crossing steed, serving as a "psychopomp," which guides recently deceased souls to the afterlife.

Rhiannon's mythology—a painful fall from grace, accused of a heinous crime she didn't commit, and a subsequent punishment of public humiliation and serving as a beast of burden, ultimately vindicated and her honor and position restored, is a testament to female endurance. But what about her *horse*—

a magical horse that can outrun both men and horses while only walking, and can pass back and forth between this world and the otherworld? Now *that* is truly intriguing. Sadly, the horse's name has been lost to time, which Telyndru confirmed to me.

It's long past time: Rhiannon's horse deserves a rightful place of its own amongst our exploration of horse-related mythologies. Since this mysterious white mare's name has slipped through the cracks of history, I'll offer this one: Gaseg Wen (or Gaseg Gwyn), which simply means "white mare" in modern Welsh. With either translation, the two words run together sound essentially the same: Gasegwen or Gaseggwyn. The latter one looks too much like "gas egg," so I'm going with the former.

Gaseg Wen. Gwen for short. Gwennie for a nickname.

I like it.

You read it here first!

Macha

There are several incarnations of Macha associated with the revered and formidable Celtic goddess, the Morrigan. The Macha we're looking for is her final incarnation, in which she becomes the wife of a Welsh farmer, Cruinniuc.

As told by Philip Freeman in "The Terrible Curse of Macha," this ancient tale begins with a lonely and rather dimwitted widower named Cruinniuc and his sons, who lived on a farm in Ulster. A beautiful young woman named Macha comes walking along one day, enters his home, and starts doing the household chores. When night comes, she climbs into Cruinniuc's bed, they make love, and she becomes pregnant. Macha remains at Cruinniuc's home, taking care of him and his sons, and "there was never a lack of food, clothing, or anything else they needed," which I interpret as Macha becoming a very dutiful housewife. Yay.

One day, a great festival organized by Conchobar, the King of Ulster, featured a horse race, in which no challengers are believed capable of beating the king's horses. Cruinniuc sets off to the festival and Macha, who is nine months pregnant, chooses to stay back, warning her husband not to "boast or say anything foolish." Her husband ignores her and proceeds to do both by telling Conchobar that Macha can outrun any horse, including the king's horses. Conchobar, publicly slighted by this boast, demands that Cruinniuc put his Macha where his mouth is, and orders her to be brought to the horse race. Macha, with her swollen, pregnant belly, is brought before the king. She pleads mercy, as she is going into labor, but is denied.

The race begins, and the swift Macha runs alongside the king's chariot and crosses the finish line ahead of his horses, whereupon she falls to the ground screaming in labor pains and gives birth to twins. As she screams, she curses Conchobar and his men, proclaiming that from that moment forward, whenever the king and his warriors faced grave danger, they would also fall to the ground in terrible labor pains and be unable to fight. The curse sticks.

Freeman says the moral of this story is about what happens when men refuse to listen to and honor women, take them for granted, and are punished for their lack of sympathy for pregnant women.[18]

Brigid

While the mythology of Eiocha and Epona are indisputably directly about horses, and the stories of Rhiannon and Macha are clearly linked to horses, all fall short of illuminating Horse—the metaphysical kind. It's wonderful that we have horse goddesses, but we need a Horse goddess—one who captures that fiery, powerful, multifaceted, multitalented Horse energy. I'd argue that we find that in the Celtic goddess Brigid. After all, according to that Celtic creation story, Brigid is a descendent of Eiocha herself! Horses are in her bloodline!

True, Brigid (also Brigit, Brighid, Bride, and St. Brigid after the Christians arrived) is not typically associated with horses. Nearly everything but, it seems. Her classic associations are fire, forging, light, poetry, music, fertility, the healing arts, agriculture, and farm animals, particularly cows and sheep. She is celebrated on the Pagan holiday Imbolc (February 1 or 2), and in Kildare, Ireland, on St. Brigid's Day (February 1) where a sculpture was created to hold her flame, burning as a beacon of hope, justice, and peace for Ireland.

Now, wait just a hoof-pickin' moment.

Aren't horses also farm animals? And very much associated with agriculture? Horses, along with oxen, were used to till the ground—particularly large tracts of land. Once the crop was harvested, both were used to transport large amounts of those crops by cart to the marketplace.

---

18. Freeman, "The Terrible Curse of Macha."

That horses are excluded in Brigid's mythology is curious. Is it because "horse as tool" was so routine and ordinary that horses weren't worth mentioning? Is it because horses were associated with Roman conquest, and therefore the overlay of the Catholic Saint Brigid of Kildare over the Celtic Goddess Brigid under Roman rule? Or could it simply be that all the horses belonged to Epona, and she wasn't sharing? We'll have to take our "leap of imagination" and draw lines of our own.

One Tough Goddess

Consider Brigid's association with the forge and fire. What do we create on a forge? Things hammered out of red-hot iron on an anvil. What is one of the most commonly made items on forges? Horseshoes. In addition to "farrier," what is another word for a person who makes horseshoes on a forge? A blacksmith. Which goddess is associated with blacksmithing? Brigid. There—we went full circle. Okay, horseshoes weren't invented until about 400 BCE in Etruria, but work with me here.

Blacksmiths are rugged, powerful, determined individuals. Making horseshoes is tough work, and actually putting them on the horse can be even tougher. Besides the physical demand of just pounding out the red-hot shoes with a hammer and anvil alongside a blazing forge fire, horses are sometimes not cooperative with the horseshoeing process. Nailing shoes onto a horse isn't like nailing them onto a board. Boards don't move. Horses who don't like getting shoed may bite, kick, rear, and jerk their legs away.

Blacksmithing isn't for wimps. You must be incredibly powerful to sling that hammer against the iron on the anvil, over and over. Take a hammer and bang it against your driveway to get a feel of the impact on your hand and wrist. Imagine doing that over and over for hours. To forge horseshoes or anything else, Brigid was powerful enough to cross into an occupational realm traditionally belonging to men. She's as tough as they are, and then some. She's my kind of goddess!

A Goddess of Many Talents

Brigid is a complex and gifted powerhouse, bright and bold. She is associated with fire itself, be it actual fire in her forge or firing up creativity in everything from music to poetry. In the ancient Celtic world, poetry was amongst the methods used for oral storytelling—history keeping—through the generations, so Brigid is therefore also a goddess of creative writing, history, and knowledge. Besides her physical strength, and inspirational and creative nature, Brigid stands in company with the great Mother Goddesses, such as Egyptian goddess Isis and Hindu goddess Parvati, as a divine vessel of creation itself.

Her association with Imbolc also symbolizes hope in dark times. Imbolc, which means "sheep's milk," is celebrated around the time sheep are getting ready to give birth, and their udders fill with milk. This holiday comes right about when you can detect that the days are just starting to get a little longer in the Northern Hemisphere, providing reassurance that the dark, cold winter will soon pass, and spring and warmer times aren't far off. In other words, Brigid's Pagan holiday is all about hope: be patient—it won't always be this way. Brighter times are ahead. Sometimes hope is the only thing that keeps us going. It's the precursor of courage, and courage is one of Horse's great strengths.

A "Horse" Goddess

Brigid is powerful, multitalented, and exceedingly versatile—what a perfect fit for horses, and Horse. While Epona, Rhiannon, and Macha are the classic horse goddesses, Brigid is a Horse goddess. Like Horse, she's up to any challenge or task, can easily switch from one to the other, and is seemingly limitless in her range of talents and abilities. And she is as strong as a horse!

Deities and Horses

In addition to Eiocha, Epona, Rhiannon, and Macha, and our newly discovered Horse goddess Brigid, here are more deities and mythological figures classically associated with horses:

- *Áine:* ancient Irish goddess of summer, sovereignty, love, fertility, healing and the moon. She and her two sisters, Aoife and Griane, rode their horses from underground "sidhes" when the moon was full and played in the lake called Lough Gur. They are the daughters of Manannán mac Lir and the fairy queen Fand, all of the Tuatha de Danaan, the people of the Goddess Danu—a magical pre-Christian Gaelic race. Red mares are amongst Áine's sacred animals.

- *Castor and Pollux:* greek mythological twin sons of Zeus (Greek) or Jupiter (Roman). Considered semi-divine, they were associated with horses and sports, and credited for saving those in trouble at sea. Castor in particular was believed to be a superior tamer of horses. In Roman mythology they were associated with the cavalry, and are mentioned in both *The Iliad* and *The Odyssey.*

- *Demeter (Greek), Ceres (Roman):* In addition to turning into a mare in an unsuccessful attempt to avoid the unwanted passions of Poseidon, there is a cave sacred to Demeter in the ancient Greek city of Phigaleia, which includes a statue of the goddess with a woman's body and the head of a horse. In this aspect, she is known with the surname Melaina or Melaena, which mean "black." Demeter clothed herself in black and shut herself in this cavern while mourning for her daughter, Persephone, who was abducted to be the unwilling wife of Hades, god of the underworld. From Demeter's coupling with Poseidon, she birthed the magical steed Arion, as well as a daughter whose name, according to an entry in New World Encyclopedia, "could not be uttered outside the Eleusinian Mysteries." Demeter is associated with grain, agriculture, harvest, and the fertility of the earth.

- *Loki:* the shape-shifting trickster in Norse mythology who transformed himself into a mare to lure away a rival's horse. He mates with it and Loki gives birth to Sleipnir, Norse god Odin's powerful, swift eight-legged horse.

- *Neptune:* cranky Roman god of the sea, able to make the waters calm or stormy, and associated with chariot races and horse racing. His chariot was drawn by a creature with the body and front end of a horse and the hind end of a fish or sea serpent—known as a hippocampus. Neptune is the counterpart of Poseidon in Greek mythology, and is often depicted holding a trident that could produce an earthquake when struck to the ground, and which he used to create horses.

- *Poseidon:* Greek counterpart of Neptune, with corresponding mythology. He is mentioned in *The Homeric Hymns*, wherein Poseidon is declared "the great god, mover of the earth and fruitless sea, god of the deep who is also

lord of Helicon and wide Aegae. A two-fold office the gods allotted you,
O Shaker of the Earth, to be a tamer of horses and a saviour of ships!"

- *Rigantona:* possibly the name from which "Rhiannon" was derived, her
  name means "Great Queen" or "Divine Queen." Some mythologies link
  her to the goddess Epona, others to Italian origin, and still others to Celtic
  origin. Her story predates Rhiannon's. While Rigantona's name repeat-
  edly pops up as a horse goddess, in an article "Rigantona & the Realm of
  the Dead" on The Druid Network's website, Rigantona's lore is not about
  horses, but about sovereignty, mourning, grief, and the ability to pass back
  and forth between this world and the realm of the dead, like Rhiannon.

- *Silili:* Like Epona, this ancient Babylonian Goddess was also known as the
  "Divine Mare," and was considered to be the mother of all horses. She
  is amongst the deities of ancient Sumer and Babylon, and is mentioned
  only once in the Epic of Gilgamesh, on the sixth tablet, line 57. Very little
  information about her has endured the ages.

- *Sol and Mani:* From Norse mythology, this sister and brother pair showed
  up when the cosmos was created. As the gods created different parts of
  the world, Sol and Mani were used to differentiate parts of the day and
  year, as well as phases of the moon. In contrast to modern Pagan mythology, Sol is the female and charged with pulling the sun across the sky in
  a horse-drawn chariot. Mani is male and charged with pulling the moon
  across the sky. Sol's horses were named Árvakr (Early Riser) and Alsviðr
  (Swift). The names of Mani's horses are unknown.

Mystical, Magical Horses

There's a cornucopia of information about horses and horse-like creatures
that may or may have not actually existed, except in the captive, curious human mind. These magical, mystical horses appear in many cultures, and the
white horse in particular appears most frequently—highly revered but also the
most likely to be used for gruesome ritual sacrifice. Here are some horse and
horse-related creatures, some fantastical and some fearsome:

- *Al-Buraq:* From the Qur'an, this white horse with wings on its hind legs
  carried the prophet Muhammad from Mecca to Jerusalem and back, and

then up to heaven to meet with Allah. Al-Buraq is sometimes depicted as having a human face. His name means "lightning" in Arabic.

- *Arion (Areion):* In her attempt to escape Poseidon's pursuits, Greek goddess Demeter changed herself into a mare. Poseidon countered this by changing into a stallion, and they mated. This union resulted in the dark-maned Arion, a swift horse of immortal birth that carried Hercules into one of his many battles and could speak. He was unruly with any other rider.

- *Biblical horses:* Horses are mentioned more than fifty times in the Holy Bible. While the four horses of Revelation get the most attention, horses are mentioned elsewhere in both the Old and New Testaments. A most impressive description of horses is found in Job 39:19: *"Do you give the horse his might? Do you clothe his neck with a mane? Do you make him leap like the locust? His majestic snorting is terrifying. He paws in the valley and exults in his strength; he goes out to meet the weapons. He laughs at fear and is not dismayed; he does not turn back from the sword. Upon him rattle the quiver, the flashing spear, and the javelin. With fierceness and rage he swallows the ground; he cannot stand still at the sound of the trumpet. When the trumpet sounds, he says 'Aha!' He smells the battle from afar, the thunder of the captains, and the shouting."*[19]

- *Bucephalus:* This beautiful black horse was wild and unmanageable when presented to King Phillip II, the father of Alexander the Great, in Macedonia in 346 BCE. An audience gathered to view the horse, but no one could get near him, let alone ride him. Young Alexander wagered with his father that if he can ride the horse, it will become his own. Noticing that the horse was afraid of his own shadow, Alexander turned him toward the sun so he couldn't see it, and in one swift leap, mounted him and rode off at full gallop. Upon his return, the King gave the horse to Alexander, who named him Bucephalus. Alexander rode Bucephalus into every battle from Greece to India.

- *Centaurs:* With the legs and body of a horse, but a human torso, arms, and head where the neck should be, centaurs were iconic in Greek mythology. They were considered to be wild, lustful, and lawless, and ruled by animal passions. Amongst the best-known centaurs is Chiron, characterized as

19. OpenBible, "100 Bible Verses about Horses: Job 39:19."

more civilized than the others. Centaurs are sometimes believed to be the result of the mating of the mythological Centaurus with Greek mares.

- *Enbarr of the Flowing Mane:* Associated with the Celtic sea god Manannán mac Lir, Enbarr was a beautiful white horse that traveled like the wind over land and sea. Manannán mac Lir lent Enbarr to his foster son Lugh, also a Celtic god, after whom the Pagan celebration of Lughnasadh is named, signifying the beginning of harvest in early August. Enbarr was crucial to Lugh's success. Lugh is associated with the Tuatha de Danaan, and mentioned in the Celtic *Origin of the Universe* creation story.

- *Four Horsemen of the Apocalypse:* In the Book of Revelation in the Holy Bible, the Lamb of God (Jesus) opens a book with seven seals. Each of the first four seals unleashes riders upon horses, representing the beginning of the Apocalypse. The first horse is white and represents conquest. The second is red and represents war. The third is black and represents famine. The fourth is described as "pale" (possibly grey) and represents death by way of war, famine, and plague.

- *Gaseg Wen (Gaseg Gwyn):* the mystical white mare ridden by Celtic goddess Rhiannon, in this world and into the otherworld. Although it traveled only at a walk, no other horse or human could keep up with it or overtake it. (Name humbly created by this author.)

- *Hippocampus (Hippocamp, Hippokampoi):* Not to be confused with the area of the brain by the same name, the hippocampus was a Greek mythological creature with the head, neck, and forelegs of a horse and a fish-like or serpentine tail. The creature is often depicted pulling Poseidon's (Neptune's) chariot across the surface of the sea. "Hippo" is the Greek word for "horse."

- *Hippocrene:* a well on Mount Helicon, in Boeotia, Greece, formed by the hooves of Pegasus and sacred to the Muses of Greek mythology, which inspired artists, philosophers, musicians, and writers. The name means "Horse's Fountain," and its water is believed to be a source of poetic inspiration.

- *Hippoi Athanatoi:* immortal horses of the gods, believed to be the offspring the four Anemoi (Wind Gods) who, while assuming the shape of horses, drew Zeus's chariot.

- *Horse (Chinese zodiac):* People born in the Year of the Horse, which occurs every twelve years (as do all signs of the Chinese zodiac), are considered to be energetic, passionate, and independent. They are social and enjoy the company of others. Known to be honest and frank, those born in the Year of the Horse can go to the extreme and become outspoken and verbally offensive. Some of their downfalls include impulsivity, recklessness, rebelliousness, unruliness, and a dislike of obstacles.

- *Kanthaka:* powerful, athletic white horse belonging to Crown Prince Siddhartha, who rode him in battle. When Siddhartha renounced the world, he escaped from the palace riding Kanthaka, leaving behind his wife, child, and a life of luxury. After his escape, he dismounted from Kanthaka for the last time and continued his journey for enlightenment on foot as the Buddha. Kanthaka died of a broken heart but was reborn as a Brahmin (Buddhist priest) and continued to serve the Buddha, becoming enlightened himself.

- *Kelpies:* Of Scottish folklore, these demonic water horses haunted deep rivers and streams, and were able to come ashore and shape-shift into horse or human form. If a horse, their hooves were backward, and if human, they had hooves. Some believed kelpies protected small children from drowning, others believed quite the opposite—they appeared as tame ponies by a stream, luring children to get onto their backs, from which they could not escape because of their sticky hide. These trapped children would be dragged into the water and eaten. Kelpies appearing in female human form would do the same, while those appearing in a hairy male form would crush humans to death. The only way to defeat a kelpie was to grab its bridle. Kelpies may be the origin of the legends of the Loch Ness monster.

- *Longma:* winged dragon horse from Chinese mythology covered in dragon scales and considered to be wise and auspicious, and also able to fly. Horses and dragons had similar characteristics in ancient Chinese mythology.

- *Pegasus:* The immortal winged horse of Greek mythology, Pegasus was the child of the sea god Poseidon and the monstrous Medusa, from whose neck he sprung after she was beheaded by Perseus. Pegasus could create streams wherever he struck his hooves. He originally belonged to the Greek hero

Bellerophon, who tamed him with a bridle given to him by Athena. When Bellerophon was disrespectful to Zeus, he sent a gadfly to sting Pegasus and throw Bellerophon to his death. Pegasus flew to Olympus and belonged to Zeus thereafter. A constellation in the night sky is named after Pegasus.

- *Seven-Colored Horse:* There are Puerto Rican, French, Russian, and Israeli versions of this story, involving a little boy charged with guarding a cornfield at night, and witnessing a magical horse with a coat of seven colors galloping down from the sky at midnight to eat the corn. The boy lassos it, and the horse begs to be let go on the promise that he will return to help the boy whenever he calls. The boy agrees, on the promise that the horse will not eat the corn anymore, and a bargain is struck. True to his word, as the boy deals with tricks played upon him at the hands of his cruel brothers, the horse rescues him each time, helps him to marry a beautiful girl, and delivers the brothers into well-deserved exile.[20]

- *Sleipnir:* eight-legged horse birthed by the shape-shifting trickster Loki and given to Norse god Odin as a gift. Grey as a cloudy sky, his many legs allowed him to soar along mid-air, as swift as the wind, and he was Odin's most prized steed. The fearless Sleipnir carried Odin on many quests and was faster and stronger than any other horse. Sleipnir was additionally a helpful shamanic spirit to Odin.

- *Sun Chariot horses:* The mythologies of several cultures included mighty Gods that were credited with pulling the sun across the sky, amongst them Apollo (Greek and Roman), Belenus (Celtic), Helios (Greek), Ra (Egyptian), Sol (Norse), and Surya (Hindu). In these stories, the gods are given credit for this job, but without the horses, those gods would still be stuck on the ground at sunrise. A little credit for the horses, please.

- *Tangle-coated Horse:* This Celtic myth features a massive, unattractive "tangle-coated" (extremely shaggy and unkempt) horse discovered by the warriors of Fionn mac Cumhaill—a folkloric hero—who are at first so startled by him they attempt to spear him, but the spears just bounce off.

---

20. Hausman and Hausman, *The Mythology of Horses: Horse Legend and Lore Throughout the Ages,* 244–251.

The horse is merely amused by the pathetic efforts of the men. The horse could also shape-shift into a beautiful silver horse.[21]

- *Tianma:* Chinese mythological horse, also called the "heavenly horse" that flew through the heavens. Tianma has a Chinese constellation named after it.

- *Tibetan Wind Horse:* This horse is the most common symbol seen on strings of colorful Tibetan prayer flags and is believed to be a powerful energy that carries prayers to the gods on the wind. Known as *lung-ta* in Tibetan, it is believed that hanging Tibetan prayer flags with the Wind Horse symbol from two points where they can flutter in the breeze increases positive energy for all in the surrounding area. Each flag color represents the Tibetan perspective on the elements: blue is sky and wind; white is air and clouds; red is fire; green is water; yellow is earth.

- *Tulpar:* winged horse of Turkish mythology, mentioned in the *Epic of Manas.* This swift flying horse was created by God to help the valiant and opens its wings only in the dark. If someone sees his wings, Tulpar will disappear. This winged horse appears on the state emblems of Kazakhstan and Mongolia.

- *Uchchaihshravas:* In Hindu mythology, this king of the horses rose from the churning ocean. Horses in Hindu scriptures symbolize a force that carries another force, as horses carry riders, and the life current and senses flowing between the brain and the body. Uchchaihshravas was a white, seven-headed horse, and the name was also associated with one of the Hindu sun god's horses.

- *Unicorn (traditional):* white, blue-eyed horse with a single horn on its forehead, mentioned in ancient mythologies of India, China, and Greece, and even mentioned multiple times in the Holy Bible. This strong, fierce beast symbolizes purity and innocence, juxtaposed with masculinity and power, and can only be tamed by a virgin maiden. Arguably no other horse-related image has been spread as far and wide as that of the unicorn, which appears on a vast array of commercial items. Along with the lion, the unicorn appears on the royal coat of arms of the United Kingdom,

21. Hausman and Hausman, *The Mythology of Horses: Horse Legend and Lore Throughout the Ages,* 226–231.

and is the official national animal of Scotland, representing the Scottish fight to remain unconquered.

- *Unicorn (American):* This white, whimsical unicorn snorts glitter, poops rainbows, and is often used as a term to describe someone who is completely unique, unusual, or very odd. It often has a rainbow mane and tail, and its image is on everything from T-shirts to tennis shoes. It sometimes has wings as well and may also be a cat.

- *Vogelherd Horse:* Carved of mammoth ivory during the Ice Age, this thirty-five-thousand-year-old figurine is the oldest known sculpture of a horse. Discovered in the Vogelherd Cave near Stetton, Germany, it depicts a stallion with a strong, curved neck and appears to have symbols engraved along its neck and back.

— II —
THE SPIRITUAL
HORSE

Chapter 4

ELEMENTAL HORSES

Earth, air, fire, water: These four elements make up our planet and our own bodies. They are associated with specific directions and times of day, as well as with symbolic Elemental Horses, each skilled at doing certain types of jobs on the metaphysical plane.

In this exploration of the elements and Elemental Horses, we'll use the Pagan angle on the four elements. There are other perspectives of the four elements (some have five) as well, including Native American, Buddhist, and Hindu spirituality, all just as valid and meaningful. The Pagan version, however, is most familiar to me.

We'll also use some meditations to meet the Elemental Horses to really illuminate each one in your own mind, solidifying quick access to mental cues to call each one forth.

Elemental Horses Are Specialists

Each element—earth, air, fire, and water—is associated with certain symbols, strengths, and energies. The Elemental Horses aren't the element themselves, but they represent them, just as a particular stone or color might. Each Horse is uniquely talented for helping you to access the energies and qualities of its element, in a particular fashion. Each is naturally gifted for a particular task: power, speed, courage, or grace. Earth Horse is large, powerful, and muscular, excelling at tedious, demanding, laborious work. Air Horse is slender, swift, and light, able to cover distances and overcome obstacles, requiring precision, swiftness, and agility. Fire Horse is courageous, bold, and athletic, ready and able to take on any challenge. Water Horse is graceful, smooth, and polished, mastering skills or abilities that require time, effort, and patience. Each Horse brings you right to the elemental energies you need, by using mental imagery as well as a thorough understanding of each element's energies.

These horses aren't decorations, they are doers. Their motto is "get 'er done," each with its own special method of "gettin' 'er done." However, they won't get anything done on their own. Just like real horses, they'd rather graze. They require human direction to do a job. You *must* participate. Your Elemental Horse will keep you focused and moving forward in the right direction, but you have to do the actual work. Horses of both the physical and elemental type will pour their energy into the task at hand, but only if asked to do so. The human's job is to communicate the task, and the horse's job is to obey. They don't do the job for us. They manifest our intentions. Whether real or metaphysical horses, we must be riders—not passengers.

The Elemental Horses serve as mental bumpers, keeping us moving forward in our desired lane rather than wandering all over the place and getting lost in the weeds. Whether we seek to get a bachelor's degree, free ourselves from a bad relationship, build a redwood deck, or move past anxiety, we have a stable of precisely skilled Elemental Horses to prompt us to stay focused and on task until the job is done.

To work with Elemental Horses, you first need to define what you want to do: study for a test, organize your closets, learn to play the violin, ask for a raise, etc. This is your intention. Then, you call forth the image of the particular Horse you need, absorb its powerful energy, and employ it as a mental prompt to keep you on track. Mental imagery engages the right half of your brain, which is visual and thinks in pictures and montages, and addresses and solves problems differently than your verbal left half. You can understand the difference by thinking about how you remember to drive to a certain place. Do you tell yourself in words, "turn left at the red barn and right just after the fruit stand," or do pictures flash in your mind of the red barn and the fruit stand? If you use words, that is your left brain; if pictures, your right.

Horse Has All the Energies

I was searching for the term "Horse Spirit" one afternoon and landed upon a website called "Spirit Animal" that listed these characteristics for Horse: "personal drive, passion, and appetite for freedom." It also mentioned that Horse represents strong motivation; "a driving force, what you thrive for that carries you in life"; a balance between instinct and domestic; sexual energy (particularly masculine energy); and "strong emotions, passionate desires."[22]

These are all aspects of Horse energy, but they're only a few tiles and not the complete mosaic. The site notes that the meaning of Horse "varies depending on whether this animal spirit guide is represented as wild, tamed, moving freely, or constrained." They're so close, but in my opinion, it's still a swing and a miss. Props, however, for recognizing that defining Horse in one aspect doesn't suffice, even if they weren't able to put their finger on "why." Here's where to push the pin on that caveat: on the word "or," which I'd argue should be changed to "and." Horse is wild, tamed, moving freely, *and* constrained. Horse can be all that, and more. Anything and everything. One, some, or all. Calling on Horse energy is all about what you want to do, and which elemental aspect of Horse that best suits that purpose. Horse, in its totality, is versatile, mobile, and multifaceted, and the Elemental Horses are all components of Horse.

The Elements Connect on the Solar Cross

To get a better mental picture of how the elements connect and interact, imagine the four elements occupying a position on the rim of a circle, each emanating a line straight across to the other side, creating a plus-sign-shaped cross in the middle. This shape is called a "solar cross" (see figure 1). Earth is at twelve o'clock, air is at three o'clock, fire is at six o'clock, and water is at nine o'clock. Note that these are the positions on a clock face, not the corresponding actual times of day, which are midnight, dawn, noon, and dusk, respectively. The solar cross looks similar to the Native American Medicine Wheel, where the elements are directions, and have different colors.

The center, where the straight lines cross, is "spirit," not technically amongst the physical elements. It is our own ethereal, spiritual core or consciousness, the "you" that you recognize and connect with in your own heart and mind; your true self, in your heart of hearts. We'll get to spirit later. First things first: the four earthly elements.

---

22. Harris, "Horse Spirit Animal."

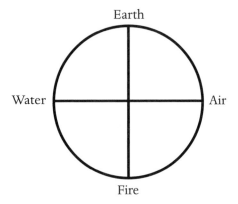

Figure 1: Solar Cross

Earth

The direction of earth is north, its time is midnight, and its season is winter. Its colors are greens, browns, and black. Its symbols include rocks, gems, and crystals, as well as mountain, forest-dwelling, and burrowing creatures. Its zodiac signs are Taurus, Virgo, and Capricorn, and its tarot suit is pentacles. It is a feminine, receptive energy. Earth is our body, our health, and our material possessions.

Like the ground we stand on, earth is our foundation. Think of the word "grounding." When we're grounded, we feel calm, safe, and stable. When someone says, "Get your feet back on the ground," it means to let go of confusing, whirling thoughts and frenetic activity, and get back to a rational, calm, focused center. When we plant our feet on the ground, it means we're stable and steady, and cannot be knocked off balance. We become the mountain that can't be moved.

Earth is fertile ground, from which green life springs up, and it is also protective, like caves and burrows where animals dwell and hibernate. It's the cool, dark forest. Just imagining the scent of rich soil or fresh pine trees can induce a feeling of calm.

Earth is substantial and solid, slow and measured, taking whatever time it needs to progress. Life springs up from the ground in a methodical way, and returns to it in a methodical way, and cycles back again with the passage of each season. You can't force a bud to open or will a tree to turn its leaves orange. They will do these things in their own time, at their own pace. While most always stable, still, and predictable, earth has a destructive side too. When tension builds, or the load is finally too much to bear, earthquakes and landslides can destroy everything in earth's path, and reduce massive structures to a pile of rubble and dust. Luckily, it takes a *lot* to push earth to that point.

The horse that represents earth is slow, steady, and powerful—the "heavy horses." Earth is symbolized by the massive, muscular draft breeds that pull plows through fields or felled logs from the forest. These are *big* boys. However, despite their impressive size, they are particularly docile, tolerant, and obedient, which is important. A two-thousand-pound animal that is unruly or flighty would be exceedingly dangerous.

Heavy horses are cooperative team players, sometimes pulling carts or wagons in teams of two, three, four, or more, controlled by a single human wielding long, skinny leather reins. If someone tried that with six skittish Thoroughbreds, they may be just as likely to run away in panic from the rattling contraption "chasing" them as they are to pull together for a common goal. Heavy horses are the descendants of the massive medieval European warhorses bred to carry a knight in full armor into battle, while wearing armor of their own. Medieval humans singled out the warhorses with calm, easygoing temperaments, and used their bulk and muscle for plowing and pulling, leaving the fiery, spirited ones for the battlefield.

Earth Horse's motto is "Keep pushing forward." Like big old Boxer from George Orwell's *Animal Farm*, they have a job to do and through snow, heat, mud, hills, and ruts, they'll keep putting one hoof in front of the other until the job is done. No point getting all bent out of shape about the task at hand—just get going, and keep going until you get there. Like all the Elemental Horses, Earth Horse prompts you to "git 'er done" in its own special way: dig in, keep going, and don't give up. And also, no whining.

Do any of the following characteristics sound familiar?

- Do you "put off today what can be done tomorrow," but tomorrow never comes?
- When faced with a difficult task, do you complain or become crabby, cranky, or snippy?
- Do you usually do something that's fun instead of what you need to do?
- Are you more of a hare than a tortoise? More of a grasshopper than an ant?

- Is your house full of clutter or piles of things that you just can't seem to put away or organize?
- Do you have a lot of unfinished projects? A better starter than finisher?
- Do people sometimes call you a "hothead" or "troublemaker"?

If you find yourself chuckling or nodding your head in recognition, hitch your cart to Earth Horse. Look up images of heavy horse breeds online and save images that really impress you, or draw one. Watch videos of heavy horses competing in pulling contests or working the land to get an idea of their raw power.

Mold an image of your own perfect Earth Horse in your mind, which you'll call upon when you need to access the energies of earth. It doesn't need to be a particular breed, just big, muscled, and powerful. For a little extra inspiration, find one in an earth color: dark brown or black. My metaphysical Earth Horse is a deep, dark bay Shire, massive and muscular, with a white blaze and white feathers on all four legs. He is alert, powerful, and willing, ready to dig in and work for me whenever I call upon him.

Stay on Task

While writing this book, I wore a harness brass on a ribbon around my neck. Earth is my weak spot. I often have trouble staying on task, because... squirrel! A harness brass is a flat brass medallion, which is attached to the harnesses of working draft horses for good luck and protection, or to decorate a harness for a parade or show. They can also be mounted on a leather flap and attached to the browband of a bridle, resting right on a horse's forehead. The physical sensation of the brass against my body was a tactile prompt to stay focused whenever I'd get the urge to scamper off and do something else.

I found my harness brass on eBay, and strung it on a sturdy cloth ribbon to create my "harness," which I wore around my neck to prompt me to stay focused, and keep my butt in the chair and my fingers moving over the keyboard. When I put on my "harness," it's time to get to work. I didn't allow myself to "look at Facebook for just a minute" (hours) or "just one cat video." Adorable kittens are the gateway drug for wasting obscene amounts of time.

Grounding with Earth and Earth Horse

When you need earth energy, think of your Earth Horse, wear earth colors, and carry or wear stones, pebbles, crystals, geodes, or seeds. Get outside and feel the solid, cool ground under your bare feet. Dig up a handful of dirt and crumble it between your fingers, and smell its thick, rich scent. Grow a plant on your windowsill or plant a new tree or bush in your yard to draw in earth energy. Go for a walk and find a large stone, one that feels cool and heavy, and place it in a conspicuous spot to remind you that you—not others—will define your own pace in life.

Air

The direction of air is east, its time is dawn, and its season is spring. Its colors are yellow and pastels, like the early sunrise. Its symbols include birds, flying insects, feathers, wind chimes, spinners, and any creatures that fly. Air is connected with tall or high places—mountaintops and pinnacles—as well as the sky itself. Its zodiac signs are Gemini, Libra, and Aquarius, and its tarot suit is swords. It is a masculine, projective energy. Air is our mind, thoughts, and communication skills, both written and verbal.

Air is the realm of the intellect. It is directed, logical, rational, and innovative. Air energy is for defining and solving problems. Actual air oxygenates our blood, and intellectual air "oxygenates" our mind. Although very light, air can lift and carry things like leaves and seeds on the breeze, or, in its full terrible force, whirl into a tornado or hurricane, and toss houses and pickup trucks around like toys. Air can be gentle and it can also be very destructive—just like words.

Air cleanses and refreshes. Sometimes we say, "I need to clear my mind" when too many thoughts are tumbling around in our brains. Air clears out the haze and allows us to step back, view our challenges, and plan a strategy for overcoming them. Or, there's "let's air it out," meaning we need to sit down and talk about our issues and disagreements, rather than bottle them up. Turns out, we really *are* airheads! And that's a good thing!

Air knows no boundaries, and few barriers can contain or stop it. Likewise, Air Horse is the same. It sees the barrier and soars over it. Barriers? What barriers? Air Horse helps you strategize about the task at hand, carrying you to your destination swiftly and accurately, defying gravity all the while. Air Horse commits to the planned strategy and won't be distracted or "blow" randomly from one different course to another. It will help prevent you from finding yourself lost in the tall weeds of "How come I'm sorting socks when I was supposed to be washing the car?" Air Horse prompts mental willpower.

Ask yourself these questions:

- Are you easily distracted or have trouble staying mentally focused?
- Are you easily blown off course by your personal problems, feelings, or emotions?
- Are you a "drama queen"?
- Do you struggle to choose a course of action?
- Do you have trouble sticking to a plan?
- Are you stuck on a problem, or problems, that you just can't seem to solve?
- Do you make decisions with your heart rather than with your head?

If you see yourself in these questions, let Air Horse carry you. While Earth Horse keeps your nose to the grindstone, putting one foot in front of the other until you're finished, Air Horse prompts you to evaluate a difficult situation, identify the barriers, and then create a logical plan to overcome each barrier until you arrive at your destination. That sounds a bit like Earth Horse, but there's a qualitative difference. To use a military example, Earth Horse would be the hard-working soldier, who follows orders and keeps trudging along no matter what. Air Horse would be the general coming up with the strategy and commanding the troops.

Air Horses are swift as the wind and defy gravity. They are the racehorses, steeplechasers, jumpers, hunters, and eventers. They tend to be light and sleek, and may be a variety of breeds. The versatile Thoroughbred could be a representation of the quintessential Air Horse, able to fly over the ground or soar over most any obstacle.

Know Your Obstacles and Make a Plan

When calling upon Air Horse, we take a step back, assess the obstacles in our path, and plan a strategy. When I rode show jumpers, we didn't just trot merrily into the ring and start jumping things at random. We first studied the course, memorized it, and noted any sharp turns, tight squeezes, or particularly challenging jumps. By the time we rode into the show ring, our strategy was set. It's too late to plan a course of attack, or change it, when you're already moving. Once you're in the show ring, it's "go time." There are no do-overs; go off course, and you're excused from the ring.

Besides knowing your course, you must also set your eyes where you want to land. Your horse can sense where you're looking, and that's where it'll take you. If you stare *at* the jump, that's where you'll end up—head first into a plywood brick wall. Been there, done that. You must focus your eyes beyond the jump, where you want the horse to land, and that's where it will go. Air Horse is like that too. If you get distracted, it will too. Wherever you focus is where you'll end up. Air Horse prompts you to really *occupy* your mind, rather than getting swept away in the currents and eddies of swirling thoughts. In working with Air Horse, don't focus on the barriers. Remember your strategy, and focus on clearing them.

Attracting Air and Air Horse

To bring Air Horse into your life, gather images of horses you like, in the colors associated with air: pastels, white, creams, or gold. My personal favorite Air Horse representation is the rare Akhal-Teke breed, particularly in the rare color called "cremello," an ethereal, shimmering pale gold. The national emblem of their birthplace, Turkmenistan, the lithe and leggy Akhal-Tekes are stellar jumpers. They can soar over any obstacle, and do so with breathtaking grace. What will your Air Horse look like?

To access air energy, imagine your Air Horse and collect, carry, or wear feathers, chimes, or bells. Wear clothing in the pastel colors of air. Get outside and inhale some cleansing fresh air, oxygenating your brain and body. Burn incense or use a scent diffuser to fill the air in your home or office with a scent that clears your mind, like peppermint, citrus, or rosemary. Find a little clear, blown-glass horse, put it on a windowsill and let the morning light shine through it. Maybe find one with wings like Pegasus, which is the ultimate Air Horse. Whatever inspires air or Air Horse for you, put it in a visible place as a reminder of the energy you need.

Fire

The direction of fire is south, its time is high noon, and its season is summer. Its colors are orange and red. Its symbols include flames, the sun, deserts, canyons, wide-open plains and prairies, candles, campfires, hearth fires, volcanoes, and animals that "burn" (bite or sting) or have fiery, aggressive temperaments. Its zodiac signs are Aries, Leo, and Sagittarius, and its tarot suit is wands (or rods). It is a masculine, projective energy. It is the seat of our athleticism, sexuality, and courage.

Fire is stamina, skillfulness, and athletic prowess, be it on a sports field, battlefield, or open range. Fire is warrior energy. It is fearless, inexhaustible, enthusiastic, and a very versatile and useful tool. In our earliest days, it offered a warm, soothing hub for gathering and bonding, and a weapon for keeping away wild beasts. Later, it became a way to cook food or clear brush. When controlled, fire is extremely useful. When out of control, it's a monster. It consumes everything in its path, leaving nothing but scorched earth. When we say, "You're playing with fire," it means watch out, you're about to get hurt.

Fire's "git 'er done" angle is all about athleticism, determination, speed, precision and most importantly, immediacy: "Git 'er done *now*."

The heart of fire energy is courage, so our symbol for Fire Horse is the working horse. These horses have a job to do, but as compared to the earthy heavy horses, which trudge mightily forward until the job is finished, working horses have to move quickly, doing jobs that require them to override their own instincts and trust their riders more than they fear what's happening around them—without hesitation.

That's asking a lot of an animal that's evolutionarily hardwired to flee from danger and predators. It's not a horse's nature to stride through a surging crowd of screaming rioters or protesters, or stare down huge, uncooperative cattle and cut them from a herd, or gallop for miles over rough terrain to deliver a satchel of mail. The inexhaustible, fiery working horse will obey its rider over its own instincts, and keep going until it collapses.

If you need to do the impossible, and do it quickly, Fire Horse is your ally. It doesn't hesitate, balk, or question, it just gets moving—enthusiastically. Give Fire Horse a challenge, and its immediate response is "I'm on it!"

Do you need some Fire Horse energy? Let's take a look at that:

- Do fears, phobias, depression, or anxiety prevent you from doing things?
- Do you feel sluggish, sad, bored?
- Do you need to get in shape or lose weight?
- Is getting started on a task harder than actually doing it?
- Are you faced with a task that seems impossible?
- Do people describe you as "uptight"? A "stick in the mud"?
- If circumstances change, is it difficult to quickly shift to a new strategy?
- Do people complain that you are lazy or too slow with projects?

If you're holding up your hand and saying, "Guilty," let Fire Horse ignite you. Check out some videos of working horses cutting cattle or barrel racing so you can get a feel for just how quick and precise these horses are. Our iconic Fire Horse is symbolized by a cutting horse, ready to charge in and chase down those cows. It's a muscled athlete, and so skilled at its job that its rider must loosen the reins and let the horse do the work, because a horse can react to a cow's attempts to escape far more quickly than a human. By the time a human figures out the next move, a skilled cutting horse has already done it. The horse's job is to cut the cattle. The human's job is to manage to stay in the saddle while the horse is doing it.

Do you need to accomplish a big task at top speed? Maybe your dinner party is in three hours, and your house is a mess? Crazy packed schedule at work, plus three conflicting evening commitments, and you need to be in three places at once? Saddle up Fire Horse and get moving! You can do it!

Maybe you need to get in shape or build up your strength and stamina, and it just seems overwhelming. Rather than get sucked into the pit of inertia by excuses and rationalizations, Fire Horse tells you, "Just start." It sparks you out of inertia and gets you moving. One step is a start. Then all you need is a series of first steps, and before you know it, you've walked a whole mile.

Help Me, Fire Horse!

In writing this exact chapter, I had a burst of inspiration and energy about Elemental Horses, because working with the elements is right in my wheelhouse. I use the elements to make sense of all sorts of things, from jobs to other people to myself. Simmering with inspiration, I sat down at the keyboard, my fingers flying, pumping out sentences and paragraphs like a high-speed word machine.

I wrote for seven hours straight and never came up for air. I was just getting to "Water" when my brain ran out of gas. Just like a car, it slowed, sputtered, coughed up some dust, and rolled to a complete stop. I had written myself into a stupor and, worse yet, into a corner. I had a big, fat, hot mess that wouldn't make sense to anyone but me.

After getting some sleep, I started pondering what I was going to do about the problem I'd created for myself. I looked at the totality of my predicament and a single solution slowly materialized: I must cut large chunks out of this section. In other words, a whole lot of work after already having done a whole lot of work.

Sadness.

I faced an entire day of cutting and rewriting, rather than launching into new material. I didn't want to, but it had to happen. And that was that. No point whining, crying, and pouting. Just dig in and do it, now.

I had a huge cutting job ahead and I needed a swift cutting horse. I saddled up Fire Horse in my mind, and we cut those "cows" from the herd. I charged right in and didn't look left or right. I didn't stop to feel sorry for myself or throw up my hands and cry. There was no time for that. I just "got 'er done." It took all afternoon. Yes, my butt was aching from being in the "saddle" all day, but when I was finished, all the "cows" were separated into the corrals where they belonged.

Igniting Fire and Fire Horse

To ignite that fire energy, put a photo of a cutting horse in action on your wall, and in your mind. Collect, carry, or wear lava rocks or red stones—like carnelian or red jasper—burn red or orange candles, or grow a little cactus plant. Wear big, bold, fiery in-your-face colors, like orange, red, or hot pink. Wear cowboy boots! Play some rock music a little too loud and get yourself moving. Yes—dance! And do it like no one's watching! Get out and walk, run, or hike. Get comfortable with being in your own body. Move your body! Make something with your hands, particularly something that involves tools or building something. Seeing a tangible thing that you built yourself fires up your confidence.

Water

The direction of water is west, its time is dusk, and its season is fall. Its colors are blue, turquoise, and purple. Its symbols include seashells, fish, and creatures that swim and live in the water. Its zodiac signs are Pisces, Cancer, and Scorpio, and its tarot suit is cups. It is a feminine, receptive energy. Water is the source of emotion, intuition, artistic creativity, and empathy.

Water is where our feelings dwell, and they can be bright and sparkling or dark and murky. This element is highly changeable and adaptive, and can be frozen or boiling, and everything in between—just like emotions. Emotions are what drive artistic creation that bubbles up from water's depths—drawing, painting, poetry, dance, writing, and music. Water is the home of a dizzying array of marine animals of all shapes, colors, and sizes, symbolic of the unlimited creative potential swimming around in our subconscious depths. Think of a jellyfish—Mother Nature poured a little extra creativity into that!

Because of its intuitive, psychic, and often moody and mysterious nature, water is associated with the moon, which, of course controls the ocean tides. All life on earth initially evolved from water creatures, making water the womb of all life. Inside the actual womb, we float peacefully in water. Whether the evolution of life or the beginning of our own, it all began with water. Our own bodies are about sixty percent water, and sometimes the moon tugs on that too.

Our Water Horse encompasses the calm, serene nature of flowing water, as well as the patience of water: It takes an immense amount of time for flowing water to smooth rocks or for ocean waves to tumble jagged broken glass into sea glass. It takes time and effort to smooth out rough edges. As contrasted with the lightness and speed of Air Horse, and the lightning-quick reflexes and courage of Fire Horse, Water Horse is all about patience and practice.

Water Horse's message is "git 'er done, gracefully." Relax into the process with acceptance rather than resisting it. Go with the flow. Creativity itself has a flow; it can't be forced or contrived. It flows at its own pace as if channeled from the universe itself. That experience of many hours elapsing, unnoticed while we're focused on painting, writing, or polishing a piano sonata is even called a "flow state"—total immersion in the creative process, tapping into our own inner limitless well of inspiration and expression. That takes time, or in other words, practice.

We don't become ballet dancers or write novels or paint masterpieces over-night. These things require patience and practice, and there are no shortcuts. Creativity and perfection take however long they take. Patience is the soil from which practice emerges. You can't have one without the other, and you can't create amazing things without both. Water Horse prompts us to embrace the creative process, practicing and polishing ourselves each step of the way.

Practice and Patience Make It Happen

Consider the training of a Lipizzan (or Lipizzaner) stallion. To be consid-ered for the world-famous Spanish Riding School, young colts spend a leisurely first three years out at pasture. The most promising ones are selected for train-ing and taken to Vienna, where the school is located. Lipizzans spend up to eight years in classical dressage training, which includes the mastery of the "le-vade," which is balanced in a reared-up position; the "courbette," similar to the levade, but hopping forward on the hind legs; and the "capriole," leaping into the air with forelegs tucked and at the top of its leap, kicking backward with the hind legs.[23] All of these moves are difficult and unnatural for a horse, even a Lipizzan. Patience and practice, rinse and repeat.

Even regular dressage horses must go through hours upon hours to perfect the controlled, ballet-like movements, such as the *passage* (a slow, springy, trot), the *piaffe* (a slow, high-stepping trot almost seeming to occur in place), and the *half-pass* (moving forward and sideways simultaneously, with hind legs and forelegs crossing over each other). For our purposes, our iconic Water Horse is a dressage horse: grey like a cloudy ocean day; always striving to create beauty, grace, and perfection, and taking the time it needs to achieve it.

Learning to Dance

While walking Penn around the ranch, I'd see all those dressage riders spending hours and hours perfecting their moves and techniques. It's beauti-ful and mesmerizing to watch! I wanted to try it myself, so I took a dressage lesson. Dressage is the language that Penn speaks, and I wanted to learn *his* language.

---

23. Morris, "Lipica: The Original Home of the Lipizzaner."

During that lesson, I discovered that despite my many years riding English, dressage techniques were far more difficult than they looked. The cues all seemed backward to me, and sometimes having a muscle memory for doing something a certain way is a hindrance when you're trying to learn something new. You have to remember *not* to do something the old way before doing the new thing you're trying to master.

Just simply turning Penn in a circle at the walk the "dressage way" (using the outside leg and inside rein) required a lot of mental focus because it was the exact opposite of how we navigated a turn in show jumping (using the inside leg and rein together). I found myself thinking, "This is ridiculous. Who cares how I cue Penn to turn as long as he turns?" Part of me wanted to give up. But if I did, I'd never learn dressage.

I was practicing a "leg yield" one day, which is similar to a "half-pass," where the legs cross over one another. My pal Sarah watched my clumsy efforts. She told me I wasn't ready to do this at a trot. In fact, I wasn't even ready to do it at a walk. I needed to practice from a standstill, just moving Penn's hindquarters. And, that's what we did. I had to accept a slow and steady approach, and that was that. Never mind all the fancy gals on fancy horses prancing past me. I'm not doing this to impress them. It's not about them. It's about me. My goal isn't to compete in the show ring like them. It's simply to "dance" with my horse.

Take the Time to Learn and Feel

Is there something you'd like to learn or accomplish, but you're discouraged by the time and effort it will take? Yoga is a perfect example. You can't just launch into thirty sun salutations right on the first day and expect to be anything but sore, tired, and frustrated, and that's if you're even able to do one sun salutation at all without throwing your back out.

If you aren't limber and strong, and have never done yoga, you need a lot of patience with yourself when you're beginning, and a lot of practice doing simple, modified movements, often with blocks or straps, until you can achieve a pose, learn to relax into it, and breathe. However, along the way, you discover that mastering poses isn't the goal. It's the process itself that's the goal and being centered in the moment during that process.

This is the gift of Water Horse: just be in the moment—not the past, worrying that you've always failed before, and not in the future, where you imagine yourself failing again. Just be in the present moment, fully aware of what you're doing right now, at this moment in time. "Be here now" is the mantra of the present moment, and when you hold yourself there, free of past disappointment and future anxiety, you find serenity.

Water Horse's grace and patience helps our true feelings to flow, whether between people or in artistic endeavors. Without feelings and emotion, relationships and all creative expression—from art to writing to dance—couldn't exist. To be empathetic or creative, we have to acknowledge and fully experience our true feelings. You can't feel another person's pain if you've never allowed yourself to feel your own, or write a romance novel if you're afraid to truly love. If you "stuff your feelings" and avoid expressing them, Water Horse encourages you to break down the dam that holds your feelings back.

Help Water and Water Horse Flow to You

Do you need to call upon Water Horse? Let's see:

- Do you prefer logical decisions over emotional ones? Do you trust your head more than your heart?
- Are you impatient with others or yourself?
- Do people accuse you of being insensitive, rude, cold, or hard-hearted?
- Do people call you a "cold fish" or an "ice queen"?
- Is it extremely difficult to express tender feelings, like love, empathy, or affection?
- Does saying "I love you" seem terrifying?
- Are there things you'd like to try, but the commitment turns you off?
- Have you always loved art, music, dance, or creative writing, but avoided studying them because they aren't "practical"?

If you see yourself in the answers, Water Horse can help you. To help water and Water Horse flow into your life, collect or wear seashells, find pictures of fish, waves, water lilies, and—of course—seahorses, or anything associated with flowing water. Wear watery blues and purples. Get out and be near water if you can, or relax to an ocean soundtrack and imagine horses galloping along the shore, the waves your breath and the hooves your heartbeat. Get out and look at artwork, take a dance class, listen to beautiful music that makes your heart feel full.

Become inspired by Water Horse with an image of a prancing dressage horse; better yet, exercise your creative talent and draw one! My own iconic Water Horse is a beautiful, graceful, dappled-grey dressage horse, prancing through the surf. What would your Water Horse look like?

Meditation to Meet Your Elemental Horses

Although represented by various horse breeds in real life, Elemental Horses don't exist in the physical world, only the metaphysical. Therefore, we must travel internally to meet them.

We'll build upon our "Meditation to Meet Horse" in chapter 1 by adding in a breathing technique promoted by integrative medicine guru Dr. Andrew Weil, called "4-7-8 breathing." To practice the technique, inhale deeply and slowly through your nose to a relaxed count of four, hold for seven counts, exhale forcefully, but slowly, through your lips with a "whoosh" sound for a count of eight. This triggers your autonomic nervous system to relax.

To begin our Elemental Horse meditation, have a notebook and pen handy to jot down images or insights you want to remember afterward. Again, get out in nature if possible, away from human-generated noise. If that's not possible, earbuds and a long ambient nature soundtrack will do. Sweet, simple quiet works as well. As with the first meditation, read through the entire meditation first, and record it if possible so that you can relax into the imagery and not worry about remembering details.

Before beginning this meditation, take note of where north is, and from there, all the other directions: east, south, and west. You should be able to "turn" in that direction in your mind.

Sit or lie down in a comfortable, quiet space where you can breathe, sink into relaxation, and let your mind float like a leaf on a gentle current. Feel the support of the chair, bed, or ground upon which you sit or lie. Tell yourself, "I am completely safe," and sink into that, letting it serve as a trigger to let go of stresses or concerns.

Breathe easily, and when you're ready, move to the 4-7-8 breathing to help relax you into an even deeper state of peacefulness. After a few times you'll feel your heartbeat slow down. Now, just breathe deeply, easily, and slowly, imagining your breath coming into and out of your navel.

When you're feeling calm and receptive, visualize yourself standing in a large, flat, circular clearing. Turn your attention to the north, earth. There's a deep, thick, green forest there. You make a short, sharp whistle... calling. You hear a rustling that grows louder until brush sways. From that thicket emerges a massive, dark-colored draft horse, wearing a harness and tacked up to pull a load. Look at the horse and take it all in. Does it have white markings? Male? Female? What is its energy like as it steps toward you, its heavy hooves clopping on the ground? How do you feel as this huge horse approaches?

The horse stops about ten feet away from you, its ears pricked toward you, waiting for a greeting. You approach it, hold out your hand, let it nuzzle. Feel the tickle of the whiskers and note how small your hand looks next to its massive head, as you are next to its back—too tall to see over. You walk to its side and run your hand down its tall, thickly muscled neck and over its rounded shoulder... down a sturdy foreleg, down to a mighty hoof as big as a dinner plate. Feel how sturdy and connected to the earth it is. It's as solid as the ground it stands on. Stand and stroke its long, strong, tall back, and think: *Earth Horse.*

Give Earth Horse a firm, friendly pat on the neck, and return to the center of the circle. It knows to stay where it is and patiently await further direction.

Return to the center, and turn your mind's eye clockwise to the east, air. There's a vast open field, with several fences stretching across, the grass gently rippling in the breeze. Make that quick, calling whistle again. The breeze picks up and tickles your hair and skin, and you hear distant cantering hooves growing closer. In the distance, a light-colored horse canters up over the rise, heading toward you, effortlessly soaring over every fence as if carried on the wind. It clears the last one, then slows to a trot, stopping about ten feet away from you.

The horse is breathing a bit heavily from its dash toward you, but is bright and alert, and ready to keep going. It wears a jumping saddle and bridle. It looks at you with inquisitive, curious eyes. What color is it? Does it have white markings? Male? Female? Feel its energy as it tosses its head and dances upon long, slender legs as if to say, "Let's go!" How does it feel to take in the majesty of this horse?

You approach and hold out your hand in a greeting, and relish the feel of the velvety, trembling lips in your palm. Run your hand down its silken neck and your fingers through the tidy, trimmed mane, feeling the well of energy pulsing in this horse, ready to carry you anywhere. Tell yourself: *Air Horse.* Hold your palm to it and let it nuzzle again, and return to center. Air Horse knows to stay where it is until called upon.

Once again in the center, turn your mind's eye clockwise to the south, fire. You see a bright orange and gold desert plateau, dotted with large boulders and stretching cactus, scarred with deep ravines. You whistle quickly, sharply, and loudly. From one of those ravines rises a cloud of dust as you hear thundering hooves coming closer. Up from the rim of the nearest one pops a fiery, copper-colored horse, leaping up over the edge and hitting the ground at full gallop. It wears a Western saddle and bridle, and the shoes on its hooves clink against rocks as it barrels toward you, launching a spray of dust as it slides to a stop just in front of you, head high and snorting. It rears and paws the air in excitement, and then lands solidly, watching you, waiting for direction.

You approach and hold your hand out in greeting, and it gently lips your palm, hoping for a treat. What sort of markings does it have? Is it male? Female? How does it feel to approach such a formidable creature? Stroke its hot, damp, tossing neck. Note how the light shimmers gold in its red coat like ripples of tiny flames. Hold the reins for just a moment and feel the power surging at the other end as this horse prances and shimmies, eager for you to swing into the saddle and get going. Feel its surge of energy and excitement and think: *Fire Horse.*

Gently stroke the side of its velvety nose, conveying to it that its turn will come, but for now it must stand and wait. Dancing in place, Fire Horse obeys, and you return to center.

Turn your mind's eye clockwise to the west, water. You see an ocean inlet there, its waves gently lapping the shore. You whistle. A rolling sea mist billows over the water and then, as you peer even closer, you see the outline of a grey horse coming through that mist at water's edge. It wears a dressage saddle and bridle, and picks its feet up high as it prances, as if it has springs in its hooves, side-passing toward you with gracefully crossing legs, seeming to float over the ground until it stops in front of you, its neck arched perfectly as if posing for a photo, its large brown eyes soft and focused right upon you. What shade of grey is this horse? Does it have dapples? White markings? How does it feel to stand before this ethereal creature?

You approach and greet Water Horse with an outstretched palm, which it sniffs inquisitively, and you wrap your arms around its warm neck. You feel its neck curve over your back and its head push gently against you, returning the hug, and you rest there, feeling serene and calm and thinking: *Water Horse.* You'd like to stay there for a long while, feeling safe and close, but it's time to return to center. Water Horse watches you retreat, patiently awaiting your directions.

Back at the center, you turn your mind's eye clockwise, back to Earth Horse, admiring its power and might; then to Air Horse, ready to chase the wind; Fire Horse, pulsing with vitality and energy; and Water Horse, strong, graceful, loving. Soak in how it feels to stand in the center of this elemental circle of equine power and spirit…how it feels to realize that each of these Elemental Horses is tacked up and ready to go, just for you, willing to take on any challenge or task. All you have to do is ask. Each will respond to your touch the moment you pick up the reins and settle into the saddle or onto the wagon. Their only desire is to manifest your wishes and dreams, and they will carry or pull you tirelessly until they succeed. These are *your* Horses. Your very own spiritual elemental herd. They will not appear exactly as they are in anyone else's mind but yours. These are yours and yours alone.

Absorb the feeling of freedom and power in having these spiritual equine allies available to you at all times, for any task or goal. Settle into that newfound knowledge, and when you feel ready to return to the physical plane, give a short piercing whistle and wave your arm in farewell to each Horse, one at a time, releasing it until you call upon it again, watching as each canters away and disappears from whence it came.

The circle is just yours again.

Return your mind to focus upon your breathing, down in your belly button, and train your thoughts to that spot. When you're ready, return your attention to the physical space around you, breathe peacefully, and open your eyes. Jot down any impressions or messages you received during this meditation. Note the images and your feelings, and any thoughts inspired by the meditation.

You'll imagine and call upon these Elemental Horses when you're struggling with a task, situation, or person. Decide which qualities or strengths you need to succeed…which cluster of elemental traits would be most helpful? That will tell you which Horse to call upon. In time, just flashing an image of your Elemental Horses will trigger your mind to know exactly how to deal with the task at hand. Your Horses are always there for you, no matter where you are, or what difficulties you face. They won't let you down.

Attracting Elemental Horses

Each morning, you can set your intention for the day and invite your Elemental Horses to prompt the energy you need to accomplish that. Wear colors, clothing or jewelry that correspond to the element you need. It's a visual, tactile reminder of your intention. When you notice your prompts throughout the day, imagine your corresponding Elemental Horse too.

Me, I prefer stones and crystals. They have a vast array of energies, and one for every intention. They also fit in your pocket, and tumbling one around in your fingers feels reassuring. Some of my favorites include agate or jasper for earth, citrine or selenite for air, tiger's eye or carnelian for fire, labradorite or fluorite for water, and clear quartz crystal or moonstone for spirit. There are a gazillion healing and energetic correlations for stones; this is but a tiny sample. However, what matters most is that a stone triggers your intention and the energy you need.

Stone or crystal bracelets, pendants, and rings are particularly helpful because they're easily within your visual field at any time, reminding you to stay focused, be assertive, or just keep the image of your Elemental Horse in mind. The point isn't whether or not the stones actually generate healing or change themselves. It's that they keep you focused on your intention so that you can actively choose your responses. It doesn't matter *why* it works; it matters *that* it works. And trust me, it does.

Maybe it's not just a random day or you're doing something out of the ordinary, like visiting difficult relatives. You're dreading the drama, bickering, and sniping. But you have to go. You'll need patience, so you call upon Water Horse and dress in water colors or tuck a seashell in your pocket and rub it gently like a worry stone when you need to—a tactile reminder of the water energy you need to get you through this visit.

The visit will take as long as it takes, your relatives will be as annoying and frustrating as always, but they are what they are, and there's no point trying to control it. When the usual family drama starts simmering, close your eyes and breathe for a moment; imagine the gently rolling gait of Water Horse beside the calm rolling ocean. Just nod and smile to whatever they're saying, and remind yourself that you don't have to participate in every squabble you're invited to. You're not going to change them anyway, so why frustrate yourself trying?

When they say ridiculous things, pretend it's just noise … seagulls squawking on the shore as you're riding Water Horse in your mind, right there in front of them. They won't have a clue what's going on in your head, only that you aren't joining the dysfunctional family dance. They're just noisy seagulls. In your mind, go *bawwwwk* when they speak. You may find yourself stifling a chuckle, and they'll all wonder what you're up to. You don't have to tell them.

Wear Your Horse

Because I'm a huge believer in and practitioner of setting intention, most every day, I use symbols, colors, and jewelry to attract the element or Elemental Horse I want. I have a small wardrobe of horse-themed T-shirts, and I wear the one that represents whatever Elemental Horse I need to ride that day. I wore them while writing this book! One T-shirt is bright pink with a kaleidoscope horse, and prompts me to have an endless burst of energy and creativity—a combo, fire and water! Another has a horse silhouette and underneath, it says, "Mobile Device," prompting me plow forward and stay on task until the job is done. Let's get going, Earth Horse.

I accent my T-shirts with my harness brass and a pendant with a galloping horse in the middle. When I put all these things on together, it's like strapping on cleats, shoulder pads, and a uniform. It's "go time," and it feels that way. If you've ever played sports, you know the rush of adrenaline you get when your uniform is on and it's time to play. Your mind is in a completely different place than if you were wearing street clothes. Writing is my "sport," so I have a uniform, and when I put it on, it's time to "play."

Spirit

The last point on our Elemental solar cross is arguably the most important: spirit. It's right in the center, where the straight lines cross. Spirit isn't an earthly element. It's not an element at all. However, we include it when discussing the elements because it's the gravitational pull that keeps everything moving smoothly and cohesively. It's the heart of the matter.

Spirit is our divine connection to the energies of the universe, or Goddess, or God, Spirit, Source, your Higher Power, or whatever word you use for that cosmic energy that sparked life and creation, and flows through us all. Spirit isn't seen or felt like the other elements. Instead, it's experienced and internal. It's the "you" that you know and recognize in the privacy of your thoughts and feelings. Spirit is our true essence. Its color is crystal clear or white. It's neither male nor female energy, and it's both male and female energy. It is All, which is yet another term for God, Source, the universe, etc.

The center of our elemental solar cross, spirit, is where we find Spirit Horse. (Just a reminder, Spirit Horse is a specific metaphysical horse, as opposed to Horse Spirit in general.) Unlike the other four, Spirit Horse doesn't do any job for us. We don't ride it, although it may allow us to get on its back. But it won't be to do a job that *we* determine. Spirit Horse takes us where *it* wants to go and shows us what it wants to show us—not vice versa. We don't "do" with Spirit Horse, we just "be." Spirit Horse helps us recognize when our true, honest selves are being dulled by anxiety, grief, resentment, or fear, and prompts us to come clean with ourselves, and remember and rediscover our true, pure nature.

In the Celtic creation story, the divine white mare Eiocha emerges from the sea to walk on land, and thus began life on Earth. Eiocha perfectly symbolizes Spirit Horse. She rises from our turbulent, murky, depths—our subconscious—and materializes on land where we can see her—our conscious mind. With Spirit Horse, we find congruency between our subconscious and conscious minds, and our internal and external selves. But first, we need awareness and acceptance of what's really going on inside of us, both consciously and subconsciously. It's stressful to be serene on the surface if you're turbulent inside, particularly if you don't know—or won't face—the source of that internal conflict. You might fool someone else, but you can never fool your own heart.

Denying your true thoughts and feelings, your dreams and desires, creates chronic stress. It's a psychological pressure cooker, set on "high." Chronic stress prompts the body to release cortisol, and when our organs are constantly bathed in cortisol, we start having physical symptoms. Stress kills. It just does it slowly.

Spirit Horse helps us recognize the internal incongruities that cause our stress, and to develop a different coping strategy rather than simply keeping a lid on them until they finally blow. It takes us through our dark forest of painful feelings and negative, self-defeating thoughts and beliefs, and walks us out into the sunshine—or divine-shine—from where our Spirit energies can radiate. By helping us bring our own true dreams and desires into focus, and keeping us honest with ourselves, Spirit Horse helps us recognize which of the four other Elemental Horses we need to call upon to make change, and to make our dreams come true.

We Face Reality, and Ourselves, with Spirit Horse

Sometimes we end up doing things we never intended to do, like getting stuck in a mind-numbing job. All day long, you're pushing paper or staring into a computer monitor or doing tasks you don't really care about, in exchange for a paycheck. Many of us accept unfulfilling jobs to get the bills paid, and that goes double if we have kids. Then years drift by, many of them, and one day, the fact that this isn't a dress rehearsal bops you on the forehead: *Crap! Time's running out ... what am I doing with my life?* We call this a "midlife crisis." It prompts people to quit their dull, stupid jobs, sell their homes, and set off to climb Mount Everest, or buy a red Corvette, or run to a divorce lawyer like their hair's on fire. Unfortunately, although we've realized that time is running out, we're so far removed from our true, pure selves that we don't have a clue what the most positive change would be. So, we leave that unhappy situation, and find ourselves in a different situation but with the same problems as before.

Do you know someone who got into one relationship after another with an alcoholic or abusive partner? When we can't consciously solve the equation that led to our situation, our subconscious keeps attempting to do so by attracting us to people who will re-create that original situation so it can solve it. This is why children of alcoholics so frequently marry alcoholics. They're still trying to solve the "problem" of their turbulent and frightening childhoods. Solving that problem, or "closing the loop," is a basic tenet of Gestalt psychology: Our subconscious will keep working that problem tirelessly like a psychological Rubik's Cube until it "solves" it *or* until our conscious mind recognizes the dysfunctional pattern, closes that chapter (or Gestalt), and moves on.

When we chronically stifle our true feelings, dreams, wishes, and goals, it results in anger, sadness, and resentment. A common coping strategy is addiction: food, alcohol, drugs, shopping, social media, relationships, gambling, sex, or video games. We lean on things that provide comfort, pleasure, and most of all, distraction from our core pain.

If we've been insightful enough to know our true selves and preferences before we set out on careers and life choices, then we may not come skidding headfirst into midlife, wondering where all the time went and how we landed in this predicament. However, most of us are not that insightful when forced to make lifelong career decisions in our late teens and early twenties. We took our best guess or did what our parents or friends said we should do, and then ten, twenty, or thirty years later, start realizing that we're restless or depressed, lost, wallowing in despair, or just bored. Unless we change our course, and therefore our trajectory, we may become victims of our own coping mechanisms or addictions. We try to fill a spiritual hole with food, vodka, or porn, and still the empty hole gnaws and aches.

Help us, Spirit Horse! We're lost!

Choosing a new course, coming to terms with a stressful job or relationship, or simply feeling unfulfilled in our lives—none of these problems can be solved until we come face to face with ourselves. This is Job One, before even calling upon our Elemental Horses. When we're psychologically lost, we need to stick with Spirit Horse and find our spiritual center, our true and genuine self, or we'll shoot off in the wrong direction *again*.

Who Are You?

Spirit Horse is a wild entity that chooses to commune with us. It roams wherever it wants on the astral plane. Whether choosing to graze peacefully or snort and paw at the sky, Spirit Horse is all that it can be. It makes no apologies or excuses; Spirit Horse just *is*. It asks us, "Who *are* you?"

Who are you when you're not doing your job, or taking care of others, or sitting in church, or working out at the gym, or taking notes in class? If all your roles and titles are removed, and you're stripped down to your simple spiritual nature … who *are* you? Spirit Horse prompts you toward discovering—recovering—your own true nature, not the nature others expect of you or by which they judge you, but your own pure, pristine, perfect self. It also encourages you to stay balanced and centered—in the middle with it—rather than reacting to the same situations the same old way. When you don't react reflexively to a situation or person, if you take control of your responses rather than give that control to others, your mind is much clearer about what's really going on and what choices you should make. While the other Elemental Horses help you *do* something, Spirit Horse is quite the opposite: It helps you to do nothing at all until you're clear about what you want to do next.

Meeting Spirit Horse

Just as we traveled internally to meet the four Elemental Horses, we will do likewise to meet Spirit Horse, beginning as we did before. You'll need space, time, and quiet. Again, keep a notebook and pen handy to jot down images or insights that you want to remember afterward, and read through the meditations first, recording them if you can.

Spirit Horse Meditation Number One

For our first Spirit Horse meditation, get centered in your body, release the verbal static in your mind, and breathe slowly and deeply. When you're ready, incorporate 4-7-8 breathing; repeat until you feel yourself growing more still, calm, and relaxed. When you feel ready, return to regular, slow, deep, relaxed breathing. Be aware of your body being safely supported by the chair, sofa, or ground beneath you. Think to yourself, *I am completely safe*, and release all your verbal thoughts, words, and concerns to the cosmos. You can retrieve them later, but for now, they are somewhere else.

Imagine yourself in a pristine, private, natural setting—ocean, forest, open field—whatever setting you're most drawn to. Imagine yourself walking into a clearing or cove or up a rolling green hill, and notice the temperature of the air, the greenery, the ground beneath your feet. There's a magical mist in the air, and it feels so comforting, enveloping you. You are completely safe and supported in this setting. Nothing can harm you here.

Open your mind and heart and invite Spirit Horse to come to you. We don't whistle to summon it like we did with the other Elemental Horses. Spirit Horse will approach when it's ready. Wait quietly and patiently until you hear its steady, gentle hoofbeats. From out of a magical mist, Spirit Horse materializes and approaches. Hold out your hand, and invite it to come to you.

Spirit Horse stretches out its nose and you can feel its velvety muzzle in your hand. Its very touch makes tingles course through your body. Empty your mind of words, and just experience Spirit Horse. Stroke its silky white coat, run your fingers through its flowing mane, feel its warm breath on your cheek, and look into its deep, soulful brown eyes. Soak in its mystical, timeless energy. Stay with Spirit Horse as long as you like, just experiencing its divinity. When it's time to go, thank Spirit Horse for spending time with you, bid it farewell, and watch as it canters away, disappearing once again into the mist. When the image fades, breathe, and return to center. Write down anything you want to remember.

This is a wonderful meditation to help you fall asleep. You don't have to do anything in this meditation other than just *be*. If something does happen, it will be at Spirit Horse's direction, not yours. You aren't in charge, it is.

I use this meditation frequently when I go to bed. I decide I will journey to visit with Spirit Horse, and ninety percent of the time, I never make it that far. I fall asleep while I'm still walking down the path. Just setting my thoughts upon meeting up with Spirit Horse prompts me to relax and drift off to sleep. For a lifelong, chronic insomniac, this is a small miracle. Maybe Spirit Horse knows that the thing I need more than anything else—even a mystic romp on the astral plane—is a good night's sleep. And, it's absolutely correct. Spirit Horse is exceedingly wise.

Spirit Horse Meditation Number Two

The second Spirit Horse meditation begins the same as the first. Follow the same setup and scenario, beginning with calming yourself, breathing, and inviting Spirit Horse to visit. This time, once it arrives, ask it a question about what's troubling you: Why am I so depressed? What would give me joy? Who are the people that drain my energy? Or replenish it? What do I want from life? When you ask the question, communicate it mentally, telepathically—not with spoken words. Horses, and Horse, don't speak in words, nor do they think with words. They think and respond with images and behavior.

How does Spirit Horse respond to your question? Does it show you a clue or an answer? What images come to mind? When you're ready to go, thank Spirit Horse for its insight, bid it farewell, breathe, and return to center. Write down anything you want to remember.

Spirit Horse Meditation Number Three

This third meditation also begins just like the first. This time, when Spirit Horse arrives and you've greeted it, "ask" if you may ride it by sending it the image of you on its back. If it signals "yes," slide gently onto its back—no saddle, no bridle. It's okay to hold on to its mane if you need to. "Ask" Spirit Horse to take you where you need to go. It will wander wherever it chooses— just move with it as one.

Notice whatever you see, hear, touch, taste, or smell on your journey. Is it light? Dark? Does Spirit Horse walk slowly and steadily, or take you on a dashing gallop through fields or forest? How does it feel to be on its back? Spirit Horse may prompt you to dismount at some point, or it may bring you back to where you started. It's all up to Spirit Horse.

When the ride is over, thank Spirit Horse, bid it farewell, breathe smoothly and slowly until you feel yourself back in your body and your room or surroundings, and return to center. Write down anything you want to remember.

Spirit Horse Meditation Number Four

Our fourth Spirit Horse meditation is specifically for accessing your dreams. The ability to travel back and forth between this world and the otherworld is part of horse mythology, so we'll make use of that ability in accessing our subconscious and our dreams, and bringing their messages to conscious awareness.

Place your notebook and a pencil or pen near your bedside. Get comfortable in your bed, do all the fidgeting and blanket adjusting you need to do, and when you feel comfy, cozy, and still, close your eyes and breathe deeply and slowly ... four ... seven ... eight ... repeat ...

Travel to that special spot where you meet Spirit Horse. The more you times you visualize that spot, in as much detail as you can, the more easily and vividly you'll be able to return to that spot again and again.

When Spirit Horse arrives, greet it, and "ask" it to carry you into your dreams. "Ask" if it has a message or insight for you. Tell yourself that you will remember these details when you wake up. When you wake up, immediately jot down the images and insights that came to you in your dreams. It's important to do this right when you wake up, because you'll forget the details quickly as the day wears on. Over time, you may notice patterns in your dreams, which are clues about what's simmering in your subconscious mind.

I recently did this dream meditation and asked Spirit Horse to bring me a message. I dreamed of a bright, colorful unicorn head, floating in the vast darkness. A beam of white light from the universe shone down upon it and through it, and then fractured out in every direction like a huge firework, shooting out little rainbow orbs that floated in the blackness. Spirit Horse then said, "They (the orbs) are there, but they (the humans) can't see them," which I understood as "there's magic all around us but we're blind to it."

A few days later, my daughter threw a sixtieth birthday party for me. When I arrived, floating above a table decorated entirely in unicorns and rainbows, was a giant sparkly unicorn head balloon, just like the one in my dream! Then, relatives and friends began popping out, and more soon arrived at the front door. Instead of rainbow orbs around me, there were loving people all around me.

"Love is all around, but I couldn't see it."

I see it now.

Attracting Spirit Horse

Just like the four Elemental Horses, you can use visual or kinesthetic prompts to attract Spirit Horse so it can help you remain centered, balanced, and drama-free. That centered place is your refuge of calm emotions and clear thinking. Wear white clothing or a white scarf, or white or clear jewelry to prompt you to stay in your calm center, true to your own self, feelings, and choices. Burn a white candle, place some quartz crystal on your desk, or hang a prism in the window, where you can see it.

More and more, I'm drawn to wearing white because the older I get, the more I detest the manipulations of others. Even more than that, I detest my own propensity to give in to it. Staying centered with Spirit Horse as much as possible helps me to recognize when someone is attempting to manipulate me or when I'm about to cave in to their demands. I also love wearing a chunk of clear quartz crystal on a cord around my neck. If I'm wearing a white shirt *and* a quartz crystal, don't try to mess with me. I am solidly in place with Spirit Horse and cannot be budged.

When I realize that someone is attempting to provoke an argument with me or belittle or berate me, I imagine Spirit Horse right there behind me, its neck against my back, its head lovingly over my shoulder. Rather than engage in any of this manipulation, Spirit Horse prompts me to label the behavior (not the person) for what it is, state it, and drop it there: "That's harsh." "That's rude." "That's insulting." If it takes more to disengage myself, then I walk away. Label it, drop it, and walk away, with Spirit Horse at your side.

Taking Your Temperament

Each of the four Elemental Horses represents an element associated with a specific cluster of human traits and behavior characteristics. Each element has strengths and weaknesses. We need to understand them so we can recognize our own propensities, and moreover, when we need a correction.

These elements correlate to the four basic personality types, or "temperaments," which are the core concepts of a variety of temperament assessments, such as the classic Myers-Briggs Type Indicator. I used several personality and temperament assessment systems when I worked in the social services field, co-facilitating workshops designed to help people define their career goals. Before any decisions were made about careers, a comprehensive assessment was made of each person's unique temperament, and then blended in with experience, abilities, and aptitude, and all of this information was used to create a specific path for success.

These temperament systems were very enlightening, but something felt not quite right. Years later, as I started exploring the Pagan path, I realized that all these assessment systems had their roots in the basic energies and traits associated with the four earthly elements: earth, air, fire, and water. There was nothing new here, just new labels.

Many of these various assessment systems decree that there are four basic core clusters of traits, strengths, and preferences, and assert that we have one in particular that's dominant in our personalities, and *that* is who we are. They pigeon-hole people into one temperament or the other. You get the label stamped on your forehead: You are *this*, go forth and flounder no more. It felt contrived and hollow to me, but in particular, extremely limiting. I want to color with *all* the crayons in the box. Unlike those pigeon-holing assessments, I offer an alternate viewpoint: We are *all* of the elements, and we can *choose* which cluster of traits we need at any particular moment, for any particular purpose, and move back and forth between them at will. The key is not staying in your comfortable "default" spot, but rather, balancing in the center and choosing how you will react to different people and situations.

Spirit Is Central

Besides denying us access to the totality of elemental energies and traits available to us, many personality and temperament assessments further miss the mark because they don't address the center of that elemental temperament circle, where the two lines of the solar cross intersect: spirit. Without a central point allowing access to all the temperaments, all you have are four disconnected boxes of traits, and you're stuck in one box. Spirit connects them all.

Spirit itself isn't a temperament. It's essence—our own pure, unadulterated essence that we already had when we arrived in this particular lifetime. Spirit is also the pipeline to the universal, cosmic life energy that connects us all. We need to be centered, right there in spirit, in order to access all of the elemental energies available 360 degrees around us, to be whole and balanced, and to make the best decisions for our lives.

To get a better grasp of how the elements and spirit work together, we'll build upon that solar cross image, with the elements in their respective positions and spirit at the center. Underneath that spirit center, add a pin, like a child's top. We *are* the top. When it's in perfect balance, all of the elements are equally accessible, and the top could easily spin or tip in any direction, or just stay upright. When it's out of balance, it tips to one side and gets stuck there— your "default" elemental temperament.

If you remain stuck in that spot, you can't make use of the skills and abilities of the other three. You've reduced your options in life, relationships, and experiences by three-fourths. You need access to all the elemental energies to experience life fully. Sometimes we need to be very organized, like with our finances. Sometimes we need to engage our minds, like in school. Sometimes we need to take risks, like asking someone on a date. Sometimes we need to be tender, like when holding a baby.

If you only have one tool in your toolbox, you're going to be awfully frustrated when you attempt to saw a board with your screwdriver. You need all the tools, whenever you want them, right at your fingertips. The key is remaining balanced in the center, and tipping toward whatever element you need.

While writing this book, Earth Horse really got a workout. But over-focusing on one element can backfire. If I'd only relied upon Earth Horse to keep my fingers moving across the keyboard, I'd have produced 500 pages of *"words words words words words."* Earth Horse isn't selective. It just keeps powering forward. I needed Air Horse to keep concepts and explanations clear and logical, Fire Horse to provide me with limitless, nimble energy, and Water Horse to inspire creativity and polish, all kept in balance by Spirit Horse, enabling me to easily tip toward whichever element and energies I needed at that moment for the task at hand. I needed it *all*.

What's Your Default?

Let's explore the cluster of traits associated with each of the elemental temperaments. You may recognize yourself in one particular cluster. That's your "default" temperament—the traits and behaviors that come naturally to you, sort of like the lowest spot on a patch of land where water collects. It's the perspective from which you typically interact with the world and the people you encounter.

It's not bad to have a default temperament. The problem comes when you get stuck there. If you discover you're stuck, don't despair. You can use this information for insight and change. Knowing your default element also helps you to recognize which way you need to tip for a correction. Your ultimate goal is to default to the center: spirit.

Earth

People who default toward earth are naturals with data and procedure, and following and keeping order. They are comfortable with hierarchy. Those who tilt toward earth are risk averse, conservative in their choices and dress (they do not own any tie-dye), and are thorough, reliable, responsible, punctual, and loyal. They like to know the rules, follow them, and get frustrated with those who don't. They can be depended upon. They're hard workers and appreciate being recognized, respected, and honored for their service.

Those who are earthy work for that "gold star," and could be the "teacher's pet" in school—and also the kid most despised for being a tattletale. They are quick to assign blame and comfortable dispensing punishment. People who are inclined toward earth like very structured careers, such as government positions or managing an office or corporation. They're driven to make and save money, and may also be drawn to the banking and financial industries.

Air

The natural skills of people who default toward air include intelligence, logic, and innovation. They are inquisitive, precise, and persistent. Air types like to solve problems and can easily "think outside the box." They need to keep their minds busy, and are often employed in the sciences, engineering, medicine, academia and research, or even investigative journalism. Someone who gravitates toward air may tend to live "from the neck up" and would rather stare into a computer than exercise.

In school, an air person is in the AP classes, participates in chess club or on the debate team, and might be teased for being a nerd. They dress for practicality and comfort rather than high fashion, and are less concerned with appearances than function. They can be uncomfortable and or/impatient with very emotional people, uneducated people, or anyone they view as intellectually inferior, and are vicious in their criticism. An air person may be known as "Mr./Ms. Know It All," and will pick apart details to the death in order not to lose an argument. Because they are tenacious, logical to a fault, and loathe being wrong, they make great lawyers.

Fire

People who default toward fire have natural skills using their hands, whether it's power tools or electric guitars. Employing naturally superior athletic ability gives them joy and satisfaction. As opposed to air people, fire people live from the neck down. They are impulsive, bold, energetic, and competitive, and thrive on taking risks, which is why they get injured more than the other elements. They prefer careers where they can be physically active, adventurous, and even dangerous. Fire people love the outdoors; sitting at a desk all day would cause them agony.

Someone who tilts toward fire had a hard time sitting still in school and loved physical education classes. They could be bullies, are the most likely to break the rules, and got called to the principal's office with greater frequency than others when in school. However, fire people get away with a lot because they are often very charismatic. They are the most likely to have experimented with sex and drugs in high school.

Those tilting toward fire don't care much for reading, and will pick a NASCAR race over the symphony every time. They've had more than one speeding ticket. Football coaches, mechanics, race car drivers, professional athletes, rock stars, skydivers, farmers, and horse trainers are all ideal careers for someone who feels drawn to the fire element. They are comfortable in jeans, T-shirts, and coveralls, and don't mind getting dirty.

Water

The natural realm of those who default toward water involves emotions, empathy, and people. They are creative and introspective, and strive to be unique. Their lives revolve around expressing their true feelings. Someone who is inclined toward the water element may be dramatic and playful, may be eccentric in their dress (they're cool with the tie-dye), and have a lot of flair. They love costumes and love to play.

A water person is romantic, affectionate, and empathetic. If extroverts, they're probably huggers. If introverts, they may prefer to curl up with a romance novel rather than attend a crowded event. They are not found at NASCAR events, ever. Unless they're in love with someone who loves NASCAR, because love comes before anything else for water people, and they'll shape-shift to get it.

They're often brushed off as "airy fairy," usually by those who are unable or unwilling to understand their unique and sometimes eccentric perspectives. They must have a creative outlet to be happy, and choose careers like acting, painting, designing, or creative writing, or if driven to help people, seek careers where they can be nurturing and tender, such as social work, massage therapy, caring for animals, or working with children. Water people would rescue all the cats if they could.

Which Way Do You Tip?

In other temperament assessment methods, you'd land in one of these clusters, and that would be your label: you're this, but not that. However, couldn't you see a little of yourself in each one? We aren't one or the other of those elemental temperaments; we're all of them. It's simply a matter of degree. We are just like the planet we live on—consisting of earth, air, fire, *and* water. All factors must be present for life to exist. Take one out, and everything dies.

Likewise, when we feel like we're spiritually shriveling on the vine, it may be because we're entrenched in our very comfortable default element, and it's at odds with our situation, career, or relationships. We've created our own elemental rut, have forgotten how to climb out, and then we're stuck.

Our jobs or careers are one of the easiest ways to recognize when our internal and external selves are incongruent. If you and your job are a bad match, that doesn't necessarily mean you need to find another line of work; it means you need to tip into another set of elemental traits to feel better about it. If you're simply unable to do that because your job is too far removed from your spiritual center, like a creative water type suffocating in a dust-dull bookkeeping job, you may need to make a change.

Chronic dissatisfaction in a relationship is a clue that we may have chosen a partner who is seriously misaligned with our default temperament. Again, it doesn't mean the relationship is over. If you decide you love this person and want to make it work, you'll need to get better at accessing the other three clusters of strengths, gifts, and talents. Tip yourself, tip the relationship.

When we know which way we must tip, we call upon the correct Elemental Horse. Put the wrong Horse in the wrong job, and it may accomplish it, or do its best to try, but it's not going to work out as well as putting the right Horse in the right job, the one it's most naturally skilled to accomplish. You might get a Clydesdale to complete a jumping course, but there'll probably be a lot of shattered jumping poles in its wake. Better to let a Clydesdale do what a Clydesdale was born to do—plow that land until it's smooth—and call upon lightning quick Air Horse to get you through that course.

Balancing with the Elemental Horses

If you feel stuck in a certain element, particularly a job, relationship, or situation that drains your energy rather than replenishes or sustains it, it's time to set your elemental "top" back upright on its central pin and get in balance. This means replenishing your connection to your own true self: spirit.

Make a list: What makes you happy? What does not? Who do you feel energized by, and who drains your energy? What area of your life causes pain, annoyance, or dissatisfaction? What are your triggers? Stand balanced in the middle with non-reactive Spirit Horse, and consider how your default elemental temperament serves you—or doesn't—for each issue. You'll need to experiment a little, explore less comfortable elemental traits, and try them on for size. It's infinitely easier to do this when balanced in the center, deciding which way you'll tip in any given situation rather than setting out in the same old familiar lane that always take you to the same old place.

When you feel yourself going into reaction mode, behaving automatically rather than actively choosing a response, close your eyes and return to Spirit Horse. Decide which Elemental Horse you need, call it, and ask it to take you to the elemental temperament you need. Feel the physical sensation of being carried or pulled there and the feeling of mentally arriving at your destination. Your Horse will get you there. The rest is up to you.

Besides helping you to stop, think, and choose your response rather than automatically reacting, Spirit Horse has an extra strategy: the choice of doing nothing at all. Sometimes the best action is no action. Just because people want you to react a certain way or do a certain thing doesn't mean you're obliged to accommodate them. Spirit Horse prompts you to *choose* not to respond or participate in whatever drama is unfolding before you; do nothing at all until you're certain of how you want to respond. Stay calm at the center of the storm and just let the debris and bluster swirl around you. Don't get sucked in. You only need to step into it if you want to.

There in the center with Spirit Horse, *you* own your self-confidence, safety, satisfaction, and sovereignty, rather than leaving it up to chance, habit, or pressure from others. You don't react. You *choose*. Spirit Horse only requires that you be honest and genuine about who you really are and what you really want. It will accept no less.

Find Your Tipping Point

Another way to recognize if you're stuck in one default elemental temperament is how you feel and behave when you're nearing the end of your emotional rope and are overwhelmed. Do you:

- Become stubborn, judgmental, anxious, punitive? Engage in perpetual complaining? Become fatigued or experience physical problems, like nausea or headaches? Use words as evidence? Hold grudges for an inordinately long time? Gossip behind people's back, but never confront them directly? Get uptight and judgy? Give people the "cold shoulder"? If so, you are defaulting toward earth. Tip all the way across the solar cross to fire to access your active self, loosen up a bit, become assertive, and regain balance. Roll toward water and get in touch with your feelings and express them—water softens dirt into mud. Or, roll toward air and come up with solutions and strategies, rather than just whine and complain. Air dries up saturated ground. Imagine yourself riding the corresponding Elemental Horse and proceed accordingly.

- Become sarcastic, verbally abusive, critical? Immerse yourself in a book, activity, or task so you don't have to interact with anyone? Give people the "silent treatment"? Avoid them entirely? Cut them off, or out, of your life? Belittle others? Use words like a knife? Regret your overly harsh words later on? Plot revenge? If so, you're defaulting toward air. Tip across the solar cross to water to access your empathetic self that considers, understands, and respects the needs and feelings of others, and regain balance. You could also roll toward fire and take responsibility for initiating positive action; fire burns air. Or, roll toward earth and see if you can become part of the team and cooperate, rather than always being contrary. Earth displaces air. Imagine yourself riding the corresponding Elemental Horse and proceed accordingly.

- Become physically or verbally aggressive? Bully others? Harm others? Break rules? Break things? Rally others to rebel? Head to the bar and get hammered? Refuse to cooperate or show up at all? Use words like a bludgeon? If so, you're defaulting toward fire. Tip across the grid to earth and find your calm, stable, cooperative self. Think first, speak second, and regain balance. Or, roll toward water to get in touch with your emotions, and feel your pain rather than transmuting it into anger. Water drenches fire. You could roll toward air and use your brain to work through things rather than your fists. Air blows out fire. Imagine yourself riding the corresponding Elemental Horse and proceed accordingly.

- Become depressed, sobbing and crying? Become irrational? Exaggerate and become hysterical? Scream and yell? Make ridiculous over-the-top accusations? Go into full "drama queen" mode? Use words like a fire hose? Wallow in self-pity? Hide on your couch and eat an entire box of chocolates? If so, you're defaulting toward water. Lean across the grid toward air, dry those tears, and think with your head instead of your heart; use logic over emotion. Roll toward earth and come up with a reasonable and organized method for dealing with the people or situation. Earth dams up water. A roll toward fire could help you take responsibility for setting upon a positive course of action rather than just throwing a tantrum. Fire dries up water—or tears. Imagine yourself riding the corresponding Elemental Horse and proceed accordingly.

Again, you may do one, some, or all of these things at one time or another, but usually, one cluster of behaviors stands out. That's your default. Going forward, you can *decide* how you'll respond to various troublesome people or situations, rather than just reacting on reflex. You can take control of your reactions. You *can*.

The Elemental Horses Will Tip You Over

Trying out a different cluster of elemental traits may feel unfamiliar and clumsy at first, like walking backward or writing with your opposite hand, but that's just familiarity and practice. Just because you *haven't* employed a particular cluster of traits that often doesn't mean you *can't*. Tipping into a new set of behaviors can feel intimidating, but you don't have to do it alone. The Elemental Horses are your allies.

When you recognize the direction you need to tip or roll, choose the Elemental Horse best equipped to assist you. Whistle to it in your mind, and there it is, instantly at your side and ready to serve. Pick up the reins, hop onto that saddle or wagon, and off you go.

You can reinforce your elemental experiments by adding a physical or visual prompt. Wear clothing or jewelry in the colors of that element, or carry something representative of that element in your pocket, like a stone for earth, a feather for air, a book of matches for fire, or a seashell for water. When you need some psychological self-reinforcement and feel yourself slipping out of the "saddle," just reach in your pocket and roll that item between your fingers, or look at the stone on your pendant or the color of your shirt. Visualize your Elemental Horse, and repeat its name in your mind.

Horse Is All That

We've taken a look at the four elemental facets of Horse—earth, air, fire, and water, plus spirit. Now we'll pull it all together into one cohesive unit.

The Elemental Horses aren't five separate entities. They are facets of one whole, just as our planet and our own personalities are all of the elements combined. Think of a disco ball. It has all sorts of colorful mirrored facets on it, but the facets are all part of one thing, just like the elemental facets of Horse.

We imagined the elements as a solar cross toy top, with spirit as the central balancing pin, and earth, air, fire, and water each taking a position upon the rim in their appropriate places. Now imagine the entire top in a clear, round sphere. That is Horse in its entirety, all the wild energies of Horse, all the disciplined and domesticated abilities of Horse, all the spiritual energy of Horse; all the elements; the whole shebang, one big ball of all the energies you could ever need.

If you're struggling to grasp how one entity can have multiple facets, think about yourself. You have many "yous." There's the you that's an amazing cook, the you that works as a biology teacher, the you that's training for a marathon, the you that's learning to speak Italian, and the you that enjoys painting landscapes. Those are all you; different facets of you. If you decided you wanted to make your famous moussaka for dinner guests, you wouldn't shift into teacher mode, you'd shift into chef mode. You have access to all those aspects of yourself, whenever you want, and choose the best one for the task or desire at hand. You are multitalented and multifaceted; so is Horse.

To call upon Horse, in general, is to call upon all of that energy, all at once. Sometimes you need quick access to any elemental energy; sometimes you need "all of the above." Carrying or wearing anything that reminds you of horses reinforces Horse energy in its totality, with all the elemental energies and Elemental Horses at hand.

Horse in its totality is like a handy Swiss Army knife, with all the tools you need, right there in your pocket. If you're unexpectedly facing a difficult situation that you need to deal with on the spot, consider which tool, or element, you need and you'll know which facet of Horse to call:

- I need to dig in and power through this: Earth Horse
- I need to identify and clear obstacles: Air Horse
- I need quick, decisive action: Fire Horse
- I need to be flexible and just go with the flow: Water Horse
- I need to remain calm and centered: Spirit Horse
- Holy crap, all hell's breaking loose! I don't know what I need, but I need it now: Horse

I Need It All

When might you need access to all of Horse, in its entirety, all the time, tipping back and forth between the elements? At the top of that list, raising children. You'll need every skill you can muster, and then some. While raising children, you'll need Horse continually, because your children's job is to knock you off that Horse, every day, for about eighteen years. Just had a baby? Saddle up, pardner, it's gonna be a long, bumpy trail ride. Thankfully, you've got a great mount.

Teachers also need all of Horse, all the time. You must be organized, intelligent, energetic, and patient when working with children or teens, and their parents too.

Another example? Marriage. Yes, you're madly in love when you say "I do," but once the gifts are put away, and you're fighting over where the sofa should go or who should take out the garbage, the sparkle and shine of what you imagined marriage might be like starts to get dull and grungy and lame, and yeah, you're gonna need Horse. All of it.

Keep Horse Close

Wearing or seeing a Horse prompt—artwork, on a shelf, as your computer wallpaper, or a simple pendant with a horse on it, or maybe an actual Swiss Army knife in your pocket—is a constant reminder that all the energies of the universe are readily available to you. You are not a victim without choices. You can choose your reactions and responses, and lean on Horse for support.

As you become familiar with these Elemental Horse concepts, you'll know automatically which aspect of Horse you need in any given situation, just like when you're going to make lasagna, for example. The image of the ingredients and particular kitchen tools you'll need immediately pops into mind. That's how it will be when you need an Elemental Horse for whatever you're doing. An image of your Elemental Horse will pop right up, ready to go.

When you're astride a horse, you feel big, confident, and powerful—even on one that only exists in your own mind. When I'm in the saddle, whether physically or mentally, no one can touch me. Riding my Elemental Horses empowers me to move boldly in a certain direction or, if need be, stay calmly centered and grounded with Spirit Horse, completely in control, not allowing myself to be buffeted about by people or situations.

Chapter 5

HORSES OF THE TAROT

If you've never seen, let alone used, tarot cards before, not to worry. You don't have to become a tarot expert to get started. In fact, you don't have to become one ever. You *will* need a classic Rider-Waite-Smith deck to get started, however, and if all you want to do is use them for meditations or to reinforce the energies of your Elemental Horses, that's just fine. If you want to dive deeper into tarot, an abundance of information about tarot is available.

A Quick Introduction to Tarot

Tarot cards appeared in fifteenth-century Europe as the game of *tarocchi*, and were used for divination later on. On contract with A. E. Waite (a member of the Hermetic Order of the Golden Dawn), artist and storyteller Pamela Colman Smith created the classic tarot images in the early 1900s, and this deck is most commonly known as the Rider-Waite-Smith (or Waite-Smith or Waite-Colman-Smith) deck.

There are two types of cards in a deck—major arcana and minor arcana. The major arcana are the power cards, and tell the story of a person's journey through life. Each of the twenty-two cards represents mastery or a challenge about some aspect of life's journey. When you get a major arcana card in a reading, that's a big deal, like getting a message in all caps: THIS IS IMPORTANT!

There are fifty-six minor arcana cards, corresponding to a regular deck of playing cards, except there is an extra court card. A regular deck has jacks, queens, and kings, while the minor arcana additionally has pages. The other cards in each suit of the minor arcana are called pip cards.

Each suit also tells of a progression, beginning with the ace, through the step-by-step challenges of that suit in the pips, and up through the fuller expression of the suit in the court cards. The suits in the minor arcana correspond to playing cards: pentacles/diamonds, swords/spades, wands/clubs, and cups/hearts, and the suits additionally correspond to the elements: pentacles/earth, swords/air, wands/fire, and cups/water. In some decks, pentacles are called coins, and wands are called rods or staves.

Tarot cards can be used for divination, personal insight, guidance, problem solving, and planning. You can purchase them online or at bookstores, and most tarot readers no longer adhere to the superstition that you must not buy your own tarot cards, that they must be given to you. Nonsense. If a deck speaks to me, I'm buying it, and you should too.

While the Rider-Waite-Smith deck is the classic most everyone begins with, the Celtic Cross is the spread most people learn first. It has two sections: a circle and a straight line, composed of ten cards total. Each position on the Celtic Cross has a particular meaning, which you can research on your own, as we won't be using it for our Horse tarot readings.

If your curiosity is piqued about tarot, you'll discover a universe of resources and information available. You might also visit a local metaphysical store, where they may be able to guide you toward a trusted professional. Finding an experienced tarot reader will really enhance your learning process. Pick up a book by Mary Greer, and you'll be off on the right foot.

I recommend that you look at the following Rider-Waite-Smith tarot cards I describe online, or get a deck for yourself. The brilliant colors and iconic images drawn by Pamela Colman Smith have inspired generations of intuitive people, and are a shared language between most everyone who loves tarot. However, you'll probably want a deck of your own so you can do the spreads I'll be describing and later on and to use some of the cards on your altars.

Can We See the Future?

Tarot doesn't necessarily predict the future. It peers into the potential future by tapping into your own psychic abilities, intuition, and insight to discover or connect ideas that you might not have on your own. There are a lot of "aha!" moments in tarot. I've witnessed so many uncanny, spot-on, laser-focused insights with tarot and seen them play out in real life, I am certain those cards know something we don't.

A tarot spread shines a spotlight on your situation and says that if you do nothing at all, this is the likely outcome. For example, the cards tell you that if you're standing on top of a big hill and let a ball roll down, it's likely to hit this log, bounce off that rock, swing through this gutter, get bogged down on that pile of leaves, and then roll down and end up *there*. If you like that outcome, fine, do nothing. If not, you've been given some suggestions about what to change and where to intervene.

Reversals

Reversals are when you draw a card upside down. For experienced readers, this offers another seventy-eight ways to interpret the cards. Some people like to read reversals, some don't. Me being a Gemini, I swing both ways. Most of the time not, because stopping to think about the reversal interrupts my right-brain flow of just soaking the cards in and feeling them. During a local Pagan convention, I attended a couple workshops led by eminent tarot experts and was surprised to hear them say they no longer bother with reversals.

I recommend foregoing reversals until you're very familiar with your cards, and know them immediately when you see them. However, if you really must do it all at once, keep a reference book or website nearby that gives reversal definitions. Once you can really feel a card, and know it, you can get an idea of how a reversal feels by flipping it upside down—you may get an instant gut reaction.

Tarot Horses

In the Rider-Waite-Smith deck, horses only appear on seven cards: the knights of all four suits and the Six of Wands in the minor arcana, and Death and the Sun in the major arcana. The knights and Death signify movement, going from one place to the next, just like our Elemental Horses. The Six of Wands is finishing its movement. The Sun card isn't going anywhere—it has already arrived.

The Sun is like spirit—not amongst the four earthly elements, but existing within its own realm. It shows a joyous, carefree child reveling in the warm sunshine, enjoying the moment, astride a gentle white horse that has an expression on its face indicating that it is borderline annoyed, but tolerating all this youthful glee—just as every good real-life equine babysitter does with children. That horse won't let anything happen to that child. Here, they are completely safe.

The Knights

The horses on the Death and knight cards aren't sauntering whimsically along. They move forward with power, direction, and purpose. These are action cards. They *take* us there. Each knight rides an Elemental Horse, and his suit, like all the suits in the minor arcana, corresponds with the elements: pentacles/earth, swords/air, wands/fire, and cups/water. The Knight of Pentacles rides Earth Horse, the Knight of Swords rides Air Horse, the Knight of Wands rides Fire Horse, and the Knight of Cups rides Water Horse.

Knights signify confident movement. They are so very impressive. Knights are infused with virtue, determination, and fearlessness. They commit to their task one hundred percent, and will not be thwarted by anyone or anything. "Maybe" isn't part of their vocabulary. "Do or die" is how they roll.

Knight of Pentacles

The Knight of Pentacles sits astride a powerful black Earth Horse. Unlike the other knights, he stands still atop a mountain, as if considering the weight of each option: "What will this choice cost? Is it worth it?" Like earth, this knight doesn't charge headfirst into battle. He carefully considers the risks and measures them against their worth, and will not proceed until he is certain of his course and strategy. When he does proceed, it will be at a slow and steady pace, and nothing will be able to stop him. His helmet, the horse, and his reins are adorned with oak leaves. Nothing grows as slowly, and becomes as mighty, as an oak tree. But it takes a long time.

Pentacles represents earth energy: health, wealth, work, foundations, and being grounded; your body, your stuff, your money. What it doesn't represent is the devil, which is a common misinterpretation. Although, to be fair, an upside-down pentacle has been co-opted by those who commune with good old Beelzebub.

The points of the pentacle represent the five points of the body as well as the five elements: earth (left lower point), spirit (top), fire (right lower point), air (left side point), water (right side point). The circle represents protection, specifically, protection of a person. In some decks, pentacles are called "coins," reinforcing the idea of material reward for physical effort, which is the overarching theme of this suit.

Knight of Swords

The Knight of Swords sits atop a pale, grey Air Horse charging through the air, soaring so high over an obstacle that it can't even be seen, all four legs off the ground in mid-leap. The horse is looking backward, focused on its fierce, crazed-looking rider as if to say, "WTF, dude." On the knight's helmet is a large plume, which looks a lot like wings, and the reins are adorned with birds in flight.

Although swords represent air—intellect, thoughts, words, and communication—in the tarot, swords is the suit of conflict and difficulty, which is particularly evident in the pip cards. Why? Because words travel through the air when spoken, and words can be more damaging than fists. Words are "double-edged swords" and can leave a nasty scar. Nothing will destroy a relationship faster than sharp words. Besides verbal carnage, swords also represent your own thoughts. You can do as much damage with negative self-talk as you can when dicing someone up with criticism.

Air Horse is all about strategy and staying on course. The Knight of Swords is in the midst of that. He's barreling forward with the plan, putting that strategy into play. He's "all in." No turning back, "Damn the torpedoes, full speed ahead!" Even if your Horse gives you the side-eye.

Knight of Wands

The Knight of Wands sits upon an energetic, red Fire Horse, full of fiery energy and champing at the bit. Let's get going! The knight keeps a firm grip on his spirited steed, holding tight to reins adorned with the suit's symbolic sprouting leaves, signifying bold new growth and the irrepressible life force. His helmet and sleeves are adorned with fire-orange plumes that resemble flames more than feathers and, of course, this suit corresponds with the element of fire. Unlike the other knights, his tunic is in tatters, indicating that he's already seen some battles, survived them all, and is ready to take on the next comer. He and his horse are courageous to a fault and will go down fighting or emerge victorious.

Wands is a suit of confidence and fearlessness. When working with wands, focus on generating the fiery energy and courage necessary to set out into new frontiers, new adventures, and new horizons, even if it means taking risks. Doing something when you're not afraid isn't courage. Doing something when you are afraid—that's courage. That's fire.

Knight of Cups

The Knight of Cups is the proverbial "Knight in Shining Armor" astride his proverbial white horse. He's that romantic hero who will sweep us off our feet and rescue us from every problem. Cups correspond to water, which is the realm of love, emotion, beauty, and creativity.

This knight's helmet and heels are adorned with wings, similar to those of the Greek god Hermes (Roman: Mercury), the swift messenger of the gods, which is a bit curious, as wings would more appropriately be associated with air. However, consider the earnest determination of a message-bearer: He is compelled to take his message where it needs to go. It's all about earnestness. He *will* arrive at his destination. Love, or passion about something, can give you that determination.

The Knight of Cups carries a full cup, which is challenging to carry on a horse, but he makes it look effortless. The reins on the bridle are adorned with flowing water, like the flowing gait of Water Horse, and this horse is looking directly into the flowing river—symbolic of emotions—and is unafraid to enter or cross it. He's ready to dive deep into the river of love.

The Knight of Cups leads with his heart. He is emotion put into action. When using the Knight of Cups in your reading, keep in mind the things that bring you joy and fulfillment, from relationships and romance, to things you create: painting, poetry, music, or anything that expresses emotion or gives you a sense of fulfillment.

Six of Wands

The Six of Wands is a pip card, and the only one featuring a horse. It features a triumphant rider astride his white steed. He has a laurel wreath around his head and his wand is adorned with another. Laurel wreaths represent honor, achievement, and scholarly accomplishment. The rider is surrounded by people cheering his success, and he proudly holds his head high, savoring the satisfaction of sweet glory.

The figure on this card is "arriving" or has just "arrived." As opposed to the action cards that take us somewhere, like the knights and the Death card, this rider's work is done. He's already there. However, notice his horse's face: it's looking back at his self-satisfied rider, clearly annoyed and disgruntled, as if thinking, "Hey, buddy, remember who carried you here!" A little credit for the horse, please.

Death

Stop, don't freak out about the Death card. It doesn't mean you're going to die, nor does it mean anyone else is going to die. Consider that the Death card is number thirteen in the major arcana, which is the story of a human life, and the cards continue on up to number twenty-two, ending with the World. The story doesn't stop at Death; it continues.

The Death card means a finite ending of something. A major, inalterable change. The end of a chapter. We experience many deaths over the course of our life. Birth is the death of life inside the womb. Puberty is the death of childhood. Graduating from high school is the death of adolescence. Marriage is the death of dating and single life. When you read a book, a new chapter can't begin until the one before it "dies." The card means a complete, finite, one-way ending of one thing so that another may begin.

Let's take a deep breath and look Death in the eye socket.

Death rides a fierce-looking white horse, marching past, or over, the body of the dead king, which represents the "old guard" or the status quo; the old stage or situation. A priest prays over his body, while a young child looks on, seemingly oblivious to the horror (as in their innocence, children sometimes can be). A young girl seems to be turning her face away in sorrow. This scenario might be interpreted as "everything we knew and counted upon has ended, and we are striding toward the unknown." Yes, that's totally scary. However, focused upon all the upset, the characters on the card don't seem to notice the background.

In the background, across the waters, is the entrance to a bright, beautiful place where the sun shines. In other words, there's still hope; it just can't be seen right now. The darkest hour is before dawn.

Being "kept in the dark" about the mysteries that lie ahead is further implied by the skulls and crossbones on the reins. Traditionally, the skull and crossbones represent poison (or pirates). However, I attended a workshop led by the late Stregheria scholar Raven Grimassi, wherein he interpreted this symbol as representing the mysteries of the departed ancestors. Crossed bones signify that the mysteries are not available to the living, while separated bones signify that they are. With Grimassi's angle, Death is taking us on a journey, the meaning of which we aren't allowed to know about just yet. Maybe it's the otherworld (or subconscious), which is implied by the river. Many mythologies use the crossing of a river as the threshold between the living and the dead, the conscious and the subconscious. Besides heralding an ending, the Death card may be preparing you to consciously face your dragons. You cannot slay what you cannot face.

The Sun

Unlike the knights, Death, and Six of Wands, which signify movement, the horse of the Sun card isn't taking us anywhere, it's already there. As for the rider, it couldn't be any more different from the others. It is a young, carefree child, basking in the warmth and light of a sunny summer day, naked as the day it was born, comfortable in its own skin, astride a white horse.

A wreath of sunflowers adorns the child's head and more sunflowers bloom in the background. The child waves a bright orange banner, representing vitality, fertility, and health. The Sun is pure, innocent, complete joy. The child doesn't need to do anything, because it's already doing it: basking in the lovely moment. The Sun card represents our true pure, inner selves, our happiness, and our wholeness, and corresponds to spirit.

Horse Tarot Spreads

I've created six tarot spreads revolving around the cards with horses on them: Ask a Knight, What Must End, the Victory spread, the H-O-R-S-E spread, the Elemental spread and a variation on the Elemental spread. The first three are relatively quick and spotlight a particular situation or issue. The H-O-R-S-E spread offers insight about how to meet particular needs to enhance or change your life. The Elemental spread is a large spread using lots of cards. While the Elemental spread is a relatively big project, the others are clean, simple, and straightforward, and are perfect for tarot beginners.

Focus on gaining insight. Each card, its position, and how it interacts with the others is a little clue about what's going on with you, and the entire spread altogether may create a cohesive message. Or not. Sometimes, it's a big jumble and nothing makes sense. That's okay too. You might ask your question in another way and try again, do the spread again on another day, or show the spread to someone who knows you well and see if they have some insight about what the cards are saying.

You can also ask the cards for more information. Pick another card, and if it's still unclear, pick another. Maybe even go for three. If it still doesn't make any sense, take a photo of the spread or note the cards. It may make sense later.

Before beginning a reading, shuffle your cards until it feels like "enough." Some people like to cut them. To pull a card, take one off the top or fan them across the table and run your hand over them until a card feels like "the one."

Ask a Knight

Ask a Knight is a quick-pull exercise to get a glimpse of how your day might play out or a little on-the-spot insight. Think of a question or concern you have, and determine which elemental realm it falls into. If it's money, health, and wealth? Earth. Thoughts, mental challenges, communication? Air. Courage, power, and progress? Fire. Love, creativity, and relationships? Water. Pull the knight that corresponds with that element, shuffle your deck, and pull a card. Place it next to your knight, in the direction he's looking. He's saying, "Take a look at this."

Let's say your relationship is feeling stale, so you ask the Knight of Cups, "What do I need to know about my relationship?" Maybe you pull the Fool, suggesting a fresh start, some whimsy, and adventure. It's telling you that the "same ole same ole" has become boring. Surprise your partner with something fun and fresh.

Another variation on Ask a Knight quick-pull is to shuffle the four knight cards, and then pick one. That knight is talking to you today. What is he saying? What sort of energy is he indicating you may need today? What elemental energies will come into play? Pay attention and see how your day unfolds. A situation may arise where you'll need those elemental energies.

What Must End

The What Must End spread makes use of the ultimate ending card, Death, in combination with either the Sun or the Six of Wands. Death and the Sun cards together read, "What must end so that I can be my true, whole self again?" Death and the Six of Wands together read, "What must end so I can be successful?"

To begin this spread, place the Death card next to the Sun or the Six of Wands card, whichever you choose based upon your issue, both face up. Shuffle, draw a card, and place it below the first two cards, face up, and get a gut read on what is being suggested.

Let's say you've chosen to ask, "What must end so that I can be my whole, true self again?" using Death and the Sun. The third card gives you a clue. Let's say you draw the Eight of Swords, showing a loosely bound woman in a blindfold, with eight swords stuck in the ground behind her. This card represents feeling bound and helpless by a situation. However, the card shows that the bindings are very loose and could easily be slipped off, and the swords easily be stepped past, but the woman on the card doesn't realize it. Because swords represent thoughts and the mind, the woman's own thoughts and beliefs keep her in place. Do yours?

In this example, the answer to "What must end so that I can be my whole, true self again?" is to take charge of your own self-defeating, limiting negative thoughts and beliefs. You are the one binding you in place, and you are the one who can release you.

If you've chosen to ask, "What must end so that I can be successful?" using Death and the Six of Wands, let's say the third card you draw is the Three of Cups: three joyful ladies, with cups raised, dancing about and celebrating their friendship and good times. Lovely! However, in this instance, the cards are telling you that if you want to be successful—on the job or with a project, for example—you must cut back on the fun and frivolity, and get your nose to the grindstone. Maybe a little Earth Horse could help you out.

These two spreads give insight when we're feeling stuck or hindered, but don't know why. Sometimes we just can't figure out what the core issue is. It might be the most obvious answer in the world and we just can't see it, but the cards can!

Victory

For the Victory spread, remove the Six of Wands and place it face up on the table. As you shuffle your cards, ask, "How can I be victorious or successful in (insert your goal)?" Draw another card and place it face up beside the Six of

Wands. Maybe it's the Three of Pentacles, with one person working on a project as two others watch. The message is that you can be victorious in your new business by consulting with others—collaborating.

H-O-R-S-E

Shuffle your cards until it feels like "enough." Pull five cards, one at a time, and place them face up, side by side. The first card is "H." It asks, "Where can I find Happiness?" The second card is "O." It asks, "Where can I find Opportunity?" The third card is "R." It asks, "Where can I find Resources?" The fourth card is "S." It asks, "Where can I find Security?" The fifth card is "E." It asks, "Where can I find Encouragement?" As before, gaze at the spread as a whole, and look for patterns and connections. Then consider the cards one by one, and see if you get some insights or ideas about where to find these things you need.

Elemental

This is a big spread, the granddaddy of our Horse spreads. You're going to have a lot of cards on the table.

Take the knights and the Sun out, and place them in their appropriate spots on the solar cross: pentacles (earth) at the top, swords (air) on the right, wands (fire) on the bottom, cups (water) on the left, and the Sun (spirit) in the middle. This is a spotlight reading about blocked Elemental Horse energy. A spotlight reading means that you aren't asking a specific question. Instead, you're asking the cards to show you something to consider about each element and spirit.

With your five cards in place, shuffle your deck until you feel it's enough. Hold your cards and ask, "What's blocking me?" Pull a card and place it face up horizontally across earth (like a little cross), then do the same for air, fire, water, and spirit. First, just take it all in. Do you see a lot of a certain suit? Your issue may lie amongst that element. Do you see a lot of major arcana cards? Remember, that's a big message in ALL CAPS. Do you see a lot of the same numbers or colors? Do you see a lot of men? Women? What does that mean to you? What does the totality of it look like to you?

Begin with earth: the horizontal card reveals what blocks your power, health, and wealth; air—this blocks clear thinking, learning, problem solving, and strategy; fire—a horizontal card blocks your energy, enthusiasm, and courage; water—this blocks your creativity, joy, and relationships; spirit—the horizontal card blocks your sunshine, your spirit—who or what is the "black cloud" in your life?

To continue further, you can ask, "What will help unblock this energy?" and draw a card for each "mini cross" you've created and place the card next to it. This helps remedy whatever blocks your energy. What solutions or insights emerge?

The Yin and Yang of the Elements

Here's a variation on the Elemental spread: With the knights placed in their appropriate elemental spots, you have two halves: swords/air and wands/fire are male energies; pentacles/earth and cups/water are female energies. Male and female energy has nothing to do with genitalia. We all have both energies. Energy is gender fluid and we all have access to its entirety.

Male energy is hot and projective (white), and female energy is cool and receptive (black). This is the symbolism of the Yin and Yang in Chinese philosophy: the black and white swirls spin around each other, representing the balance and harmony of opposing energies, with an "eye" of each in the other.

Imagine the Yin and Yang symbol superimposed over the knights, the black swirl over pentacles and cups, and the white over swords and wands. Shuffle your cards, asking, "What energies am I attracting or receiving?" Pull a card and place it over the black swirl's "eye." Shuffle again, asking, "What energies am I causing or projecting?" Pull a card and place it over the white swirl's "eye." What are those "eyes" telling you to look at?

Intuition Through Tarot

Reading tarot cards is a great way to brighten and sharpen your intuition. Developing your intuitive abilities gives you a new tool for assessing the problems and situations that life throws at us. Many problems don't have obvious solutions and sometimes intuition must be our guide. Intuition is also an important skill for working with real, live horses, which are innately intuitive. The more intuitive you are, the more you'll be on the same wavelength with a horse and understand what it's saying or feeling.

Chapter 6

HONORING HORSE SPIRIT

In chapter 4, we looked at the elemental facets of Horse, and touched upon some ways to attract those energies. Now we'll kick it up a notch and create visual prompts that do the same. As you create and try out these spiritual tools, don't be surprised if you start noticing horses all over the place. You're attuning to Horse, inviting it in, and Horse will start tapping you on the shoulder in all sorts of places.

Horse Altars

An altar is a special spot in your home that serves as a constant visual reminder about your needs, desires, or goals. It should draw your attention and be a reinforcing presence. You can even have more than one, for different or reinforcing purposes. All that matters is that when you look at it, the altar prompts the particular energy you'd like to fortify.

I have altars all over my house, and most people don't even realize what they are. They just look like pretty little collections, or assemblages of unusual or interesting items. However, each altar is very intentionally created, with a specific purpose.

There are working altars, which are used in magickal Pagan practices and rituals and often include specific items.[24] We're going to focus upon attraction altars instead, which are designed to draw in, attract, and welcome a particular energy—in our case, Horse.

---

24. Pagans spell magic with a "k" to contrast their practices from magicians who pull rabbits out of hats and do card tricks.

Choose the right spot for your altar. Look around and find one you're drawn to. Move your items around on your altar until it feels just right. Your altar might include a little statue of a horse goddess, an image of one of those magical, mystical horses mentioned earlier that caught your fancy, or any item that represents a Horse energy.

Anything "horsey" in general will attract Horse, such as horse-themed artwork, figurines, sculpture, fabric, and collectibles. If something says "Horse"— get it. You could also paint it, photograph it, or make it. Symbols for the Elemental Horses, such as stones, shells, feathers, incense, or candles, could also be included.

A Horse altar could include actual horse tools, like a hoof pick or currycomb, or the all-time classic symbol for horses and good luck: a horseshoe. Horsehair is a nice touch, but be sure it was respectfully gathered from a living and well-treated horse.

You can further attract Horse toward your altar and your life by placing a tempting treat there: a piece of carrot or apple, a sugar cube, oats, or a handful of hay or fresh grass. Be sure to refresh perishable treats when they wilt or look brown. Wilted offerings on an altar are a huge metaphysical "party foul." No deity will grace you with their presence if you offer sad, tired, wilted offerings. You wouldn't serve spoiled food to a guest, so don't offer it to Horse either.

Fairy lights are another nice touch on altars. My altars seem to come alive in their gentle glow. Most of the items on my altars are things I already had, and repurposed for a specific intention. Meaningful, personal items are perfect for an altar.

The scope of your altar is limited only by your own creativity, passion, and space. When you look at your altars, you should feel inspired and energized. They're reminders of what you want to attract into your life. They can be big or small, simple or elaborate. Regardless of size or ornamentation, your altar should feel alive. It should really mean something to you and not be just a random collection of stuff. It's also important to keep your altar clean and free of dust or clutter. Energy moves more freely when things are neat, clean, and in place. Energy hates clutter.

Elemental Horse Altars

Sometimes you need more than simple attraction. You may have a specific need or goal, so you create an altar for a specific element or Elemental Horse. As you make it and look at it, concentrate on your need for action and manifestation. You aren't simply attracting energy—you need that Elemental Horse to do a job.

An Elemental Horse altar sets an intention, and puts a spotlight on it. You're alerting the universe that you need something specific: solutions, change, resources, movement.

Earth Horse Altar

To welcome earth or Earth Horse energy, collect figurines or photos of draft horses, or draw them yourself. Items with earth energy include things from the ground: pebbles, gems, seeds, geodes, or even a tiny jar filled with soil. Salt lamps or candles also have the calming energy of earth. A horse figurine carved from onyx or tiger's eye would make a fine Earth Horse symbol. Items in the colors of earth—brown and green—also enhance earth energy. Put the Knight of Pentacles tarot card on your altar.

Earth's realm includes health, wealth, work, finances, and physical security. Maybe you want to buy a house or find a new apartment. Put a photo of a perfect house or apartment for you on that altar. If you already know the specific place, use a photo of it. Maybe you need more money. Scratch a dollar sign into a green candle, and let it burn there. Having a health issue? A little potted plant could represent growth, health, and thriving.

Air Horse Altar

Air Horse travels on the wind, so things that do the same will welcome it to your altar: feathers, dried leaves, and seedpods, the scent of potpourri, incense, or candles in pastel colors. A figurine or drawing of Pegasus, the ultimate Air Horse, would be perfect for an Air Horse altar. Keep the feel of this altar light and airy, encouraging energetic movement. Because air is the element of communication, you could also write phrases or mantras that are meaningful to you on bits of paper and place them there. Put the Knight of Swords tarot card on your altar.

Air Horse's realm includes strategy, learning, and verbal communication. Maybe you need to finish your college degree. Put something on the altar representing that field of study, like a lab book or protractor. If you're struggling with a particular problem you can't seem to solve, write it on a piece of paper, concentrate on it, then burn the paper in a small, fireproof dish or bowl. Let the smoke carry that problem through the air. Let the universe find the solution. Scratch the name of what you need—"focus" or "memory" or "strategy"—into a yellow candle, light it on your altar, and let it burn out.

Fire Horse Altar

A figurine of a rearing or running red sorrel horse would be a perfect adornment for a Fire Horse altar. You might also gather lava rocks, candles, or matches there, and maybe a little potted cactus. Go out for a walk, gather some twigs and create a miniature campfire. Include bright orange or red items, the colors associated with fire. Include things that *spark* your imagination! Put the Knight of Wands tarot card on your altar. Scratch "courage" or "energy" into an orange candle, light it on your altar, and let it burn out.

Fire Horse's realm includes courage, athleticism, sexuality, and enthusiasm. Sex life sad and dusty? Put a sexy little thing there to spark interest and desire. Facing a situation that will require extraordinary courage? How about a small stick or wand, like the one the Knight of Wands carries? Wishing to learn to play the drums? Place a drumstick there. Fire energy is adept with tools. Include any tool you might use for your desired goal, or an image of the thing you wish to make.

Water Horse Altar

All water—oceans, lakes, rivers, or streams—will enhance a water altar. Use items that come from those places: a little bottle of beach sand, or pictures of fish, waves, or water lilies. Blues and purples are water's colors. Include stones and gems in water colors, or blue or green glass aquarium stones from a craft store to create a watery feel. Your Water Horse representation might be a drawing or photo of a seahorse, a dressage horse, or a Lipizzan stallion. Put the Knight of Cups tarot card on your altar.

The realm of water is love, kindness, empathy, and creativity. Anything heart-shaped will serve this purpose. A piece of rose quartz—the gemstone of love and tenderness—in a heart shape is perfect. If the kind of love you're seeking is more of the romantic nature, a red heart is the iconic symbol for love. If you want to become a painter, put a paintbrush on your altar. If you want to learn to play the guitar, put a guitar pick there. Scratch "kindness" or "creativity" into a blue candle, "love" on a pink candle, or "romance" on a red candle, and let it burn out on your altar.

Drape a blue or purple cloth—something soft or shiny like velvet or silk—all around your altar to give a feel of flowing water. If it's an appropriate spot, put a little fishbowl there. As you tend to the fish, tell yourself that you're feeding your creative, kind, emotional water energies.

Spirit Horse Altar

A Spirit Horse altar should feature things that look pure, clean, and clear, like quartz crystal, and in particular, any clear item that refracts light into rainbows, such as prisms or cut crystals. A sunny windowsill where beams of light pass through them and cast rainbows into the room is a fantastic spot for a Spirit Horse altar. When those rainbows dance around the room, spirit is dancing with you!

The Great Mare should be represented on this altar, as she is our divine Spirit Horse. A little white or clear glass horse figurine is perfect. Include anything that you find spiritually uplifting or inspiring—poetry, photos, mementos—anything that reinforces the "you" that you alone know, in your heart of hearts. Place the Sun tarot card there too.

Because Spirit Horse guides you toward clarity in your own thoughts, feelings, and desires, something that symbolizes wholeness or balance is a nice touch—maybe a lotus flower, which rises up from the mud and muck and blossoms in the light, and symbolizes a pure mind and heart in the Hindu culture. If you can find a crystal lotus flower, that's perfect for a Spirit Horse altar.

Horsehair Charms and Trinkets

Horsehair is just about the cheapest, most versatile, and most readily available item for a Horse altar, to place on your dresser or desk, or keep in your pocket. I created a simple horsehair altar adornment myself—a miniature horsetail that I made while trimming Penn's tail—which we'll learn how to make in chapter 10. On another altar, I have a little lock of Penn's tail hair, wound into the infinity symbol, which represents everlasting love, wisdom, and insight, and looks sort of like a skinny eight on its side. That's a lot of symbolism to pack into one little lock of twisted horsehair, but it illustrates how something so plain, simple, and inexpensive can be very meaningful to you.

Besides altar adornments, you can put some horsehair in a locket or small leather pouch (mojo bag) or braid it into a bracelet. It can also be twisted and wound into a very simple and comfortable ring, fashioned into a brooch, or used to adorn jewelry, hats, or hair accessories. You could also put a loop of horsehair in your pocket or purse, and when you're facing a difficult person or situation, roll that horsehair around between your fingers for reinforcement.

Horsehair is cheap and easy to find if you know someone with a horse. If not, you could call or visit a stable and explain you need a little horsehair for an art project (all true—an altar is a project, and it's very artistic). Ask if you could come by and collect some from a brush or comb, or if someone would be willing to collect some for you the next time they trim a tail. Some horse people might think that's a pretty weird request, but probably won't mind helping you out because it's just horsehair, and after grooming horses, it gets thrown out anyway.

You can also find horsehair online, and it's often shown collected into long swatches used for paintbrushes, jewelry, and art projects. Before purchasing any horsehair online or from craft stores, however, consider that it was likely collected from a rendering plant or slaughterhouse, and that's not the energy you want to bring into your altar, particularly one for Horse. Horse will run the other way from slaughterhouse energy.

Be sure to ask how the hair was collected, and don't just fall for "humane" either, because technically, it's humane to collect hair from a dead animal. The best source for horsehair is a living, happy, well-loved horse. That's the energy you want you want to welcome, and the energy that will attract Horse.

Horseshoes Aren't Just for Hooves

Nothing says Horse like horseshoes. They feel powerful, like the animals that wear them, able to withstand the pounding weight of a horse. They're perfect for any Horse altar, but can be used as decor anywhere in your home to soak in all that wonderful and powerful Horse energy. Besides their association with horses, horseshoes are the classic good luck symbol. Used or new horseshoes are readily available and inexpensive. If used, they're free. Most of the time, they're discarded, and you can ask the same person who gave you the horsehair if they can spare a used horseshoe or two. You could also inquire at a local stable or contact a farrier.

Used horseshoes are pounded and shaped by the weight of a horse, and therefore are shaped by the actual, real energy of a horse, and that's an energetic bonus. But, new horseshoes are fine too, can be found anywhere that sells general livestock equipment, and typically cost less than three dollars apiece. A farrier should also be able to supply you with both new and used horseshoes.

When hanging a horseshoe, there's disagreement about whether they should be positioned heels up or heels down. If up, it's believed that all the luck stays put. If heels down, it's believed that the luck runs out. However, some folks believe that hanging a horseshoe heels down over your front door showers good luck upon all who enter. Hang it in the position that appeals to you. Make sure you affix it well to the wall, or it will be very bad luck for whoever's head it lands on!

You can create a lucky four-leafed clover by taking four horseshoes, representing the four elements and Elemental Horses, and placing them flat on a table, heels together, for an altar or table centerpiece. If you want something solid that can be hung up, ask a local farrier or blacksmith to forge the heels of the horseshoes together.

Whether hanging or as a centerpiece, it's fine just the way it is, full of Horse energy. Just be aware that horseshoes will eventually rust when exposed to moisture and left standing, so paint or seal them if they're going to be outside. You can find sealant that discourages rust at most hardware stores. You can also paint the horseshoes with regular paint primer and then a topcoat of paint in any color you wish. The Rust-Oleum brand of paint is particularly great for metal that will be exposed to moisture or inclement weather. Before applying sealant or paint, brush away any visible rust with a metal brush or sand it with a metal fiber scouring pad.

You can also decorate your horseshoe cloverleaf. An easy adornment is to put a candle inside the curve of each shoe, maybe in the color associated with each element, add a little seasonal greenery if you like, and *voilà*, you have a Horse centerpiece for your dinner table. Even I, the craft-challenged, can do that. You could also embellish your cloverleaf with symbols of each season or holiday, like a perpetual centerpiece. The horseshoe frame stays in place, and the decorations change whenever you wish—bunnies and birds in spring, sunflowers and fairies in summer, autumn leaves and nuts in the fall, and evergreen and holly in the winter.

Horseshoe Nails

Horseshoe nails are cheap and easy Horse energy items. They're flatter than regular nails, because they're pounded in from the bottom of the horse's hoof. through the walls. The sharp tips pop through the slope of the horse's hoof, whereupon they're snipped off and filed smooth. You can simply keep a nail in a mojo bag or pocket (file down that tip first), put one or some on an altar, make a decoration or mosaic with them, or spell words out of them for your altar. They also make very interesting and impressive jewelry. Search "horseshoe nail jewelry" online and hundreds of Etsy links will pop up. You can also bend a nail into a pinky ring or a loop to hold a pendant on a chain.

I had a friend with a very mystical looking pendant made of three horseshoe nails, bent into a triskelion, an ancient Celtic symbol consisting of three matching symbols, all rotating from a center point. Her pendant was more than just interesting. In her family's lore, if you were given a horseshoe nail triskelion pendant, it was meant as a symbol of fidelity. As long as you remain loyal to that person, all is well—the triskelion remains as is. If you cheat or commit adultery, the nails will spring open and pierce your heart. Ouch! This is an interesting allusion to the Three of Swords tarot card: three swords piercing a heart and representing heartbreak, which is often the result of infidelity.

Also, consider the purpose of a horseshoe nail: It binds a strip of iron to the hooves of a powerful horse and holds it there, through whatever terrain or activity lies ahead. Use a horseshoe nail when you really need to "nail something down." Write your need on a piece of paper, or get an image of it. Place it on a piece of wood or cork, and envision achieving that goal as you pound that nail through that paper or image. Place it on an altar and surround it with things that symbolize the energy needed to make it happen.

Other Ways to Attract Horse

Here are some more ideas for attracting Horse to your life, that you can wear or put in a visible place:

- *Artwork or photographs*: Any painting, drawing, or photo of a horse that makes your heart leap with joy is perfect for attracting Horse energy to you and your home. Horse artwork and photos are in abundance online and in gift shops, and photos you take yourself are especially wonderful. Go for a drive in the countryside where there are horses grazing, or to a horse stable, racetrack, or horse show to "lasso" some horses with your camera or cell phone. You could use your photos to "paint your cave wall."

- *Jewelry:* Whether made of horseshoe nails or not, jewelry is an easy way to keep Horse with you throughout the day. Horse pendants are ubiquitous, as is jewelry with horseshoes. You could even go to a beading store and create a necklace or bracelet in colors that attract a particular elemental energy, and adorn it with horse or horseshoe charms. When you make something yourself, it's more meaningful and powerful. If crafting isn't your thing, there's an abundance of horse-themed jewelry to be found, online, in department stores, tack stores, gift shops, thrift shops, and garage sales. A locket with a picture of a horse or some horsehair inside and worn around your neck could be a Horse magnet.

- *Mojo bags:* Medicine or "mojo bags" are another easy item to put around your neck before heading out the door, or keep in your pocket. A typical mojo bag is a small fabric or leather pouch, usually closed with a leather or satin lace, into which you put items representing your magical or spiritual intentions. Your Horse mojo bag might include some horsehair, horseshoe nails, pebbles or shells, feathers, or any combination of things that you choose will draw a particular elemental energy toward you. You can even fold up a small picture of a horse and place it in there, and wear it around your neck—your heart's desire!

- *Stones:* Smooth or polished stones are easy to find, come in just about every color imaginable, and are perfect for mojo bags or pockets. Gemstones also have energies associated with them, just like the elements and colors.

Particular gemstones are associated with particular elements, and therefore, Elemental Horses. Brown and green stones like agate or malachite are associated with earth; pale, clear, or yellow stones, like citrine or yellow quartz are associated with air; red stones such as red jasper or carnelian are associated with fire; and blue and purple stones such as turquoise or amethyst are associated with water. Clear crystals, like clear quartz or zircon, are associated with spirit.

One gemstone outlier is rose quartz. Although not in the colors associated with water, rose quartz is especially known for love, kindness, and healing, particularly for oneself, and can also represent the energies of water when self-acceptance, love, and personal healing are your central concerns.

- *Candles:* Candles are a common way of setting an intention, and are great for attracting particular energies. Small colored "spell candles" are perfect for this purpose and are available at most metaphysical stores or online. Pick a candle in the color of the element or Elemental Horse you wish to attract, or a white one for Spirit Horse. Infuse the candle with your own energy and intention by focusing on your need and breathing a particular goal or intention into the candle. Scratch a word or phrase representing that need into the side of the candle. Place it on your altar, shelf, or dresser and let it burn all the way out, knowing that the universe, and Horse, will take it from there.

- *Equestrian wear:* Equestrian clothing comes in both Western and English styles. Cowboy hats, snappy blazers, tall black boots, neck scarves, tooled belts, and big silver belt buckles are about the easiest thing on earth to find. Look no further than a local tack shop. If you don't have one nearby, there are multiple virtual tack shops and equestrian wear outlets available to you with the click of a mouse. You don't have to own a horse to wear horse-related clothing. If it makes you feel happy and horsey, that's all the reason you need.

Cowboy hats are wonderful, and available all over the place, from boutiques to tack shops. Wherever they sell hats, you'll probably find them. Of all the equestrian wear, however, there's nothing like cowboy boots. Cowboy boots are always in fashion, and come in a huge variety of styles, sizes, colors, and price ranges. You can easily find cowboy boots at boot stores, online, or at places that sell farm and livestock equipment or horse tack.

Wearing cowboy boots immediately shifts your energy. They're instant attitude. Just try some on and you'll discover a newfound swagger in your step. You literally walk differently when wearing them, with power and confidence. Cowboy boots aren't for shrinking violets.

Tattoos

A tattoo is the ultimate in wearing Horse energy. I have one created by my daughter, who is a tattoo artist. She wanted to give me a tattoo for Mother's Day. I wanted something that inspired joy whenever I looked at it, so I thought about that ... what inspires joy? The image of Penn's big old nose, poking out over the top of his paddock gate every morning, greeting me, snuffling a little "good morning" nicker flashed into my mind. Almost nothing gives me greater joy than that!

Penn's nose has a large, oddly shaped snip between his nostrils. I gave a photo of it to my daughter, and asked her to transform the mark into crystals in the colors of the chakras. The resulting work of "skin art" is unique and beautiful, and also impossible to identify. People always admire it and ask what it is. I tell them I'll give them ten bucks if they can guess. So far, that Hamilton remains in my wallet. The most common guess is Italy, Chile, and my favorite, a skinny Africa. I love to reveal the answer by whipping out my cell phone and showing the photo of my tattoo next to Penn's nose. It always makes people laugh and sigh with delight.

Besides being a beautiful, one-of-a-kind tattoo, this one has multilayered symbolism—my own storybook horse, who changed my life; the creativity, talent, and love of my daughter; the love and support of my husband; and Sarah, who brought Penn and I together. Positioned on my left, receptive, forearm, it draws these energies toward my heart, where I hold them all dear. That's a lot of work for one little tattoo, isn't it!

Think of the many images we've discussed that would be amazing tattoos: the Uffington Horse, Pegasus, Epona, any of the Elemental Horses (or all of them), a horseshoe—let your imagination and creativity run wild until you get a gut feeling. Work with a tattoo designer to incorporate the images that are meaningful to you—don't just point to a generic picture of a horse on the wall at any greasy old tattoo parlor. You are unique, and your tattoo should be as well. It's going to be on your body forever, so spend the extra money and work with a tattoo designer. Think of it as an investment—in Horse!

How About a Horse Chest?

A "horse chest"—similar to a hope chest—is the ultimate item in attracting Horse, and in particular, for attracting a real horse into your life.

When I was in high school in the 1970s, the feminist movement was dawning, but old-fashioned values were still lingering. In high school, girls still took home economics courses and boys took woodshop classes, and that's the way it was, except for a few plucky rebels. When girls graduated, we each received a little redwood box—a miniature hope chest, made by the manufacturers of real, full-sized hope chests in the hopes that we'd run out and buy a big one from them.

If you're too young to know what a hope chest is, prepare to cringe: It's a large cedar chest, in which teenage girls collected all the things they'd need to be a good wife and housekeeper, such as towels, kitchen utensils, dishes, and the like. Because getting married is all a girl needs to hope for, right? Find a man, get married, pump out some babies, and spend the rest of your life putting everyone else first! Who could ever want more! Look how well that turned out for our goddess Macha!

I wasn't hoping for a husband when I was in high school. My hope chest was a collection of stuff for me to move out and go to college, and I certainly didn't need any man for that.

A traditional hope chest foretold that, "The man of my dreams is just around the corner, and when he sweeps me off my feet, I'll be ready to set all my hopes and goals aside and devote myself to fulfilling his every need and desire!" This wasn't a goal I had or agreed with, but there's something to be said for having everything in place so you'll be ready when the time comes—acting "as if" until you get there, like the motto of every Girl and Boy Scout: "Be Prepared."

Acting "as if" scoots you from "I wish" to "I will." When you just wish for something, you're putting it completely out of your control. It literally frames your desire as something you're unable to accomplish on your own: a wish. "I wish to get married" or "I wish I could have a horse." You can almost hear the implied helplessness.

Wishing is like being the flower, stuck in place, sitting and waiting, hoping the bee will come to you. Willing is grabbing that bee by its tiny little short hairs and dragging it into your petals. Don't just sit there waiting for that bee to come along. Show it who's boss! Moving from "I wish" to "I will" is empowering. Try it. Say to yourself: "I wish I could have tacos for dinner tonight." Then say, "I *will* have tacos for dinner tonight." See? Feels totally different. "Will" is "wish" on steroids. If you really want a horse, *will* it to be so. Say it to yourself: I *will* have a horse! (Trust me, they're way better than tacos.)

How did that feel? Did you get a little of tingle of "Oh, yeah, this is going to happen"? Hold on to that feeling of *will* and let it fuel your intention. Don't get bogged down with negativity about having a horse. Stay in *this* moment: "I *will* have a horse." It doesn't mean you'll have a horse five minutes from now, or tomorrow, or next week, or next year. Maybe it will be more than a year. But it *will* happen. Just trust in that, and let the universe and Horse work out the details.

Until it does happen, we'll dust off that sad, tired old hope chest and repurpose it into something wonderful: a horse chest. Instead of preparing for a man, we'll prepare for a horse!

Get a large box or footlocker, and gradually collect items and store them inside. Fill it with things you'll need when you *will* have a horse: lead rope, currycomb, mane comb, grooming brush, tail brush, hoof pick, spray bottle, washing mitt, scissors for trimming hair, a shower or grooming caddy (good for carrying all this stuff around), a feed bucket, hay net, and an equine first aid kit.

You don't need to get everything all at once; just pick things up as you can, one here, one there, no rush. The really cool thing is that these items are necessities and you'll actually use them. You won't have wasted a dime. Even the footlocker can be taken to the barn for holding your horse supplies.

If you're wondering why no bridle, halter, or saddle for your horse chest, it's because not all tack is appropriate for all horses, and not all tack will fit all horses, just as not all shoes will fit all people. You purchase these things when you actually have your horse, and decide what you actually need, in the correct size. Even halters shouldn't be purchased in advance (unless it's strictly a spiritual Horse prompt) because what will you do if you've purchased a halter for a draft horse and you end up with a delicate, fine-boned Arabian?

Each time you place something in the chest, say "For my horse!" to reinforce that you *will* have a horse of your own. Don't be wimpy or timid about it. Say it with absolute conviction. It *will* happen.

— III —
THE PHYSICAL
HORSE

Chapter 7

SO, YOU WANT TO GET A HORSE?

The ability to pass between worlds is part of Horse mythology, and this is where we've arrived, this liminal spot, having traveled through an evolutionary, cultural, mythological, and spiritual exploration of Horse. We've been in the metaphysical realm, and now, we'll cross the threshold into the physical realm of real horses.

That said, you don't *have* to move on to real horses. At this point in our journey, you have a huge spiritual toolbox to embrace Horse and work with its energies to manifest the change you seek in your life. You could end right here, and you'd have all you need to welcome Horse into your life and benefit from its strengths and power. You're already equipped to immerse yourself in Horse right now, without ever seeing, handling, or owning a real horse. All of Horse is at your fingertips. How cool is that?

But what if you want more? Even if you believe it's utterly impossible, what if the desire for a horse burns in your heart and will not be denied? What if you've never handled a horse and have no idea where to start? Well, let's cross the threshold and transition from the spiritual to the actual, from doing something in spirit to taking action. This is where we've arrived.

Are you ready to saddle up?

Can I Afford a Horse?

Full disclosure, if horses could just eat cash, it would be a lot quicker and simpler. Accept that you'll watch your hard-earned money ultimately become manure, which I find hilariously symbolic.

Buying a horse is the smallest expense. The real cost is the ongoing expense of supporting it. Unless you are well-padded financially, you'll need new strategies to juggle and stretch your money. However, horses inspire a new relationship with money. The things you value start to shift. Time with your horse becomes priceless, and the money starts to matter less and less. It becomes a vehicle for enjoying time with your new companion.

You must enter into this potentially expensive situation with your eyes wide open. You can cut corners on some things, but there are certain basics you *must* pay for, like board, quality feed, veterinary care, and farrier care. You cannot scrimp on these. When you get a horse, you are entering into a spiritual bargain to care for that horse's every need, which luckily, are relatively few: a safe, clean place to live with protection from the weather; plenty of fresh, clean water; nutritious high-quality food; routine veterinary care and immunizations; regular hoof care; grooming; exercise; and most important of all, love, empathy, and kindness. Also carrots. Lots of carrots. I buy them by the forty-pound bag.

Is It in the Budget?

First, analyze your budget. How much could you budget for a horse every month, right now? Decide upon an amount, then call around and find out what things cost in your area. Prices change depending on where you live.

Come up with an estimate for the total cost of boarding, feed, veterinary care, and farrier care. How does that compare with the amount available in your budget? If it falls short, what can you eliminate from your monthly expenditures that are worth less to you than having a horse? Magazine subscriptions, makeup clubs, gym memberships, shopping sprees, and a trip to Starbucks every day aren't nearly as wonderful as a horse. Adjust those cuts into your horse budget, and if you still fall short, don't panic. There are ways to get creative and chip away at some expenses. But first, let's look at the necessities.

Board

The big ticket item for horse owners is board, unless you're lucky enough to have a large patch of ground (at least one acre) that could be fenced for a horse. If you have property, keep in mind that horses aren't happy living alone. They are herd animals and need to be in a herd to feel safe, even if it's a herd of two. You may need a companion animal for your companion animal. However, you might find a companion for your horse by boarding someone else's in your newly fenced horse pasture, and that will reduce your own expenses. Ultimately, don't keep a horse all by itself; it will never be happy.

Heading out of town, I often pass by this old white horse on a little strip of land next to the freeway, surrounded by orchards and cars whizzing by. He's all alone, not another horse for miles, and I've never seen a person with him once. He isn't underweight, so someone is taking basic care of him, but he's still alone and lonely. In his paddock are several junker cars at one end. He often stands near the cars, his nose brushing against them. Those cars are his "herd." Heartbreaking. How do you look at that every day and just carry on?

If you don't have a piece of property to transform into your own personal horse haven, join the club. Most of us must board our horses. The cost of board varies based upon what services and facilities are included, and by area. In California, where I live, everything seems to be more expensive, yet I pay about one-third of what it costs to board horses in the Northeast, where snow and long, cold winters make everything more difficult and therefore more expensive. A stall or shelter in the Northeast is absolutely necessary, unless you have an Icelandic pony. If you live in a mild climate, horses can get by in pasture year-round, but they do need shade from the hot sun and shelter from the rain. They'll often inexplicably choose to stand in the rain anyway, but at least they have the option to get out of it if they want.

If you live where there's lots of rain and/or snow, you'll need access to a stall. Not only is it undesirable for your horse's health to be cold and soaking wet for weeks and months at a time, their paddocks will quickly turn into mud soup. Then your horse will roll in that mud, just because it can, and you'll have a muddy, stinky horse when it's too cold to bathe it. The optimal situation is access to both a stall and pasture, or a paddock with shelter. A place with a covered arena is wonderful, particularly if you live in snow country, a place with heavy rainfall, or in a summertime broiler as I do in California.

If your horse will have access to a pasture, make sure it has well-maintained fencing specifically for horses. Sure, barbed wire will hold them in, but it can also cut them. Horses will stick their necks through wire to get at grass on the other side, slice up their heads and neck, and you'll have a fat vet bill on your hands. Avoid barbed wire.

Hog wire (sheets of wire with large, square holes) is a definite "no" because horses can put a hoof through the holes, which are the perfect size for getting stuck, thrashing about, and causing all sorts of bloody injuries, and yes, vet bills. Truth in advertising: horses are spectacularly creative at injuring themselves on anything and everything. You should scour your horse's pasture or paddock and clear it of anything broken, sharp, or remotely dangerous. If a toddler might get hurt on it, then a horse will too. Horses are heat-seeking missiles for things that hurt them.

Another downfall of hog wire fencing is that horses will sometimes paw at it, catch the backs of their horseshoes, and pull them right off. You can't ride a shoed horse that's missing a shoe. Continually replacing horseshoes gets to be a real drag, and expensive too.

Thin, flat electrified tape is a fencing option, by itself or strung along the top of a fence. The first time I saw this tape while Penn was staying at a nearby ranch during a fire evacuation, I scoffed. That thin little tape didn't look like it would hold in a horse. Then one morning, my hand brushed against the tape. The jolt made me jump two feet backward, making me a believer. Apparently horses are too. They only need to get their nose buzzed once, and after that, they'll stay away from that fence.

Electrified tape is the new and improved "hot wire" for horse enclosures. Hot wire still exists and will work if you need to keep your horse away from the fence. Like the tape, it will give you a nasty jolt if you touch it. I'm personally not a fan of hot wire. I'd rather install a proper fence than use hot wire on my property. But then again, I live in an area where one spark can ignite a raging wildfire in a snap.

Stalls are convenient for people and optimal in the winter, and most horses tolerate them just fine—for a while. Horses get a little stir-crazy after several days, unless you can exercise them or turn them out in an arena or pasture to burn off some steam. A stall is really boring for a horse and rubs against their natural instinct to be able to flee at any moment. That in itself can be a stressor for a horse. Bored horses show stall stress with particular behaviors like "cribbing," which is holding the edge of the stall door (or anything they can grasp) in their teeth and gulping air into their bellies, or weaving back and forth incessantly from one front leg to the other, or continually pacing in circles, sometimes to the point that they work themselves into a lather.

Horses evolved to keep moving, and a horse that is weaving or walking ruts in its stall is expressing that need. Weaving or pacing are one thing, but cribbing is a pain in the butt to stop. Sucking in air makes horses high, like when you hyperventilate, so they're essentially self-medicating to relieve their boredom or stress. A cribbing junkie is an ongoing management problem, because air in the gut can cause gastric distress and more vet bills.

Weighing All the Options

While exploring your boarding options, in addition to cost, note what services and amenities are included, and balance this against your own time and abilities. Local boarding options may range from a grassy pasture with no assistance from the property owners, where you have to feed and shovel manure yourself, to fancy, full-service boarding stables, where stall cleaning and feeding is included. Like anything else, you get what you pay for.

Weigh the positives and negatives of each boarding option, beyond the cost. Take a hard, honest look at how much time you have to take care of your horse. Besides money, time is also a precious commodity. Are you able to feed your horse and clean its stall every day, or do you have a full-time job that will make that difficult? You might need a stabling situation that does all that for you, unless you're willing to get up really early, every day, rain or shine, or finish your work day at the barn.

Are you hoping to take riding lessons? A stable that offers lessons on site is an easier option than trailering your horse for every lesson, which additionally means you'll need a truck and trailer, and probably lessons in pulling a trailer. Trailering a horse isn't like hauling a boat. Boats are still. Horses aren't. They move around, get upset, and can lose their balance while you're chugging down the road. Horses can also be spectacularly uncooperative when it comes to trailering, so consider the hassle factor of trailering when choosing a boarding facility.

Other Expenses

Here are some "must haves" that you'll need to factor into your budget. For each of the following needs, do some research online and visit local feed stores to see what options are available and what they cost.

Besides the items in your horse chest, you'll need a halter, feed bucket, and a blanket for very cold weather, and a saddle, saddle pad, and bridle if you intend to ride. If you take care of these things, they'll last a long time and won't be ongoing expenses. You can often find these things used. You'll also have a few other minor ongoing expenses, like saddle soap, sponges, horse shampoo, fly spray, hoof dressing, a salt lick, and ointment for cuts and scrapes.

Feed and Supplements

Don't think of high-quality feed and supplements as expenses. Think of them as preventative measures against racking up huge veterinary bills. Feed is cheaper than a vet visit. And, it's actually pretty interesting to research equine nutrition, apply it, and watch it slowly create positive, healthy change in your horse. However, it takes time and patience to see the results, in particular, when using supplements. If you're supplementing for a shiny coat or strong hooves, you'll have to wait for all the new growth to see the results.

Hay is a horse's most basic need because they evolved having free access to endless amounts of forage. Grazing all day is what their stomachs have evolved to do. When a horse is only fed once or twice a day without access to pasture, its stomach still produces enough acid to digest grass all day long. Without a constant flow of roughage through its system, a horse can get ulcers or colic. A great way to mitigate this is to get a slow-feeder hay net. Your horse can only pull a few straws at a time though the small holes, which cuts down on stomach distress, and alleviates boredom.

Unless your horse is working hard—galloping and sweating on a regular basis—it doesn't really *need* grain. A diet that's too rich is actually not desirable, and creates health problems of its own. Barring special dietary needs, like pregnancy, underweight, age, or certain health issues, more hay is probably a better option than adding grain. Consult your vet to see what your horse needs.

As for supplements, you can spend a small fortune on prepackaged or premixed supplements. You can do some research and find out what the key ingredients are, buy them individually, and just feed those—usually much more cheaply than buying the prepackaged option. That's my approach. Penn gets a whole cocktail of supplements for his various "old man" issues. I get his supplements online in bulk, and discovered that supplements for horses are sometimes way more expensive than the same product packaged for people, and that the people products work just fine. Just check the label carefully to make sure it's the same thing. You don't always have to go straight for the expensive, long-term medication. With some research, trial and error, and patience, you might find a cheaper and healthier option by mixing up a special supplemental "cocktail" for your horse on your own.

Veterinary Care

One of the first things you must do when you get a horse is establish it as a patient with a local veterinarian specializing in equine or large animal care. Your doggy doc won't do. Get recommendations from other horse owners, and set up a "new patient" exam. You must be established with a vet because in addition to routine veterinary care, you need someone to call in an emergency when moments could be a matter of life and death. When your horse is bleeding profusely from a cut or writhing on the ground with colic, those aren't the times to start searching for a vet.

Your horse will need veterinary checkups at least once a year, but optimally twice, because horses need seasonal vaccines in the fall and spring. At one of those visits, the vet will likely "float" their teeth, which means sedating the horse and putting its head in a rather medieval-looking device that holds its mouth open while the vet files down sharp edges on the molars with a special drill. Vaccinations and dental care are the absolute minimum of veterinary care for a horse.

Those are the planned veterinary expenses. It's the unplanned ones that'll get you. Unless you're exceedingly lucky, you'll have some. Just embrace the fact that unexpected veterinary expenses, from injuries to illnesses, are part of the horse ownership gig. Don't be surprise if you have to bust out your credit card from time to time.

Hoof Care

Horses need their hooves trimmed, and shoes replaced if they wear them, about every six to eight weeks. If you're not doing intense riding, showing, or trail riding, and not habitually walking your horse over rough, rocky terrain, find a farrier that specializes in barefoot trims. It's a bit of a hassle going from shoes to bare feet, but in the end, it's worth it. It will also save you some money, and is better for your horse's hooves.

A horse's hoof evolved with some flex to it, and shoes prevent the hooves from flexing naturally. The hooves then take on the shape of the rigid shoes, which can have a negative effect on the horse's soundness or conformation over time. Without shoes, the hooves can have a natural shape and will get better blood supply because they'll flex as the horse walks.

If your horse has always worn shoes, be very patient as your horse adjusts to being barefoot. Their bare feet over gravel feel just as ouchy as yours would. Hoof boots with bottoms can help get you started, particularly after trims, when your horse's hooves are the most tender. Cracking and chipping is normal during this transitional phase. A moisturizing hoof dressing can help, as will hoof supplements. It takes at least a year for a horse to grow new healthy hooves. It took Penn nearly two, but the results are worth it.

What If You Can't Afford It?

So, you've worked up a budget, analyzed the expenses, and no matter how you slice it, affording a horse just doesn't pencil out. Don't throw your hands in the air just yet. Let's think outside the box a little.

Share a Horse

Is there someone who might be a good partner in sharing a horse? The key to making such a situation work is good communication. You'll have to agree on a schedule for spending time with the horse, and use the same methods for groundwork and discipline so the horse doesn't get confused.

Don't worry that your horse will get exhausted by multiple handlers, particularly a companion horse. They're perfectly capable of interacting with people for more than a couple hours per day, and if there are carrots involved, will probably welcome the attention. It takes some orchestration to co-own a horse, but the upside is that pooling resources brings the overall cost down.

Leasing

Leasing a horse is another option. Lease conditions and prices vary from horse to horse, and occur for all kinds of reasons: a horse owner recovering from illness or injury, military deployment, a teenager going away to college, needing to care for a sick loved one or elderly parent, or a job layoff. Horse owners, just like anyone, can find themselves in a "temporary long-term" situation. Suddenly, they're unable to spend time with their horse or afford them, but they can't bear to sell their horses, so they lease them.

Leasing is a great opportunity to "test drive" horse ownership, and with a horse that's clearly loved. Just don't forget that no matter how much you love that wonderful horse, it ultimately belongs to someone else. Don't become hopelessly attached.

Learn to Ride

Take some riding lessons. Western? English? Dressage? Does one appeal to you? Maybe give them all a whirl and then decide? Besides developing a new skill, lessons expose you to horses and horse people, and some stables may allow you to come brush the horses on their down time, as well as walk and graze them. Some may actually welcome it. Also, those hard-working school horses would surely appreciate a little extra love and care. You don't have to own the horse to have a loving companion experience. And, should that school horse need to retire, that horse you've grown to love and care for may be delivered right into your own hands!

Horse Shows and Expos

Go to horse shows and horse expos, which are held all over the country, and watch, listen, learn, and enjoy. Soak up all that amazing Horse energy. Most expos feature workshops with horsemanship experts, where you'll see a variety of methods for both riding and groundwork.

Expos are an opportunity to get useful information, network with new horse people, and learn about all sorts of horse-related issues, from health care to handling to new products. Some expos feature demonstrations with rare breeds that you might not get to see elsewhere, such as the Draft Horse Classic, held every September in Grass Valley, California. It's a cavalcade of "heavy horse" power and beauty—a whole world of real live Earth Horses!

Volunteer

Whether a horse rescue operation or an equine therapy facility, most need volunteers. At a rescue operation, you might help care for neglected and abused horses, maybe with the goal of finding them homes—maybe yours! Habitat For

Horses and Red Bucket Rescue are just two of many horse rescue organizations. If they're too far away, you can help support the horses with donations.

As for equine-assisted therapy, horses are emerging as the newest, most effective assistants for helping humans with both physical and psychological disabilities and challenges. Equine therapy facilities are springing up everywhere. If you'd like to help autistic children, teens at risk for juvenile delinquency, or veterans with PTSD, there's a program for that. Here's a side bonus: Besides being near horses, you'll probably discover that helping others with their therapy turns into therapy for yourself.

Search for an equine-assisted therapy facility near you. If you can't love on a horse of your own just yet, love on some people who desperately need it. You may even discover a new career path and source of income: equine-assisted therapy.

Vacay with the Neigh-Neigh

Horse therapy isn't all about rehabilitation and disabilities. There are programs for grief or anxiety, and others with a lighter aim, like simple stress relief or self-enlightenment. Or just plain fun! Yoga with horses? There's a retreat for that. Writing with horses? There's that too. There are also "dude ranches" where you can play cowboy or cowgirl, and ride real cattle horses. Horse recreational retreats are fun and rejuvenating. Don't you deserve a little vacation anyway? Why not spend it with horses?

Start a Business

Speaking of vacations—horse owners need them too. It's one thing to get a pet-sitter for your cat or dog. It's a little trickier finding one for your horse. You might get a friend from the barn to feed your horse while you're away, but what if you want more than that? It's a tall order to ask your friend to also clean your horse's hooves, brush it, apply fly spray, clean its goopy eyes, take it out walking, talk to it, and give it lots of carrots.

Check around—there may be a horse-care niche that needs filling, and you might discover a new source of income or even a new career. Some busy horse owners even pay people to care for their horses and ride them because they don't have time, which seems pretty crazy to me. Why have a horse if you don't have time for it? What's the point? Wouldn't it be quicker and easier to just flush your money down the toilet?

Before starting any horse business, you'll need experience handling them first. Once you're confident, get the word out that the "Horse Nanny" is ready and willing to help. How ironic is that—you can't afford a horse right now, but you can find people who will pay you to be with theirs!

Horse Videos

If you can't go to the horses, the internet will bring them to you. Become a YouTube junkie. If you can think of a horse question or topic, there are YouTube videos about it, from conformation, recognizing signs of lameness, teaching a horse tricks, to the finer points of equine massage (also a potential career path involving horses).

Explore horsemanship videos and take notice of which style or expert really resonates with you. Follow their videos, visit their websites, and read their books. Many offer in-person workshops that you can attend, even if you don't have a horse. One of my favorite online resources is Equitopia Center, which focuses on the needs of the horse *first*, and also has a website and a library of videos.

If you only watch one horse video, make it the two-part PBS documentary, *Equus—Story of the Horse*. It's a lovely, gorgeous overview of horses and their relationships with humans, and is packed with amazing historical, evolutionary, cultural, and behavioral information. The segment on how horses can read human facial expressions is a mind-blower. Also, comb through Netflix or Hulu or any other video streaming service, and watch all the horse movies and documentaries you can find.

Read, Read, Read

There are a gazillion books out there on just about any horse topic you could imagine, from history to particular breeds to horsemanship to equine history, and many are available right in your local library. Look for the ones that focus on horsemanship, rather than riding, as these will get you on the right track for a companion horse. For some reading ideas, check out the bibliography in this book.

Get Creative

Besides horses, art is another therapy that heals the soul. Draw horses or take a painting class and learn to paint them. There are people out there who still want oil paintings of their horses! Make jewelry, mojo bags, horse-themed gifts: any creative expression, from ceramics to stained glass, could focus on horses. Who knows—you may develop into quite the equine artisan and, once again, discover a new revenue stream for yourself.

Recap, Review, Meditate

If you're really financially or physically stumped in finding a path to horse ownership, go back to Part II in this book, and immerse yourself in Horse, the mythologies and deities of Horse, and the mystical, magical horses. Deepen your relationship with your Elemental Horses, as well as your understanding of the elemental energies. Learn more about tarot, which is yet another universe of exploration. The more you learn, the more depth your Horse tarot readings will have.

Keep practicing the Horse meditations to relieve stress and carve out some time to feel calm, grounded, and relaxed. You can pick your favorite meditations and when you arrive at your special "meeting spot," rather than calling any of the Elemental Horses, ask the universe to show you the perfect horse for you. When you're sitting calmly in that safe, secluded place in your mind, tell the universe, "This is who I am…" Breathe until you feel connection to the astral energies. Then say, "Please show me my horse." Keep breathing. See what images emerge. Note the color, breed, and personality of the horse. Spend as much time as you like with it. When you feel ready, release your horse to graze, and bring yourself back to your physical surroundings.

In that image, the universe has given you a suggestion. Take note when you see horses matching the image of "your horse." Keep focusing on the goal of "your horse" rather than all the obstacles keeping you from it.

If You're Just Stumped

If it seems like every roadblock is popping up on your path to horse ownership, dial it back a few notches. Focus on enjoying the experience of exploration. Let go of the search for an actual horse for now. You aren't abandoning your dreams, just putting them on pause. Just because you can't make it work right now doesn't mean that you won't be able to make it work in the future. Situations can change, finances can change—stay in the moment, keep loving horses and learning about them, and sink into Horse.

Hand your desire over to the universe, and let it work on it for you. If it takes awhile, that's okay. Just assume that the universe is carefully searching for a perfect horse for you, and fill yourself with gratitude that you are just so darned special that the universe doesn't want to throw just any old horse your way. Many times when we push hard to solve a problem and continue hitting roadblocks, it's because it's just not the right time. We usually don't know why until much later. But the universe does. Trust the process.

Safety First

As you explore the horse world, if you plan to handle horses, you must know the safety basics. Your life depends upon it. Even the gentlest, most well-mannered horse can become 1,500 pounds of explosive fear and panic given the right set of circumstances. Controlling a horse with a halter and lead rope is an illusion, really. If a horse really wants to overpower you and get away, it will, and if that means injuring you in the process, it will do that too. There's a good reason to put safety first because when it comes to horses, if it isn't first, anything else you do first might be the last thing you ever do. The best way to prevent injury, or worse, is to have a thorough grasp of horse safety.

If you think you'll never get hurt while handling or riding a horse, you need to either reframe that notion or not get a horse at all. Even just handling a horse, just brushing it and leading it around, there's always a possibility for injury. You can get stepped on by the kindest of horses, or they can throw their heads unexpectedly because flies are stinging their eyes and knock you flat. You have to learn to keep one eye on your horse at all times, just like taking a toddler near a swimming pool.

While injuries are always a possibility, don't let that scare you away from horses. Knowledge about horse safety greatly reduces your chance—and your horse's—of injury. You're likely tougher than you think, but have never really had an opportunity to discover that. Can you get killed while handling a horse? Sure, but you're a lot more likely to get killed every time you get in your car, yet we don't give that a second thought because it's so familiar. In time, horses will become that familiar. You're more likely to get hurt slipping and falling in your own shower than just about anything else, so keep your worries in proportion.

One morning while driving out to the barn, I was pondering the potential danger, and thinking that yes, it was possible that I could get thrown and die that very morning. It's not like these things give you a heads-up. They just happen. Did I turn around and head for home? Nope, I just shrugged and told myself, "Yeah, but it's *so* worth it." However, I'm not an idiot. I never tempt fate. I'm ultra cautious, and at this age, will only ride if all the planets are in alignment. I make sure I feel rested, healthy, and alert, my horse seems calm and quiet, there aren't a bunch of riders in the arena taking jumping lessons and galloping about, and—this one may surprise you—the wind isn't blowing.

Many horses (Penn at the front of that line) get very goofy in the wind, because wind carries sound and smells, and a horse's ears and nose are always scanning the surroundings for potential predators. It's in their DNA to do that, like biological radar systems, regardless of how well trained they are. You can't train a horse's survival instincts out of them. Take extra caution on windy days.

I can walk Penn out in the field to graze on a calm day and it's completely peaceful. Walk him out when the wind is gusting, in the very same field where we've walked ten thousand times, and his head will be up in the air, his eyes will be ringed with white and he'll be making that little "uh-oh, I'm very nervous" purr-snort every time he exhales. This behavior means your horse is anxious about something, and you may not have any idea what it is. You don't see your surroundings the same way your horse does.

When your horse is giving signals that it's getting nervous and paying less attention to you than your surroundings, it's very important to breathe and ground yourself, and convey the message that everything is fine. You have to be the calm leader in this situation, because if you're not, your horse will decide it needs to be the leader and take matters into its own hooves. I already know that Penn gets more wound up than I want to deal with when the wind is blowing. Walking him out in the field on a windy day is like trying to hang on to a 1,500-pound kite with rocket jets for a tail, so I just don't.

Knowing the limits of your abilities and evaluating your circumstances—sometimes very quickly—is vital to staying safe. I developed some severe tendinitis awhile back in my upper right arm that left it extremely weak. Any pulling or jerking motion felt like stabbing a knife into my deltoid. One day, I tried leading Penn with my left hand, but we were both too clumsy at this to go out into the field, so I took my chances with my weak arm, and followed Sarah and her two horses out to graze.

It was an idyllic day out on the grassy green hillside near the stable under crystal blue skies. The horses were grazing peacefully, and Sarah and I were having a grand time charting all the ways that horses were better than men. Then, we heard a rumble and a clatter down the hill.

There's a bridge that spans a creek to get to the field, and it's the only way in or out. Rumbling over that bridge was the old red barn tractor, its bucket loaded with scrap wood, winding down to the big burn pile below. The load was dumped, and then the stable hand hopped out, walked to the pile, and lit it. A thin flume of smoke snaked up into the blue sky above growing orange flames getting larger by the moment.

The only way out of the field was to pass right by the fire. Some horses get nervous around fire, some might be fine with it. Mine is not. He doesn't like the tractor in the first place, and gets nervous every time it goes by even though he sees it about three million times a week. He also associates fire with panic because of the chronic wildfires in our area of California. Legions of machines screaming by, air choked with smoke, visibly approaching flames, utter chaos, sirens, helicopters, and air tankers overhead, as well as a bad experience with an emergency evacuation have left Penn with a fire phobia.

Penn's head was already up high watching the smoke with his big white-ringed eyes, snorting his anxiety. Sarah's horses, meanwhile were happily grazing on their own a ways off and weren't bothered. However, even horses that don't flip out over fires can be more difficult to handle around them. We tense up, so they tense up too.

Factor in my injured arm into this situation, and there was only one way to look at it: oh, *shit*.

If I absolutely had to, I would have powered through the pain to keep Penn under control, even if it meant shredding that angry deltoid tendon and starting physical therapy over from scratch. Thankfully, I wasn't alone.

Sarah quickly did the calculation: big nervous chicken horse; friend with a bad wing; her own horses running loose; crackling, smoking burn pile fire growing bigger by the second; and no way out but past it.

"Okay, this is really happening," she said, and asked, "Do you want me to take Penn?"

I nodded, because all the arrows pointed to something really bad. I handed the rope to her, and Penn tested all of Sarah's experience and strength, panic-prancing, pulling, balking, and snorting the whole way to the bridge, where she handed him back to me and ran back for her own horses. Keeping our heads about us and making quick, rational decisions kept this situation uneventful. Uneventful is the goal when you're handling horses.

What this story illustrates is that the most peaceful, perfect outing with your horse can spin on a dime into a potentially dangerous situation. You always have to be alert, be aware of your own shortcomings, and not let your ego get in the way of handing the lead rope to someone else if you're in over your head. Ego and safety are poor bedfellows, particularly around horses.

Be Prepared and Ready to Think Fast

Every day when you go to spend time with your horse, be prepared. Have a plan about what you're going to do that day, even if the plan is just walking around and grazing, and be ready to scrap that plan should you need to adapt to sudden circumstances. Forcing your own agenda in the midst of less-than-optimal circumstances is a young rider's game and also the perfect cocktail for getting hurt. There's nothing you need to do that day that's worth risking your own safety or your horse's.

Here's another story of how an easy-peasy morning spun around one hundred eighty degrees in a blink. I'd turned Penn out in the pasture and was walking back to the barn. We'd had a stretch of rain and the horses were stir-crazy after several days cooped up in stalls, so Penn was out there burning off excess jet fuel, galloping, bucking, snorting, and farting (horses often fart when they buck—jet propulsion).

It was a rare stormy spring day, with billowing grey clouds rolling across the sky. Just as I reached the barn, a bone-rattling clap of thunder crackled from that bank of incoming clouds. Thunder is rare in this area, and it really freaks some horses out. I analyzed my situation: Hmmm... 1,500-pound chicken, already zipping around like a maniac, and an incoming thunderstorm. What could possibly go wrong? Oh, pretty much everything.

I hustled back to the pasture to retrieve him, power-waddling, not running, because running can cue anxiety in horses. Thankfully, there wasn't another thunderclap while leading him back to the barn, because one was all it took to put Penn into dance-prance-snort mode: *Mama! The sky is exploding! We must flee!* He would have jumped into my arms like a big, frightened damsel in distress if he could have.

In addition to always being ready to scrap your plans should things change, you must be the one with the cool head at all times. Calming your own fears and emotions is a crucial horse safety skill. If you panic, your horse will lose its shit, sometimes literally. Horses often poop when they're nervous—less weight, easier to run away from predators.

When your horse is wound up, breathe deeply, calm your mind, and exhibit the behavior a calm lead mare would. Adopt a "no big whoop" physical and mental state, keep the image of calmly continuing on your way in your mind—not potential disaster—and give a long, deep sigh, as if you're bored to death. You can also flutter your lips as you exhale, mimicking that sound horses make when they're bored. Penn remained reasonably calm because I was communicating to him that this situation was boring as dirt. Had I not, this situation could have whirled out of control in a nanosecond.

Horses don't interpret *why* you're tense, they only interpret *that* you're tense. If their two-legged lead mare gets nervous, they will too. If you're scared, they're scared. Thinking fast and remaining calm is a key safety skill.

I'm not trying put fears into you, only some reality. A horse isn't a bicycle. It's a living, thinking, reacting animal that may not have the same agenda or perceptions as you. You'll have to think fast if a potentially dangerous situation pops up, and realize that this could happen when you least expect it.

I also want you to embrace the idea that you'll probably get some horse-related bumps and bruises along the way. It's just part of the gig. You learn to tolerate minor discomforts when you're around horses, from cuts and scrapes to minor injuries. Horses will teach you how tough and resilient you really are, as well as how dirty you can get, and how comfortable you can become with that.

If you absolutely never, ever want to risk injury of any type, that's okay. However, if you feel that way, don't get a horse yet. Find ways to observe and handle horses, baby step by baby step, until joy starts nudging your fears aside. Experience will desensitize you to your fears.

That said, allow me the indulgence of tempering your fear: safety is an illusion. An asteroid or airplane could crash through your roof or a truck through the wall, and squish you right in your own living room. As someone who has battled the "anxiety dragon" her entire life, and obsessed about horrific scenarios that most people couldn't and wouldn't even imagine, and then based her life decisions on those unlikely situations, trust me on this: fear is a shackle. It prevents you from living your life. The trick is acknowledging the fear, but proceeding with what you want to do anyway. If you never feel the fear and do something anyway, you may extend your life, but you won't be living it. "Safety" in the end is mostly just really good luck. And plenty of preparation.

Some Safety Tips

Your best weapon against fear and injuries is knowledge. Specifically, knowledge about how to handle a horse safely. These are the "super basics" you must know before you even have a horse—just going to visit a barn or stable, taking riding lessons, or interacting with horses:

- When offering a horse a treat, keep your hand flat. Fingers feel just like carrots to their sensitive lips, and may be treated as such. Fingers are good, so strive to keep all of them. Also, don't give a horse any kind of treat unless you're sure it's not toxic to a horse. Walnuts, for example, are great snacks for people, but toxic for horses. Acorns can be lethal. Don't guess—research it first.

- Don't fling your arms around a horse's head. When one horse wants to tell a horse of lesser stature to move, it will fling its head to herd the other horse out of its way. Your arms suddenly flying up mimic that body language, and the horse is likely to fling its own head into the air or attempt to escape because you're "telling" it to move. When you're around horses, speak their language, not yours.

- Always wear sturdy, closed-toed shoes—but not steel-toed boots—around horses. You can get stepped on by even the gentlest horse. Going barefoot or wearing sandals is an absolute "don't." The day I got my first pony, Comanche, I hadn't yet developed that "third eye" to constantly watch a horse's every move. Good old Comanche stepped down square on my foot, and I squalled in pain. When I pulled off my little cowboy boot later, the smallest three toes on my right foot were black and blue, but still intact. Had I been in sandals, my toes would surely have been crushed.

This illustrates why steel-toed boots aren't optimal around horses. If you think that little steel toe will sustain the weight of a thousand pound animal, think again. That steel toe will be crushed and worse yet, could be bent at an angle and cut the blood flow right off from your toes, or maybe cut them off completely. It's not like you'll be able to pull the boot off then and there. You'll have to make it all the way to the emergency room where they can cut the steel. Whether or not they can save your toes relies entirely on the talents of the surgeon. Toes are also good; strive to keep all of them too.

• Never wrap or tie the lead rope or reins around your arm or wrist with the foolishly mistaken notion that you'll be able to hang onto your horse better that way if they suddenly bolt. You won't. Instead, you'll get dragged along like a child's pull-toy. Getting dragged is the most dangerous of all situations. Your body dragging behind may trigger a horse's flight response. It will run and run from that "predator" until it physically can't run anymore. By then, you'll be a big sack of hamburger. The rope or reins must be *grasped* in your hand *only*, never wrapped.

• Never walk up behind a horse without first making a sound, clucking or calling to it, making sure it knows you're coming. If you aren't familiar with that horse, don't walk up behind it at all. Come in from the side, talking softly all the way. Even your beloved old bombproof horse may kick in panic if it doesn't know you're there or you catch it by surprise.

I was once out at the barn, chatting with a friend who happened to be standing right behind his very gentle horse while it was preoccupied eating hay. At one point, he playfully smacked his horse lightly on the rump. That horse kicked out its hind legs in a millisecond and sent him flying. That smack could have been a predator from the horse's perspective.

• When walking or standing behind a horse, stay very close to its body. If it kicks, you'll be pushed away rather than launched into the dirt. Whenever I go behind a horse, from one side to the other, I stay very close and trail my hand along its sides and rump so it knows where I am.

- Don't leave a horse tied up without using a "quick release" knot or latch. Horses sometimes pull back when tied and some are chronic pullers. Sometimes it's an isolated incident, like the rope caught over the horse's head. That feeling of their head being trapped causes instant panic, and the horse will throw all its weight and energy into escaping. If you've tied a regular knot, the sheer power of that animal will pull it too tight to undo in two seconds. You'll need to have a pocketknife handy to cut the rope.

    Pulling like this can injure a horse's head or neck, and in a panic, they can loose their footing and slip, opening up a new universe of injury. Also, despite how they do this in the movies, never tie a horse by the reins. If a horse pulls back with a bit in its mouth, it can severely damage the tongue and mouth. If the horse is wearing a bridle and needs to be tied, put a halter over the bridle and tie it with a lead rope.

- Don't run around horses. They're acutely sensitive and hypervigilant, and if you're running, they may think they need to run too.

- When riding in a saddle, wear boots meant for that style of riding. They are more than flashy fashion statements. The heels of riding boots prevent your foot from slipping through the stirrup, which is immensely dangerous if you get thrown and your foot gets stuck. Even worse than getting dragged by a rope wrapped around your wrist is getting dragged by your foot stuck through the stirrup. In that position, if your horse takes off, your head will bang on the ground the entire way, right near those powerful, frantically galloping back hooves. Even with a helmet on, you're likely to sustain a horrific head injury. Getting dragged by the stirrup is the worst-case scenario. Get the boots; they're an important safety tool.

    Tall English boots protect your shins from getting rubbed raw against the stirrup straps. Cowboy boots, although safe enough for English riding, won't protect your shins. However, their pointy toe makes it much easier to catch the stirrup if your foot falls out of it.

    Athletic shoes are acceptable for riding bareback, but not in a saddle. There's no heel to keep your foot from slipping through the stirrup. Hiking boots are also not safe in the saddle, because the knobby soles could hang up on, or through, the stirrup. Riding boots are completely slick on the tops and bottoms to allow your foot to slide right out if you get thrown, rather than getting caught in the stirrup.

You could get away with going barefoot while riding bareback (and I did a million times when I was a kid). However, if you're out on the trail, and your horse picks up a rock or throws a shoe and you have to walk it back, or you fall off and can't get back on, you're going to have some pretty raw, tender feet by the time you get back to the barn. If it's summer, you'll be astounded by how hot the dirt on that trail is, and you haven't even reached the asphalt yet. Just wear the shoes.

- Don't ride alone. I see people do it all the time, and it's because they haven't had their close call yet. Riding alone is like swimming alone. You might get away with it a thousand times without incident, and then the thousand and fifth time, you hit your head on the side of the pool, get knocked out, and drown. Horseback riding is the same. I say this from experience, because I rode alone all the time back in the day. Then came my one thousand and fifth ride.

I was eighteen, in peak condition, an excellent rider, confident in my abilities, and decided to take my sweet old mare, Rosie, out for a ride at dusk on the bridle trails near my home. She was a kind, obedient, well-mannered old gal, and also very tall.

Off we went, just before sunset, all by ourselves. We were having a marvelous time, with the park practically to ourselves, and were gently cantering along the trail. I felt so relaxed and comfortable, I had her on a "loose rein," meaning the reins were slack and I was making no attempt to slow her down. There we were, rocking along, and all of a sudden, she gave a gentle little tip of her back end, as horses will do when feeling playful. However, a little tip on a big horse ends up being quite a large movement. Because I was *doe-dee-doe* cantering along, my mind wandering elsewhere, she caught me completely off guard and launched me head over heels into the air. I landed head first in a pile drive, and then the lights went out.

When I came to, it was pitch dark. I was completely alone, no one was in the park, and those were the days before cell phones. It was about a mile walk back home. I was woozy, stunned, and aching, but thankfully, nothing seemed broken. I got up, looked around, and there was Rosie. She'd stayed right by me the whole time, grazing on some weeds about ten feet away. She looked up as if to say, "Well, it's about time you quit napping."

I was too dizzy and disoriented to get back into the saddle, so I gathered up the reins and steadied myself by hanging onto the saddle and walking alongside. Rosie knew the way home, and she trudged slowly along, never faster than I could manage. She knew something wasn't quite right. Horses are astonishingly intuitive.

Would having someone else with me have prevented me from getting thrown? Probably not, but there would have been someone to go get help had I cracked my skull open or broken my neck. Had an injury like that have happened while riding alone that evening, I probably wouldn't be here today writing this book. I was ridiculously lucky to have survived that fall with nothing more than a mild concussion, which brings us to our next safety "must":

- Always wear a helmet when riding. Helmets are just as necessary on a horse as they are on a bicycle or motorcycle, and worth every penny when you consider what they're protecting. Is there any helmet at any price that's worth more than your brain? The answer is no. Get the best one you can find, designed specifically for horseback riding.

  Back in my early riding days, nobody wore helmets except in the show ring, and they were just cheesy little velvet hardhats meant more to complete our fancy hunter-jumper ensemble than serve any real purpose. Equestrians have gotten a lot smarter since then, although in the Western riding world, the switch from a cowboy hat to a helmet is lagging behind. The cowboy hat is just so iconic. You rarely see cowboys/girls wearing helmets in the show ring, even though they're chasing down cows and racing at top speed around barrels, and even more surprising, while riding bucking broncos in rodeos. The person who finds a way to hide a helmet in a cowboy hat will be a millionaire.

- Take off all your jewelry before riding or handling a horse. Earrings that dangle, necklaces, or bracelets can get caught on tack or in a mane, and horsehair is tough. If your big hoop earring gets caught in a mane, and the horse tosses its head, your earlobe will lose that battle. Rings can easily get caught in manes too. Wear them at your own risk, or wear riding gloves.

- If you wear glasses, take them off if you can. Some people can't or they'll walk into walls. If you intend to be around horses a lot or ride, consider getting contact lenses, LASIK surgery, or at the very least, safety glasses. The last thing you want to be wearing on your face around big, unpredictable animals is glass. Also, if you wear glasses out on the trail and they fall off—or you do—and get broken, you'll have to ride back with impaired vision. Do you trust your horse to know the way home? Get the contacts. I've worn them almost the entire time I've been around horses. Get the soft kind: dirt under hard lenses is very painful!

- Never handle or ride a horse if you've been drinking, period. Alcohol and horses are a disastrous cocktail.

- Never, *ever* smoke in a barn or near a haystack. One stray ember in the wind and you've got a blazing emergency on your hands. When you see someone smoking in a barn, rest assured, you're looking at an idiot. The words of a true idiot are, "Well, I do that all the time and nothing ever happened."

    Yet. It's all about the "yet."

    A fire that ignites in a barn is an immediate crisis. Barns are loaded with combustible material, from hay to stall shavings to the structure itself. If the barn's on fire, will you have time to lead each horse out? Or throw open all the stall doors in hopes that the horses will run out themselves? They may not—they may feel safer in their stalls and refuse to leave. If the fire is between the horses and the door, you won't be able to get the horses out at all. Is it worth a cigarette to hear those horses screaming as they burn to death? Good lord, I hope your answer is "no." If it's not… find a different hobby, preferably one that doesn't involve living, sentient creatures.

Safety Tips for New Horse Owners

All of the previously mentioned safety tips are things you need to know before handling or riding horses. There are a couple more crucial concerns for when you do get a horse:

- Never attempt to load, haul, or unload a horse from a trailer without expert guidance and practice, even if you've pulled a trailer or boat before. Pulling a loaded horse trailer isn't the same thing. Your load is alive.

You must corner extremely slowly so the horses can adjust to the shift in weight and angle, and brake even more slowly. If you corner or brake too abruptly and your horse falls down in the trailer, you've got a big, dangerous, deadly problem on your hands. Nothing struggles more mightily than an injured, fallen, panicked horse.

While trailering, you need nerves of steel and eyes behind your head for the jerks that rush up on your tail, honking because you're going too slow, and then passing in a big huff and cutting you off, forcing you to slam on the brakes. These jackasses put your life and your horse's life at risk. May there be a special place in hell for them. Also, bear all of this in mind when you're stuck behind a slow-moving horse trailer and getting frustrated. The driver isn't poking along to annoy you, they're doing so out of concern for their horses.

• Be prepared for natural disasters in your own area. Although earthquakes get all the buzz, in California, wildfires are the biggest concern. Elsewhere, it may be floods, mudslides, hurricanes, or tornadoes that create instant calamity. Whatever sort of natural disasters occur where you live, you must have an evacuation plan for your horse, and you must practice it before you actually need it.

For the last four years, we've had at least one major wildfire every summer near Penn's stable. Some of the horses are adjusted to the chaos, and others panic at the smell of smoke, the sight of flames, wailing fire engines, and roaring water-dropping helicopters swooping overhead.

While most horses get a little uncomfortable around fire, Penn has a full-blown fire phobia. Just the sight or smell of smoke, even from an innocent campfire across the creek, launches him into DEFCON 2. I'm not sure if it's the fire itself, or his bad evacuation experience, or both. During an emergency fire evacuation a few years back, he panicked and balked, refusing to get in the trailer. The person trying to load him figured that the best way to convince a terrified horse to get in a trailer during a fire evacuation is to beat it. Eventually, he got Penn in the trailer, but it left lasting emotional scars. Fires and trailers hit all of Penn's triggers. And dang if one recent summer, he didn't have to face them.

By pure coincidence, while sitting out at the barn one day on fire watch for the latest blaze scorching the nearby hills, Sarah and I were

working on desensitizing Penn to the trailer because we didn't have anything else to do. We pulled the trailer out and walked Penn to the ramp.
He was trembling the whole time, but Sarah had some skillful loading
tricks and lots of patience, and he finally, tentatively stepped into that
trailer, eyes wide as saucers and snorter on high. But he did it and I could
tell he was so proud of himself.

We were passing time as the billow of black smoke grew and grew,
choking the air and finally blocking out the sun until it was only a glow-
ing orange ball in a blackened sky. We could see the wall of flames licking
the top of the ridge and wondered if maybe we should start evacuating.
The decision was suddenly made for us. Unbeknownst to us, the wind
had shifted and was picking up, poised to sweep the fire right over the top
of us. Sheriff's deputies came onto the property and ordered, "Evacuate
now." That's what we did. Forty horses had to be loaded and trailered to
safety, with only one road in and out. Fun times.

I gathered up my nervous horse, and Sarah led him up to the trailer,
just like we'd practiced. Shaking like a sapling in a hurricane, he stepped
into the trailer, snorting and white-eyed. It wasn't merely a success, it was
heart-touching. Penn had decided to trust us more than his impulse to
flee. When a horse trusts you above his own instincts, it's huge. It's putting its life in your hands. That's a big statement for a prey animal.

Don't wait until a natural disaster strikes to find out how your horse
will react to trailering. Practice ahead of time. Have your emergency
plan in place well before you need it. Know where you can evacuate your
horse, and if you don't have a truck and trailer, prearrange with another
horse owner to evacuate your horse in an emergency. Contact your local
sheriff's office to find out the process for emergency large animal evac-
uations. In our area, the local county fairgrounds is the last-resort evacuation spot for horses. Where is that place for you? You must know this
before you actually need to know it.

• Create an emergency card for your horse, and post it near its stall, paddock, or in the barn. The card needs to include your horse's name, age,
breed, a good full-body photo, your veterinarian's name and phone number, and your phone number. It also needs a designee to make decisions

about your horse in case an emergency situation occurs while you're out of town or unable to get to the barn in a hurry.

- Know the signs of colic. Colic is the dreaded monster of horse ownership. Colic in horses isn't the same as colic in infants. When babies get colic, they're cranky and miserable. Colic in horses is severe and potentially lethal stomach cramps. When a horse gets colic, it's a veterinary emergency. Sometimes it's caused by fecal impaction, but the bigger danger is when an intestine twists. The latter is most always fatal, and will probably require euthanizing your horse unless you're willing to spend about $5,000 or more on a surgery that probably won't work anyway.

Colic can happen to any horse at any time, at any age. I saw two horses colic and die at Penn's barn one summer, and it's a horrifically agonizing death. If the vet can't get there right away, there's not much you can do but walk them around to keep them on their feet. Their natural instinct is to roll the belly pain away; however, that means their impacted intestine can twist, and that's lethal.

There is an injectable drug called Buscopan that can be administered in an emergency if your horse colics and the vet can't get there right away. However, this means you'll need to learn how to give an injection, and where to give it. The drug relaxes the gastrointestinal muscles and temporarily eases the pain, but won't cure the problem. You can purchase a vial and some syringes from your vet to keep on hand for an emergency.

You must know the symptoms of colic, because time is of the essence. A horse that colics won't eat, looks back at his stomach, and may lie down and roll, which you must prevent him from doing. The horse may also paw at the ground, sweat, kick at its stomach with its back legs, start lying down more than usual and not want to get back up. A horse that colics may sweat, its veins may protrude all over its neck and chest, and agonized distress will be obvious on its face. If you see this cluster of behaviors, call the vet *immediately*.

Your Horse Pre-Ownership Checklist

We've covered a lot of ground in this chapter, so here's a checklist of what you'll need before getting a horse:

- A safe place to board that has the services and amenities you want
- Basic understanding of what and how to feed a horse
- Familiarity with local feed stores and tack shops, and what they sell
- List of local veterinarians
- List of local farriers, and maybe a specialist in barefoot trimming
- Basic grooming and first aid items, plus a lead rope and halter in the size your horse needs. If you plan to ride, you'll need a bridle, saddle, a saddle pad, and riding boots appropriate for that style of riding, and a helmet.
- Winter blanket if you live in an area that drops below forty degrees at night, or has long, cold winters
- Thorough understanding of safety concerns and cautions
- Emergency card and evacuation plan in place
- Being familiar with the signs of colic
- Experienced horse person to guide you if necessary
- Practical, physical experience handling a horse. At the very minimum, you must know how to lead and groom a horse, pick its hooves, and how to tie it safely. You cannot learn this from a book. You must have someone teach you.

Chapter 8

READY FOR A HORSE—
BUT WHICH ONE?

In this chapter, we'll explore the vast array of horses available, for sale, for lease, and sometimes for free. We'll discuss the value—and urgency—of considering rescue horses, as well as the plight more horses than you could imagine face every day. We'll also consider breed, age, and background, which are factors in choosing a companion horse.

So Many Choices

So, you've worked out a budget, decided owning a horse is do-able, checked off everything on that pre-ownership checklist, and you're ready to start searching for your own horse. Congratulations! The good news is that there are thousands upon thousands to choose from. The bad news is that there are thousands upon thousands to choose from. The more you look, the more dizzy you'll get because there are just too many choices—like picking one grain of sand from the beach. If you go searching for "brown gelding," you'll get about ten thousand more brown geldings than you want. Let's refine your search, taking into consideration your own needs and desires, and physical and financial realities.

Once again, it's all about safety first. The type of horse you choose is also a safety consideration. You must consider age, breed, soundness, temperament, and the training and veterinary history of that horse, all balanced against your own age, strength, fitness level, physical difficulties or impairments, and experience handling and riding horses. You'll also need to decide what you want to do with your horse. Do you want to ride, or just walk around and spend time with a horse, or maybe a little of both? Whatever your desire, there's a horse out there to fill it, maybe hundreds.

If you think riding is on your horizon, consider your own circumstances: Do you have access to an arena? Trails? Riding lessons? A trail horse will likely do just fine in an arena; however, a horse that spent its entire life in an arena may be very jumpy out on the trail, just like my Penn. When I first got him, I imagined us going for trail rides, but discovered that he was afraid of bushes, birds, logs, and pretty much anything he never saw in his constricted arena world. I've abandoned the idea of hitting the trail with Penn. It's just not what he is, and forcing him to be something he's not will lead to trouble. I'm too old for trouble. This is why matching the type of horse to the type of activity you want to do is important. Not all horses are good at—or appropriate for—all things.

The One Word You Must Know

If you're a beginner and looking for your first horse, or are an older rider, or have a physical condition that limits your ability to handle a horse safely or withstand a fall, there's one mandatory word to include: "bombproof." It means that this horse has seen it all, done it all, is patient, good-natured and tolerant (particularly with newbie mistakes), and doesn't buck, kick, or bite.

Horses with the bombproof label are often backyard pleasure horses, trail horses, or "school horses," which have spent years being used for riding lessons and have tolerated just about everything. They'll put up with novice riders mounting with their feet backward in the stirrups, bouncing like clumsy sacks of cement on their backs when they trot, yanking on the reins as if they're meant to help them hang on rather than guide the horse, and landing in front of the saddle, hugging their necks for dear life to keep from falling.

A former school horse—if not sour after years of lessons—is a great first horse. Backyard horses that have been mostly handled and ridden by kids, as well as seasoned trail horses that have experienced all sorts of unusual circumstances, like joggers coming up on them or walking over fallen logs or through water, are both great first horses. For beginners or older riders, bombproof is the only way to go.

Do You Plan to Ride?

If riding is your goal, what kind of riding will it be? How often? Do you want to ride just for pleasure, or learn to barrel race or compete in shows? What's your level of riding experience? Beginner? Intermediate? Experienced? Only horse you ever rode was on a carousel? Shape your search to your level of expertise, unless you're willing to get riding lessons.

In addition to your level of experience, you must consider the hard reality of where you're at physically. The older you are, the slower your reflexes are, the worse your balance is, and the less resilient your bones are. Even a completely calm horse can trip and tumble you onto the ground. Being an older rider means taking extra precaution and choosing a calm, cooperative, well-schooled horse that has "more whoa than go."

Horse Buyer, Beware

When you start searching for a horse of your own, you'll discover all sorts of horses for sale out there, for a range of prices—some even for free—and coming from a range of circumstances. You're going to fall in love about a million times on this journey to horse ownership, so keep your head about you. Don't overlook issues like health, soundness, or behavioral concerns, and think they'll get better over time. Those issues may or may not get better. If not, prepare to make your veterinarian or local professional horse trainer a little richer.

Should you find a horse you want, be cautious. That horse owner may be as honest as the day is long, or a sly, fast-talker who wants to unload a horse with hidden problems. There's a reason that the term "horse trader" means a slimy, dishonest shark that's out to get your money: because they exist. They'll say anything to get that horse into your trailer and wave goodbye. Then you'll later discover that horse isn't sound; is much older than was stated; has chronic, nasty, or dangerous behaviors; or has a hidden veterinary issue that will require regular, expensive treatment and medication. Always bring an experienced horse person with you when considering adopting or buying a horse. In addition, always have the horse "vet checked," which means a routine examination and lab tests from a veterinarian who will inform you whether that horse is A-OK or tell you about the veterinary issues you're facing and what it will cost to manage them.

For example, an old bowed tendon can be ugly, but the horse could be functionally sound if ridden gently. However, a horse with chronic lameness or a back injury could be permanently crippled, and only able to be led around slowly and gently, which might be just what you're looking for. Other conditions, such as Cushing's Disease (a dysfunction of the pituitary gland) or simple arthritis that come with age, may not be visible except to the trained eye. Both conditions are fairly manageable, but you'll need to adapt your expectations to what that horse can handle, and may need to provide regular medication—it ain't cheap. Be aware of that, particularly when getting an older horse. Just like old people, they have health issues and need a little extra TLC.

About that older horse, here's the oldest horse trader trick in the book: "We lost his papers, but he's nineteen." Every old horse without breed registration papers—which would include a birth date—or whose papers have been "lost," is nineteen! That's because a horse's age can be roughly detected by the length and angle of its teeth up until about nineteen years of age, when the teeth reach their peak angle. It might fool you, but it won't fool a vet, who can examine the cups and grooves in a horse's teeth that change over time and give you a more accurate "guesstimate" of a horse's age.

Horses in rescue programs likely won't have breed registration papers, and wild horses certainly won't. Thoroughbred racehorses, however, regardless of age, do have one bit of evidence regarding their identities and ages: a tattoo. They're tattooed to prevent a dishonest trainer from sneaking in a dead ringer to win a race. Every Thoroughbred that races in the United States bears a tattoo on the inside of their upper lip that's linked to their registration papers. The Jockey Club, which registers Thoroughbreds, offers a free identification service on their website should you come upon a Thoroughbred of unknown origin with a tattooed lip.

To look for the tattoo, gently bend the horse's upper lip up over its nostrils, sort of turning it inside out. Most racehorses have had this done many times, and don't object much. The upper lip is very rubbery, so it doesn't cause them any discomfort to look at the tattoo.

Don't Fall in Love … Yet

This will probably happen, and you'll probably ignore my advice, but I'm offering it anyway: Don't fall in love with the first horse you see, even though that's exactly what I did when I met Penn. To my own credit, however, I wasn't looking for him. That serendipitous arrangement was guided by the universe itself. Penn was dropped into my lap!

Unless serendipity comes bopping along, leading the perfect horse right to you, you'll have to do a little searching before picking a horse. Weigh all the factors: soundness, veterinary clearance, temperament, all available information about that horse, and most important, pay attention to whether you and that horse "click" or not. Every horse has a unique personality. Some are big old lovebugs, and others are full-fledged jerks. Usually a person turns a horse into a jerk, and it's possible to rehabilitate it, but that's yet another unnecessary factor to deal with when you're just starting out.

Many Horses Need Homes

If you aren't looking for a fancy, high-end horse, consider a horse that used to be one. Sometimes beautiful, purebred horses are standing around at racing or show barns because they're aging, injured, or just not performing to their owners' satisfaction anymore. Every single day, horses pull up lame, get arthritis, get a little too old, or the kids get tired of them, and their humans are ready to move on. From a business perspective, a racehorse that can't race, a cow horse that can't cut, or a jumper that can't jump are simply money pits. But, they'd be spectacular companion horses and many could still be gently ridden. Call around at local stables and see if there's a horse that has become "useless." You may find your new equine partner there. You might also discover horses that are available for very little, simply because their owners didn't pay their board for too long and the barn owner has confiscated it. These situations exist too.

If you're thinking that you can't afford a horse, let me disabuse you of that notion. True, if you only want a purebred dressage horse at the prime of its life, you could expect to pay $30,000 and up. But look for that horse when it's ten years older, with arthritis pricking its hocks and back, unfit for the show ring any longer, and it will be substantially less. If you can offer that horse a long, loving retirement, and that horse is lucky enough to have a loving owner who wants a new horse they can compete with, you may just find yourself negotiating a one dollar "sale" (which makes it legally official) to make that horse your own. Penn's former owner isn't the only one out there who loved her old horse so much that when an opportunity arose for him to have a happy life in his golden years, she put his needs first and made that one dollar sale. Should I ever be in that position, I'd do exactly the same.

I have a friend who acquired a purebred Quarter Horse mare, simply because her days working cattle were over. She just wasn't up to the task anymore, but she was a sweet little thing, and her owner didn't want to "send her to auction" (slaughter). What do you do with a horse that can't do its job anymore, but still has a lot of life left in it and you aren't the type of person that can blithely send a horse to its certain and cruel death? You give her to someone who just wants to love her, and that's what happened to this mare.

My friend lost her first horse to colic and was aching for a new one, and although she searched and searched, she couldn't find "the one." Then, while talking with a relative about her situation one random day, the relative told her, "I know someone with just the horse for you." Phone calls were made, horse met woman and vice versa, an angel choir sang from the heavens, and next thing you know, that little mare was on a trailer headed to her new home, where she continues to be showered with love and attention, living the comfy life of a companion horse.

Just like Penn and me, or that retired mare and her new mama, sometimes the universe will bring you and your own storybook horse together without you even trying, but you must announce that you're actually looking. You have to actually *ask* for what you want! How can anyone know you want something if you don't ask?

That said, serendipity does happen, as it did for Penn and me. I was chatting with a local horse owner, an award-winning cattle-cutting rider, and he told me that he'd recently competed with his champion mare for the last time. Leading up to the event, his mare seemed less and less on her game, like her heart was no longer in it. Whereas before she was peppy and all "Lemme at 'em," they arrived at a big national cutting competition, and she just looked dull, sad, and bored. There was no more sparkle and shine in her eyes, just apathy.

He held his horse's face in his hands, took in her energy, and "heard" her say, "I'm done." He said a prayer with her, promising that however she performed in the competition that day would determine what would happen next. When the time came to cut the cows in the arena, he had to spur her hard to get her to move. When he saw spur marks on her hide afterward, that was it. His horse would never cut cows in the show ring again.

This award-winning mare had given her heart and soul to please him, and rather than turning her into a broodmare and making lots of money or sending her "to auction," he decided to honor that horse that had served him so well by rewarding her with what she really deserved: a gentle retirement. He gave her to a little girl he knew, one of those true-born Horsey Girls who have been wishing for a horse their whole life, and that little girl was just over the moon. He showed me a picture of his horse with the girl, and that mare seemed just as pleased, pure contentment on her face. The little girl was beaming. That's the way to do it, people. That's what your horse deserves when its working days are over. It has given you all it has to give, and now it's your turn to give back.

Be open to the idea that you may not need to buy a horse; someone may want to give you one. There are all sorts of situations where a horse owner desperately needs to find a home for a beloved, well-seasoned, well-trained horse, and besides being a perfect companion horse, it might also still have plenty of good pleasure riding years left. There really are horse owners out there who are more interested in their horse's welfare than stuffing some money into their wallet and will put the horse's needs before their own. It can happen! But you need to put your desire out there to find them. You must ask if you expect to receive.

You can snoop out contacts for horses in need of new homes at tack shops and feed stores. Most have bulletin boards posting all sorts of information, from riding lessons to boarding facilities to horses for sale or lease, as well as people looking for all of those things. Tack up an "ISO" (In Search Of) card with the type of horse you're looking for. You never know, some horse owner may be walking by while purchasing some grain, spot your note and think, "Oh wow, that might be a great retirement for my Lucky." Next thing you know, that horse may become *your* Lucky.

Buying a Horse

If you're too impatient for a long, careful search for that proverbial needle in a haystack or waiting for the universe to come through with a serendipitous love connection, you could certainly buy a horse. For every horse that's available for free, there are a thousand for sale, and that's probably a low estimate. They're out there, in all sizes, shapes, and price ranges. Facebook groups have become a hub for people looking to buy and sell horses, and the website Petfinder also lists horses for sale nationwide.

Expect to pay a couple thousand dollars for a relatively young, well-broke, sound horse, and a couple more if it's purebred and papered. Should you find your perfect horse, no matter how great it looks and how nice and honest its owner seems, don't buy it without having it vet-checked first. If you're planning to ride, ride it before you buy it to make sure there aren't any unpleasant surprises. If the owner won't let you test-ride it, walk away.

The Ugly Truth About Unwanted Horses

Sarah and I were chatting one day as she watched me showering Penn with adoration at the hitching post while he basked in all the attention, eyes serenely half closed in pleasure. She chuckled over how in love we were, but then she said something that stunned me, something I'd never even considered.

"You know, Penn would have ended up in a kill pen if you hadn't taken him."

How could this be? This is the most amazing, fantastical horse that ever lived! Wouldn't anyone be smitten with his wonderfulness too? I was horrified imagining my Penn standing in a noisy, crowded kill pen with his big, wide, terrified eyes, snorting in sheer panic. But Sarah pointed out that Penn was old, had become too unsound for being useful as a show horse or even a school horse, and in the horse show world he came from, that made him disposable. His options were very limited, and very ugly.

The harsh reality is that Penn is no different from thousands of unwanted horses that go to a rescue program if they're very lucky, but more likely, auctioned off for slaughter. There are literally hundreds, if not thousands, of horses heading for kill pens—where they are held for slaughter—or already there. They can be rescued, and there are many organizations that specialize in rescuing horses from kill pens and caring for them until they can find a forever home.

Besides the satisfaction that comes from saving a life, you'll save some money too. Rescue horses often cost far less than those being sold by private owners. If they're headed for slaughter, they're literally sold by the pound. There are more horses available out there than you could imagine, costing less than you'd believe, and if they're in kill pens, their clocks are ticking.

This brings us to the topic of what really happens to unwanted horses. Brace yourself, it's not a pretty or comfortable story. However, I feel compelled to shine a light on the plight of old, unwanted, or "used up" horses that will share a horrifying fate unless they're rescued by a human. You are their *only* hope.

When I was young, I knew that unwanted horses or broken down racehorses "went to auction," but I didn't really grasp what that meant. Sure, some are purchased by people who want a cheap horse. The majority are headed for the slaughterhouse. These horses, just like Penn, are no longer "useful," and have very few options, save for one, and it's ghoulish.

Show horses, racehorses, cattle horses, breeding horses, and all manner of horses that have a job to do or make money for humans all potentially face the same fate: a horrifying death. Unless someone wants to adopt them and care for them as they enter their "useless" golden years, or they're lucky enough to have loving owners who will keep them as "pasture ornaments," they go to large horse auctions, held all over the country. The "lucky" ones end up in rental riding stables or illegal rodeos—a horse version of illegal cockfights— where they'll live in misery and be ridden ragged, sort of a horse purgatory, before ultimately ending up like all the others, purchased by the pound and crowded onto a trailer headed for a slaughterhouse kill pen. After that, they'll be butchered and destined for a European dinner plate, or rendered into goop and turned into gelatin or glue. Remember the old saying about "sending a horse to the glue factory"? Turns out, it wasn't just a saying.

As for eating horsemeat, some say that we routinely slaughter cows, pigs, sheep, and chickens for consumption. Why not horses? Fair's fair. Don't all animals feel fear, panic, and pain? Don't all deserve better? I suppose that's a logical argument. Their plight is a damn raw deal too. We raise these animals with care and kindness, earning their trust and sometimes their affection, and then betray that trust and send them to their deaths—and eat them! There's no integrity in that relationship. It's a betrayal.

However, cows, pigs, sheep, and chickens are raised for human consumption, and while most Americans accept that, they are repulsed at the thought of eating horses, as much as the thought of eating cats and dogs. True, eating cats and dogs is acceptable and common in some countries and cultures, but here in the U.S., it's considered repugnant and astonishingly cruel.

I believe horses are just different from other livestock. There's wisdom and a soul in a horse's eyes, unlike those of other livestock. The only other animals I've seen up close that have such depth of soul and mystic wisdom in their eyes are elephants, dolphins, and whales. When you look into the eyes of these massive creatures, and they look back, they aren't looking *at* you like a cow or sheep does. They're looking *into* you. You're having a spiritual exchange. There's something mystical and vast in those eyes. These are intelligent beings, looking right back into your eyes and considering you as another creature, just as you are considering them. They're *aware*. Species-centric humans assume that it's only we who have a collective unconscious. What if all sentient creatures have a collective unconscious of their own? Why should humans be so special? Answer: we're not.

When you look into a dog's eyes, you see, *"I love you so so so much, how can I please you, please please please love me back!"* Cats, on the other hand, gaze back at you through a veil from some other mystical realm, through half-closed, contented eyes, and say, *"You have done well, human. I am pleased with you, and shall allow you to continue serving me."* Horses, however… it's hard to articulate the message they send, but it feels like, *"I know you."* You don't just look at a horse—you connect with it.

The Horror of Slaughterhouses

Beyond the fact that eating horses just seems intrinsically wrong, slaughterhouses are exceedingly cruel for horses in particular. Their evolutionary history as a prey species makes them bad candidates for the methods used in slaughterhouses. The Humane Society summarizes on its website why horses suffer so immensely when taken to slaughter:

"Horse slaughter, whether in U.S. or foreign plants, was never and cannot be humane because of the nature of the industry and the unique biology of horses. Slaughter is a brutal and terrifying end for horses, and it is not humane. Horses are shipped for more than twenty-four hours at a time without food, water or rest in crowded trucks. They are often seriously injured or killed in transit.

"Horses are skittish by nature (owing to their heightened fight-or-flight response), which makes accurate pre-slaughter stunning difficult. As a result, horses often endure repeated blows and sometimes remain conscious during dismemberment—this is rarely a quick, painless death. Before the last domestic plant closed in 2007, the USDA documented in the slaughter pipeline rampant cruelty violations and severe injuries to horses, including broken bones protruding from their bodies, eyeballs hanging by a thread of skin, and gaping wounds."[25]

Anyone who has ever tried to merely put a halter on a panicked horse can understand how difficult it would be to control a horse in this nightmarish situation and keep its head still in order to administer a killing blow. Even in a weakened state, horses will still fight for their lives until their last breath if they're unable to escape.

Many believe the horses are quickly shot at the slaughterhouse, but unfortunately this isn't true. It used to be that when a horse broke a leg out on a ranch or on the racetrack, the most quick and humane option was to shoot them through the head, because horses are notoriously bad patients, and few will tolerate a leg cast. Horses that end up in a slaughterhouse should be so lucky. What happens there is exponentially more horrific than a bullet.

A 2009 article by journalist Christopher Beam titled, "They Shoot Horses, Don't They?" exposes the brutality and torture horses suffer at slaughterhouses: "Horses arrive on trucks and trailers, usually after being purchased at one of the many horse auctions across the country. They proceed down a ramp, into a feeding pen, and finally through a chute that leads to a small, brightly lit room. That's where an employee holds a pressurized gun called a 'captive bolt pistol' up to the horse's forehead and shoots a 4-inch piece of metal about the size of a roll of quarters into its brain. Workers sometimes need to shoot three or four times before the horse stops moving. The horse is then dumped out a side door and strung up by its feet, at which point workers slit its throat and drain the blood. The body is then cut up and sent off to a meat company, usually in France or Belgium, where horsemeat is a delicacy."

Horror movie, right? But it's not a movie, it's real life, and it's happening every day.

Beam goes on to detail why horses are not the same as cattle headed for slaughter: "The main difference between horse slaughterhouses and cattle plants is that horses are more difficult to herd, often getting into fights en route

---

25. The Humane Society of the United States, "The Facts About Horse Slaughter."

to the holding pen. That's partly because they're raised for racing or riding, not consumption, and thus aren't accustomed to cramped quarters. (Federal transportation regulations for horses don't have a space requirement, so buyers tend to pack them in tight.) Horses also tend to be more excitable than cows—hence the blinders—and the smell of blood makes them nervous. Like other 'flight animals,' when they're scared, they try to run.

"The biggest challenge for slaughterhouse employees is getting horses to hold still in the 'kill room.' Horses don't like things near their heads, so when a worker reaches over the railing with a bolt gun, they often swing their heads around, causing the gun to fire in the wrong place. The American Veterinary Medical Association calls the penetrating captive bolt a humane method but emphasizes that '[a]dequate restraint is important to ensure proper placement of the captive bolt.' The Australian Veterinary Association, meanwhile, has dubbed the bolt 'not satisfactory for horses since firm pressure on the forehead is essential for its effective use and this tends to be resisted by the horse.'"[26]

By the numbers, this nightmare is nearly unimaginable. People for the Ethical Treatment of Animals (PETA) estimates that the Thoroughbred racing industry *alone* sends ten thousand horses per year to slaughter in Canada and Mexico. With about twenty thousand Thoroughbred foals born each year, this means half are destined for slaughter. Also well-represented in the kill pens are former working cattle horses, often purebred Quarter Horses, that have been injured or gotten too old to cut cattle on ranches or in the show ring.[27]

Although the U.S. government banned equine slaughterhouses in 2007, it didn't ban the auctions. Horsemeat brokers do a reach-around: They purchase horses at American auctions, and ship the horses to Canada or Mexico, where they're slaughtered.

Why Must We Talk About This?

After all the lovely information and inspiration we've explored about horses so far, why drop this ghoulish information into our journey now like a big fat sadness bomb? Because, this is the harsh reality for thousands of horses, every day. Their plight is immediate and urgent. In the time it takes you to

---

26. Beam, "They Shoot Horses, Don't They? No, They Put a Bolt Through Their Brain."
27. People for the Ethical Treatment of Animals (PETA), "Overbreeding and Slaughter."

read this book, hundreds, maybe thousands, of horses will die this way. Some are injured, some are old, but many are young horses with long lives ahead of them and an injury has made them financially "useless" or "disposable." The vast majority could have lived out their lives as excellent companion or riding horses.

Horses headed for kill pens in the U.S. are often beautiful, well-bred, once very expensive horses that raced, jumped, and worked hard, discarded like trash when no longer profitable or recreational for humans. Many, if not most, given time, patience, love, and proper veterinary care, could have lived out their lives—ten, twenty years or more—as companion or therapy animals, or pleasure, trail, or show horses for the cost of the price by the pound, or if rescued before they reach the kill pen, a pittance adoption fee. In other words, that horse languishing in a kill pen, or headed there, might be that perfect horse you're looking for.

Consider the story of Snowman, an unwanted, mixed-breed plow horse that was headed to the slaughterhouse when professional equestrian and horse trainer Harry deLeyer happened to notice him, already in the trailer, facing his doom. He and the horse met eyes, and deLeyer was unable to look away. There was just "something" about that horse. He bought him on the spot for $80, and that $80 "unwanted" horse started winning most every jumping competition deLeyer rode him in, becoming a national grand champion jumper in 1958.

Snowman lived for many productive years after that fateful day in the trailer—as could most horses headed for a kill pen—and was loved for the rest of his natural life by Harry and his family. There may be another Snowman out there for you.

My own beloved Penn was a kill pen candidate, ridden like a machine his whole life until his left front tendon finally bowed, rendering him useless as a jumper. He additionally suffered some sort of injury to that front leg, as evidenced by white patches of hair on his knees and a strange-looking hard lump the size of a walnut on the front of his left fetlock.[28] For jumping and showing purposes, he was unsound. Despite being a well-schooled, well-bred, very expensive horse, he had become "worthless."

---

28. The hair on horses' hides often grows back white when the skin has been severely cut or damaged.

Nearing twenty years of age and also a gelding, which is useless for breeding, Penn was a classic "disposable" horse. Goddess bless the woman who purchased him for a meager amount despite his infirmities, just because there was something special about that old red horse and she couldn't bear to leave him behind, broken and unwanted. She literally saved his life, like a guardian angel. This guardian angel loved him so much that when she was unable to take care of him any longer, she gave him to me rather than send him to auction, saving his life yet again. Penn is one lucky horse, but most are not.

Some Adoption Cautions and Options

While possibly nothing on earth could warm a horse lover's heart more than rescuing a horse from a kill pen auction, there are some concerns to bear in mind. These abused, terrified, starving horses have completely unknown histories. Unless you adopt from a rescue organization, you're adopting a wild card. They may be well trained, or they may be buckers or biters. They may be clunky-looking crossbreds of unknown bloodlines, or they may be $40,000 Thoroughbreds who just aren't winning races anymore.

Also, consider that a horse rescued from a kill pen auction may be near starvation, and look and behave completely docile, but that docility is actually due to their current physical and emotional exhaustion. It takes all their energy just to keep their hearts beating and to breathe in and out. That may be quite a different horse after months of good feed and tender loving care, full of sass and spunk, and may be more of a handful than you bargained for. Don't despair, just enlist the help of a professional trainer. That money you saved on the purchase may have to be spent on training.

Getting a horse from a kill pen auction can be risky, but saving a horse from a certain cruel death is so very heart-warming. Should you decide to pluck a horse from that maw of doom and don't know a thing about horses, you *must* bring an experienced horse person along. In fact, that goes for any horse you're considering adopting or buying, even if you're pretty experienced with horses. A second set of eyes, particularly eyes not blinded with infatuation, usually see more clearly.

For more information about finding and rescuing horses from a kill pen auction, do a quick internet search. You may discover a horse rescue organization close to where you live. There are hundreds of them across the U.S. Local animal shelters sometimes have horses too, often abused and emaciated, and desperately in need of a home.

Equine Rescue Network is a good place to begin looking for information, and horse rescue groups are all over the internet and Facebook, some of them even specializing in certain breeds. You can also contact rescue organizations like Habitat For Horses and Red Bucket Rescue, which take in unwanted, abused, abandoned, and/or emaciated horses, feed them and give them veterinary care, and place them for adoption when they're ready. These organizations also commit to keeping the horses that are inappropriate for adoption, whether because of chronic veterinary conditions or temperament, and take care of them for the rest of their days. If you can't find a horse, or can't afford one, you can still help save one by donating to these organizations.

On these rescue sites, you'll see stunning "before and after" photos. Not all of the horses come from kill pen auctions. Some were tied up and left to die, or abandoned by some idiot who thought that a domesticated horse would figure out how to survive on its own. Here's a short story about that: it won't. The stories of abuse and starvation these animals have endured tear at your heart, but thankfully, their futures are brighter. Someone is caring for them until their perfect person comes along. Maybe that's you!

Chapter 9

SO MANY HORSES

We're at the point in our horse ownership journey where we'll start considering different breeds as part of our search criteria. If all you want to do is wander happily around and become pals, you don't really need a purebred Arabian. Almost any breed would work. Remember that "bombproof" term? The older a horse gets, the more bombproof they get, regardless of breed—unless humans have made that horse mean, cranky, and dangerous. Young horses, in general, are lively, playful, and often a handful—more than a beginner could handle. The seniors are pretty much over all that folderol.

We'll contrast various breeds, "blood types," and spotlight a few that you're likely to come across in your search in the U.S. This may help you narrow down the type of horse you really want. However, keep an open mind: don't fall in love with a particular type of horse. Fall in love with your goal, and find the horse that best suits it.

We'll also talk about proper names for anatomy, coat color, and markings, so you don't say things like "I like that orange horse with the dot on its head" and get weird looks from other horse people.

Let's Talk About Sex

There are different words for male and female horses, at different ages. In general, from birth and to one year of age, both male and female horses are called foals. From one to four years of age, an uncastrated male horse is a colt. After that, he's called a stud or stallion. A castrated male adult horse or colt is a gelding. A female horse is called a filly from one to four years of age. Over that age, she is called a mare. A broodmare is a female horse that's used for breeding.

We'll begin with stallions.

If you're inexperienced with horses, here's a little story about stallions: no.

Stallions are for experienced horse people, period. In addition to the array of behavior issues and challenges a horse may present, stallions add a whole other layer of testosterone-infused concerns. If there are mares in heat nearby, you will be the last thing on that stallion's mind, and if you don't know what you're doing, bad things can happen. Stallions are wonderful to look at and watch, fiery and impressive, but should not be handled by beginners.

For the same reason, colts are to be avoided, because they grow up into stallions, unless you have them gelded. Colts become more and more rambunctious as they mature, and their hormones start telling them to gather mares and breed. Actually, young horses of either sex aren't optimal for new horse owners. When you want to spend peaceful grazing time, that rambunctious youngster is full of energy and wants to buck and play. What "play" is to a yearling could be "pain" to its two-legged playmate.

Then there are mares. Mares can be the sweetest things ever, but some are pissy-tempered—downright bitchy, even. Just like people, their hormones fluctuate too. Mares come into heat monthly year-round, except for winter, so from time to time, they can get PMS-y, just like humans. When in heat, a mare may become bouncy and goofy, and highly distracted, particularly if there's a stallion nearby. Or you may get the "mare nose": nostrils pulled up and back, ears pinned, fire and brimstone in her eyes, tossing her head at you in a bossy "out of my way" gesture. She's showing you that she's the lead mare, and you're not.

I've been lucky. All the mares I've ever had were sweet, loving, and calm. But I've seen plenty that were crabby old she-devils. Even the sweet ones have the ability to morph into Little Miss Crankypants or Little Miss Squirrelbrain when they're in heat. That's just one more unnecessary variable when choosing your first horse. The less experience you have, fewer variables are better. For a beginner, there's a perfect option: geldings.

Here's a little story about geldings: yes.

Geldings are just the best. Eliminate all those hormonal variables, and you have an even-tempered horse that will just get better and better as you go along. I am one hundred percent "Team Gelding." I'd pick a gelding over anything else, every time. Stallions are all "Let me *at* it!" Mares are like "Not today, babe." Geldings just say, "Wellllll, oooookay. Seems reasonable." For a first horse, geldings are gold. Write that on your arm with a sharpie when you go horse shopping.

Blood Types

Horse breeds fall into three categories: hotbloods, coldbloods, and warmbloods, in addition to ponies, for which the debate about which blood type they are is still open. The actual temperature of the horse or its blood type has nothing to do with these categories. The label deals entirely with typical temperament.

Hotbloods

Hotbloods tend to be high-strung, and full of "go." They have feisty, flighty temperaments and are bred to pour all that energy into speed. The classic hotblood breeds include Thoroughbreds and Arabians. A Thoroughbred—swift as the wind and ready to soar over any barrier—could represent our iconic Air Horse.

Most Thoroughbreds have Arabian blood in their distant genetics, and these sons and daughters of the desert brought delicacy and speed when bred with heavier European horses, which is how the Thoroughbred was created. It's believed that the bloodlines of all registered Thoroughbreds can be traced to one of three Arabian stallions: Byerley Turk, the Darley Arabian, and the Godolphin Arabian, whose story was told by Marguerite Henry in the classic book, *King of the Wind: The Story of the Godolphin Arabian.*

However, Thoroughbreds are routinely bred with other breeds, particularly Quarter Horses and Appaloosas, to give them greater speed or make them taller and more graceful in appearance. That dancing Appaloosa you're drooling over may have big bold spots on its rump, but it may also be more Thoroughbred—and hotblood—than anything else. A registered Thoroughbred, however, must be of pure blood.

An unregistered horse of mixed blood—a crossbred—is called a "grade horse." These are often family horses or backyard horses with unknown bloodlines, and while maybe not as fancy as a purebred, can be wonderful horses. Remember Snowman? He was "just a grade horse."

Coldbloods

Coldbloods encompass all the draft horses—the heavy horses, with bloodlines originating from European-bred warhorses of medieval times. Over time, people further manipulated the gene pool by breeding these horses for calm, docile temperaments in combination with a huge, powerful body mass, able to drag massive logs, heavily weighted carts, or pull a plow to till the soil.

Included in the coldblood category are Clydesdales, Percherons, Shires (the largest breed), Haflingers, Belgians, Friesians, and Gypsy Vanners. These big-boned, thick-bodied horses of massive size and muscle are representative of the iconic Earth Horses: built like tanks, and ready to move mountains.

Warmbloods

Warmbloods, with their origins also in Europe, were bred to keep the size and calm temperament of the coldbloods, but to have the more refined legs, body, and appearance of a hot-blooded Thoroughbred. They have calm, sociable temperaments, and graceful, rocking strides.

The classic European warmbloods—Andalusians, Hanoverians, Oldenbergs, and Trakehners—are the big ballet dancers of the horse world, excelling at dressage, jumping, and eventing, and could represent our iconic Water Horse, slowly and gracefully polishing and practicing in the ongoing quest for perfection and beauty.

There are also South American warmblood breeds—the Paso Fino and Peruvian Paso—which are smaller in size; and known for their elegant, collected, four-beat gaits; and also called "gaited" horses. The bloodlines of South American breeds trace back to horses brought to that continent by Spanish explorers in the 1500s.

American Warmbloods

In addition to fancy European and smooth, silky South American warmbloods, many American breeds fall into the warmblood category because they don't really fit anywhere else. It's the "least bad" choice. They have the more refined features of a hotblood, but the even-headedness of a coldblood. Mix hot and cold, and you get warm. However, these horses aren't the towering, willowy, graceful warmbloods that dance and prance in the show ring.

These American horses have the fire, energy, and will of a hotblood, and the sturdiness and even temper of a coldblood, minus the huge size. By default, that makes them warmbloods. They deserve their own fourth blood category: mixed blood.

While blood types are officially limited to three, there are four types of Elemental Horses, and these American breeds make perfect representations of our iconic Fire Horse: fast, smart, brave, versatile, and up to any challenge. They include the Appaloosa, Mustang, Quarter Horse, Standardbred, and the often-gaited Missouri Fox Trotter, Morgan, and Tennessee Walker.

Breeds

Although certain breeds are associated with certain temperaments and characteristics, these are generalities, and there are always exceptions. For every sweet-tempered Arabian that's calm, cool, and patient all the time, there's a cranky Clydesdale that would rather eat your face than its hay. You can't go by breed alone, or even blood, because every horse has its own personality, as well as its own history with humans, and therefore, its own opinion about them. Different breeds have clusters of typical temperaments and talents, but there are always outliers. A horse's breed won't guarantee the qualities you're looking for, but it will offer a better chance, on average, of finding a horse with the temperament you're looking for.

I did most of my show jumping on one of my parents' ex-racehorses named Lari. Thoroughbreds are about as hot-blooded as they come. Lari was a low-drama, extremely low-energy mare. When she was a racehorse, she usually came in dead last, unless another horse pulled up lame and maybe she'd beat that one. My dad commented after yet another dismal performance that she was "so far behind, she looked like the winner of the race before."

What Lari wasn't on the track, she *was* in the school ring and show ring: calm, cooperative, and always willing, as long as you weren't asking her to go too fast. She didn't buck, bite, or kick, didn't grab the bit in her teeth and try to bolt (a little ex-racehorse trick), and became the quintessential kid's horse, safe for any rider of any ability. Bombproof! Lari illustrated that not all Thoroughbreds are loopy, not all mares are cranky, and that "disposable" racehorses can be repurposed into wonderful pleasure and show horses. There are piles of stories about horses who aren't typical of their breed's characteristics. Every horse is an individual.

Which Breed Is Best?

There is no "best" breed of horse. That said, horse folks definitely have their preferences. Real horses, similar to our Elemental Horses, have different strengths and weaknesses, and whether a physical or spiritual horse, you'll have more success if you choose the right horse for the right job. Rather than create an exhaustive list of breeds (which you can easily research online or at the library), we'll focus on those you're most likely to come across in the United States.

Although you may be smitten with a particular breed, be flexible about both breed and appearance. If a ten-year-old Quarter Horse gelding with four white socks and a blaze is all you'll consider, it may take a long while to find that horse, and in the process, you may pass up a great horse that would have made a perfect forever friend. If you insist on holding out for that *exact* horse, you may have to be very patient, and you also may have to pay a lot of money for it. Maybe do a reverse selection: scratch the breeds you *don't* want off your search list. Just watch: no sooner will you write off Arabians than the most perfect Arabian horse for you will magically appear in your life, proving that the universe often knows better what we need than we do ourselves.

That's how it happened with Penn. Not only was I *not* actively looking for a horse at all, if I were, I'd have narrowed my search to horses that are small, strong, and stocky, like a Quarter Horse or Morgan, or a retired old pleasure or trail horse. It definitely would have been something a *lot* lower to the ground than Penn! Penn—a tall Hanoverian—is none of these things. I had never even seen a real live Hanoverian until I met Penn.

Had I begun to search on my own, this amazing horse and I might never have found each other. To slightly massage an old saying, "We plan; the universe laughs." Ultimately, decide which breeds appeal to you, but keep an open mind. Keep space in your decision-making for that "wild card" horse you never expected to meet. It may be "the one."

So Many to Choose From

Following is a sampling of breeds you'll likely come across in your search for that perfect horse. I list the typical attributes of each breed—typical, but not guaranteed. All horses, regardless of breed, are individuals. There are a lot of crossbreeds out there, with attributes from the breeds of their parents.

- *Appaloosa (warmblood):* It's easy to spot an Appaloosa—they have spots. Those spots can range from all-over dots like a Dalmatian, to a dainty white blanket over the rump. They are tough and athletic, were a favorite war pony of the Nez Perce tribe, and got their name from the Palouse River, which runs through Washington and Idaho. Appaloosas are more common in Western-style horse work, events, and riding, but they are also excellent show horses, jumpers, and racehorses. They are an average of fifteen hands,[29] and sometimes have funny, scrubby little tails, which was considered a positive trait when being ridden through thick brush—less to tangle. Appaloosas are versatile, level-headed, multipurpose horses.

- *Arabian (hotblood):* One of the oldest breeds of horses, these gorgeous, finely boned horses with dished, delicate faces are on the smaller side, usually fourteen to fifteen hands, and are known for speed and exceptional endurance. Arabians are very versatile, and can excel at almost anything, from trail riding to show jumping to even racing. With their long, high-crested necks; large, dramatic eyes; and huge flaring nostrils, they are the beauty queens and kings of the horse world.

- *Belgian (coldblood):* The Belgian breed originated in (surprise) Belgium, and is the powerful tank of the draft horse world, but shorter and stockier than the others. A single Belgian can pull up to three times its own weight, which on the average is two thousand pounds. They are usually between sixteen or seventeen hands tall. Like the other heavy horses, the Belgian's roots come from European battlefields. Belgians are usually chestnut with flaxen manes and tails, but can be found in other colors too.

- *Clydesdale (coldblood):* Many of use are familiar with Clydesdales. They are those amazing, enormous bay horses with flashy white blazes and feathered legs, famous for pulling the Budweiser wagon in teams. An average of seventeen hands and weighing as much as 1,900 pounds, these are big boys and girls. Although they're most famous for pulling, people do

---

29. The height of a horse is measured in "hands" and is taken at the withers (top of the shoulder blades) and on down a front leg. Each hand equals about four inches.

ride them, particularly those drawn to medieval reenactment activities; a Clydesdale makes a great mock-warhorse, perfect for a mock lance fight.

The tails of Clydesdales are usually "docked"—amputated to just a couple inches from their dock. This is allegedly done to keep their tails clear of whatever they're pulling. A horse with a docked tail will require extra attention in fly season because humans have removed its ability to swat flies itself. In addition to Clydesdales, Shires and Percherons frequently have docked tails.

• *Gypsy Vanner* (*coldblood*): These little coldbloods are taking the American horse world by storm. This breed gets its name from the hardy little horses that pulled "gypsy" carts in Europe.[30] The smallest of the coldbloods, ranging from a pony-sized twelve hands up to sixteen, this breed arrived in the U.S. very recently—in the mid-1990s. Their sweet, inquisitive personalities and plucky way of going along whether under saddle or pulling a cart make them popular. They're also astonishingly beautiful, with flashy markings—often pinto—and extremely long, flowing, thick manes, tails, and leg feathers, making every Horsey Girl heart beat a little faster.

• *Hanoverian* (*warmblood*): These big, thick horses, usually sixteen to seventeen hands, are descendants of medieval warhorses, and were selectively bred in Germany for use as cavalry horses and to pull cannons. If they broke a leg or were mortally wounded while in service, they also became dinner for the troops. Since then, with yet more blending in of Thoroughbred blood, their features became even more refined, and they are now prized as graceful jumpers and dressage horses, with friendly, even personalities.

• *Morgan* (*warmblood*): Like Appaloosas, Arabians, and Quarter Horses, it seems like Morgans can do anything. Averaging at about fifteen hands, they're small and sturdy, yet refined, with gorgeous faces and huge eyes. They are smooth-gaited, fast, and excellent for riding or pulling carriages or carts. They're the Honda CRVs of the horse world: cute, compact,

---

30. My apologies for not using the more culturally appropriate term, "Romani," but the fact is that this is where the name comes from and this is what they're called: Gypsy Vanners, not Romani Vanners.

strong, reliable, up to any task, and once you've had them, you never want anything else.

- *Percheron (coldblood)*: This breed originated in France and is a powerful pulling and plow horse with a long history in pre-mechanized agricultural use. They're about sixteen to seventeen hands on average, weighing as much as 2,600 pounds. They are typically black or grey (often dappled), and like many coldbloods, tend to be calm, obedient, and even-tempered. Percherons are amongst the most common draft horses in the U.S.

- *Quarter Horse (warmblood)*: The Quarter Horse is reputed to be the most popular breed in America, having earned that status because they can do darn near anything. In addition to show riding, like barrel racing or Western pleasure, these smart, quick, tough horses excel at ranch work and cutting cattle. They're also lightning fast. No other breed can outrun them except a Thoroughbred, and that's only after the first quarter mile. A Quarter Horse is an equine drag racer. From a standstill, they can run a quarter mile in twenty seconds, able to hit fifty miles per hour. The top speed of a Quarter Horse has been clocked at fifty-five miles per hour.

  Averaging at about fifteen hands, they have muscular bodies, hind-quarters and chests, and beautiful, refined heads. Their bloodlines began with an American Thoroughbred in the mid-1700s, but over the years, they've been selectively bred to be smaller and stockier. A retired Quarter Horse is great choice for an equine pal.

- *Standardbred (warmblood)*: Although literally a "one trick pony," Standard-breds deserve a shout-out. They aren't the Jack or Jill of All Trades like the other American breeds, and are only bred to trot (or pace), mainly for harness racing. They originated from Thoroughbred stock, and even resemble Thoroughbreds, but in general have calmer temperaments and therefore are considered warmbloods. They have superior endurance at a trot and are amongst the fastest trotters in the world.

  Because they're raised for harness racing, if adopted as a riding horse, Standardbreds must be trained to carry a rider (some have never been ridden), and must relearn how to canter because this gait is discouraged, even punished, in their harness racing training. Breaking into a canter or gallop in a harness race is immediate disqualification. However, a horse doesn't need to canter, or be ridden, to be a companion or therapy horse.

Just like their Thoroughbred cousins, Standardbreds easily become "disposable." When their racing days are over, their days are numbered.

• *Thoroughbreds (hotblood):* Sleek, tall, fine-boned Thoroughbreds are the elite athletes of the horse world. An average of sixteen hands and built like greyhounds, with long necks and refined heads, they're bred to run, and specifically to move forward, so they have low, flat gallops that don't waste energy going up and down, as opposed to the big, rocking canter of a warmblood. High-end Thoroughbreds can cost a small fortune, or far less if they run on fair circuits or small regional tracks, and way less than that at a kill pen auction.

Most racehorses start their careers at two or three years of age—far too early, in my opinion, because their bones aren't completely formed yet, making them more susceptible to injury. Most Thoroughbreds only race for a few years, which means they become "disposable" at a very young age (read: kill pen).

Besides having huge potential for being rehabbed into jumpers, show horses, or pleasure horses, Thoroughbreds coming from off the track have been handled and trailered a lot, and are exposed to a lot of hustle and bustle, like starting gates and roaring crowds. Their strength is also their downfall: They're bred to run. It's in their DNA and their training. They must learn that a human on their back doesn't always mean "gallop straight ahead at full speed."

The Little Fellers

"I want a pony," is the song of my Horsey Girl people, and was probably my first sentence. Ponies are very much like horses, but they aren't horses. They must be 14.2 hands or smaller at full growth to be considered ponies. As for what blood ponies are, there's debate about whether ponies are warmbloods or very tiny coldbloods.

Like horses, ponies have various temperaments, but overall are considered to be very smart, and full of personality and whimsy. Some people believe ponies are great for children, while others believe the very small ones, like Shetlands, are poor choices because they can't be properly ridden by an adult for training. You could make a case for both arguments.

Ponies have a stockier, sturdier build than a horse, are more tolerant of cold weather, and have plenty of endurance. They're often purchased for children, but like bunnies and baby chicks, sometimes kids get tired of their pets and don't want to take care of them anymore. That means ponies are often well represented at rescue organizations when the kids outgrow them or get bored with them. If the kids haven't soured their tempers, their background of dealing with an array of crazy behaviors could make ponies a perfect first companion horse, particularly if you find the size of a horse intimidating. Besides, if you aren't going to ride anyway, a pony will make your inner Horsey Girl squeal with delight!

My first horse was a Welsh Pony mix, a grumbly little thing, and I don't blame her for that one bit. Comanche tolerated everything we kids dished out: running from behind and vaulting over her rump to her back like gymnasts, dressing her up in hats, skirts, and veils, and riding her bareback—sometimes two at a time. Often we'd ride her to a to a nearby river on long, hot summer days, and make her canter into the water to make a big splash and soak us while we howled in delight. She'd let every kid on the block take turns riding her. Comanche would put her ears back and push her lower lip out in annoyance, but she tolerated our antics like a trooper, with never a bite or kick—and not that one or the other probably wasn't well deserved at some point. Comanche was a big, white, shaggy babysitter, and pure childhood gold.

Common pony breeds include the Chincoteague, Connemara, Dartmoor, Exmoor, POA (Pony of the Americas), Shetland, and Welsh. There are also miniature horses, "minis," that look like ponies but specific conformation features differentiate them from true ponies and from horses. Minis are teeny tiny—smaller than some large dog breeds. What they lack in size, they make up for in an abundance of personality. It's said they can even be housebroken! Gonna need a pretty big litterbox for that!

Pony Breeds

While not as large a selection as horse breeds, there are plenty of pony breeds to choose from, with a range of sizes. Here are some breeds you might run across in the U.S.:

- *Chincoteague:* Like *Misty of Chincoteague*, the first Chincoteague ponies were feral. Their lore is that they survived a sinking Spanish ship after swimming to shore on Assateague Island, located off the shore of Maryland and Virginia. Just like in the storybook, the wild ponies are rounded up and swum across a short channel to Chincoteague Island on the last weekend of every July, where the foals are put up for auction. Those that don't sell are swum back. They're scrappy little guys, not really known for warm and fuzzy temperaments, but as we know, there are always exceptions within every breed. Additionally, like Mustangs, these are young, wild animals, and will require professional assistance before becoming companion horses. They're smaller than Mustangs, but even little hooves can pack a punch. That said, who doesn't want a Misty of Chincoteague for their own?

• *Shetland:* These hardy little guys have long, deep Celtic and Norse bloodlines, and can survive bitterly cold climates. They were originally used for pulling carts, particularly in mines because they were tiny enough to fit into the mine shafts and could pull far more weight than a person. They later became the darlings of every child who ever wanted a horse, and can be wonderful little riding horses. I've heard more than one story about them developing nasty habits like biting, maybe because their tiny size makes them trickier to discipline, like a Chihuahua, but more likely from inexperienced or cruel treatment by humans, particularly small ones. A Shetland Pony (and also a Miniature Horse) could make a cute, quirky little personal companion.

• *Welsh:* The Welsh Pony (or Cob) is at the larger end of the pony scale, standing at about thirteen or fourteen hands. They're even-tempered and the perfect size for a child, but large enough for a child to grow with well into adolescence. Welsh Ponies make excellent pleasure or show horses, and can be talented little hunter-jumpers as well. Welsh Ponies are big and strong enough to carry most smaller-end adults, and could be perfect as a four-legged therapist.

What About Mustangs ?

The iconic American Mustang deserves its own discussion because those horses exist under a very peculiar set of circumstances compared to other horse breeds. There is an ongoing federal program allowing adoption of these wild horses, and it may seem very tempting to choose one. However, there are extra considerations before bringing a Mustang home.

More properly called "wild horses," due to infiltration in the gene pool by backyard mares wooed off the ranch by sexy wild stallions or strays that joined the herds, Mustangs are not "starter horses." In time, and with care, patience, and training, they could become wonderful horses, but if you're a raw beginner or even a novice, don't imagine that you're going to adopt one, saddle it up, and ride off into the sunset, because you'll probably get a one-way rocket trip face-first into the dirt, and possibly the emergency room. You must have ongoing, professional guidance to bring a Mustang into your life, and in particular, be physically up to the task.

Wild Mustangs officially belong to the U.S. government, and fall under the jurisdiction of the Bureau of Land Management (BLM). The BLM's "online corral" and holding pens may dazzle you with all the beautiful Mustangs not only available for pennies on the dollar, but even programs where they will pay *you* to adopt one. Mustangs are abundantly available, and crammed into holding pens by the thousands, where they're miserable and stressed, and the BLM is constantly wrangling with wild horse advocates as it looks for ways to unload these horses. The U.S. government views wild horses—one of our national wild treasures—as nuisances, like rats and pigeons, largely due to pressure from the beef industry and cattle ranchers who don't want the horses eating the range grasses on publicly held land. Cattle ranchers believe that these public grasslands are theirs to use for free, and that the wild horses don't belong there.

Were it not for the wild horse advocates, the U.S. government would be funneling Mustangs into Canadian and Mexican slaughterhouses as we speak. It's cheaper to sell them by the pound than to feed them. Ironically, the U.S. government has created this expensive problem by rounding them up and corralling them in the first place. The government is not their friend.

In a perfect world, the wild horses would simply be left alone. Mother Nature is quite skilled at culling herds, and chooses which are hardy enough to survive and which are not. It may seem like a cruel arrangement; however, this is how *Equus* has survived and evolved since the Eocene epoch. Mother Nature sculpted those little fawn-like creatures into the horses we see today, and will continue to do so as long as humans don't interfere. Wild horses don't need one single thing from humans except to be left alone.

Sadly, at the behest of beef industry lobbyists, the BLM rounds up wild horses by helicopter drives, herding them along, galloping in panic. Many are injured along the way, and all are traumatized. Some break their legs and are left to die, and tiny foals are trampled or left behind as coyote bait.

The BLM does sterilize wild mares, claiming the appearance of trying to solve the "problem" of too many wild horses, but rather than doing so humanely, performs a brutal procedure that involves ripping out their ovaries without benefit of sedation. In an article on the American Wild Horse Campaign website, Ginger Kathrens, director of the Cloud Foundation and Humane Advocate on the BLM's National Wild Horse and Burro Board writes, "It's obvious that the BLM wants to eradicate wild horses in the West using barbaric surgical procedures performed in an unsterile environment. Mares will suffer horrific pain and potential death. Why does the BLM continue to turn its back on proven, humane, reversible fertility control?"[31]

I'll answer you, Ms. Kathrens: Because the BLM isn't interested in what's best for those horses, as evidenced by the fact that they believe vivisection is more humane than darting the horses with birth control hormones or—just leaving them the hell alone!

Wild Horse Inmate Programs

Of the wild horses that are rounded up, a relatively few "lucky" ones end up in BLM prison inmate programs, which bring a selected few wild horses on-site to prisons, where both horses and humans interact to have a chance at rehabilitation and a better life. Prisoners undergo their own personal transformations as they work with these horses, until they are gentle enough to be released for public adoption.

When Mustangs graduate from prison programs, they're offered for sale online and at auction. However, just like criminals, there's a "three strikes" clause for those horses. Those that are passed up three times are headed for slaughter.

---

31. American Wild Horse Campaign, "BLM to Proceed with Barbaric Sterilization of Wild Mares, Despite Repeated Public Outcry and Legal Opposition."

These prison programs are rays of hope for a relatively small number of wild horses. The vast majority are not chosen for the programs, however, and just mill around in crowded, dusty holding pens. The U.S. government's preferred "solution" to the "problem" of financing the care and feeding of all these horses would be to slaughter them all, if it could get away with it.

Why Not Go Wild?

Sarah's sweet, adorable chocolate palomino, Tim, is an equine version of a living teddy bear. Although he spent the first three years of his life as a wild Mustang, he is possibly the world's most perfect horse, and the first one I rode after thirty-five years before deciding whether or not to get Penn. Obviously, it went well! He is the horse every Horsey Girl dreams of. However, Sarah emphasized to me that she didn't get him that way.

Sarah got Tim when he was "greenbroke," meaning he had some training, but wasn't experienced or polished. She said he seemed emotionally shut down after being trapped, gelded, and sent to a prison inmate program. Even though this particular program used natural horsemanship methods rather than "breaking" the horses—meaning just that: a horse's spirit is broken to make it docile and rideable—the natural methods were too traumatic for him. Tim is an ultra-sensitive guy, and it took Sarah's love, expertise, and a whole lot of time and effort before he came out of his shell and blossomed.

Sarah says Mustangs don't come like Tim. They *become* that way. They require professional training—lots of it. Even when they're obedient and polished, Mustangs are still reactive, wild animals at heart, and not appropriate for beginners or people with physical limitations. However, a second-hand Mustang that's already been with a private owner for several years, and has been handled and ridden a lot, might be a great option—not one straight from a BLM pen.

But You Still Want a Mustang

If your heart will simply break without a Mustang, well, don't say you weren't warned. Whatever you do, don't get one straight from the holding pen or inmate program without professional guidance. A wild horse isn't the same creature as a domestic horse. Mustangs aren't feral horses. A feral animal is a once-domesticated animal that becomes wild. Mustangs were born wild, and are, first and foremost, *wild animals*.

The horses that run free on the range have been honed to survivalist perfection, and have lightning-quick flight-or-fight reactions. They're very smart, and as tough as the unforgiving range on which they roam. On the other hand, because they're observant and smart, when professionally gentled and trained, they are fast learners and have sweet temperaments. And yet, they're still... different. They never really seem to stop watching for danger; it's in their DNA. Some call their behavior spooky; Sarah calls it reactive. No matter how gentle and trained they are, wild horses will never stop being aware of their immediate environment, and reacting to it. You need horsemanship experience to diffuse that.

Color

The color of a horse's coat isn't always obvious. While a true black horse is still called black, and a true white horse is white, brown horses aren't simply brown. They're called several names depending on certain factors. You can do an internet search of each of the horse colors to get an idea of what they look like.

Here's the rainbow of horse colors:

- *Bay:* brown body, ranging from a bright red, to a warm milk chocolate color called "blood bay," to deep dark brown. Bays must have black manes, tails, and lower legs—all together, called "points." Horses are called dark bay if they are a deep shade of brown or near-black, with black points. Dark bays are also sometimes called brown.
- *Black:* true black all over without any brown or tan points or other areas, such as the flank. White markings are allowed.
- *Brown (dark bay):* a deep, dark brown, with black points.
- *Buckskin:* golden body, with black points and dorsal stripes (a stripe that runs down a horse's back).
- *Chestnut:* all shades of copper and red, usually with matching manes and tails, but not always. Sometimes the manes and tails are lighter or darker, but never black, nor are there black points; that would make the horse a bay. Blonde manes and tails are called flaxen.
- *Cream (or cremello):* nearly white horses of the lightest cream color, with pink skin and often with blue or gold eyes. Because of their light-colored

eyes, these horses are sometimes mistaken for albinos; however, they do have pigment and are not true albinos.

- *Dun:* light to medium gold coat, with black points and a black dorsal stripe; more mousy in color than a golden buckskin.

- *Grey:* ranging from a nearly all-white horse to a nearly black horse, with white hair evenly distributed throughout its coat. There can be mottling on the coat, called dapple grey, or a nearly all-white coat with black flecks throughout, called a fleabitten grey. There cannot be any brown or tan patches. Black points are acceptable. Grey horses often get lighter and lighter as they age, and may be mistakenly called white in their older years.

- *Grulla:* smoky grey-tan color, sometimes called "mousy." Like a dun, it has black points and a black dorsal stripe.

- *Leopard-spotted:* a white horse with small, roundish black spots.

- *Liver chestnut:* dark brown horse with brown mane and tail of matching or similar color, without black points.

- *Paint:* Is it a white horse splashed with black, brown, or gold, or is it a black, brown, or gold horse splashed with white? It's both! A Paint is actually a breed all its own, and must have Quarter Horse, Paint Horse, or Thoroughbred in its bloodline to properly be called a Paint. However, you still hear people use the term interchangeably (and incorrectly) with pinto. All Paints are pintos, but not all pintos are Paints.

- *Palomino:* all shades of gold, from a pale straw color, to deep, dark nearly chestnut gold. The mane and tail are white, and the lower legs are not black. Darker brown coats are called chocolate palominos and may have flaxen manes and tails.

- *Pinto:* See Paint above. Unless a horse is actually a Paint breed, the correct term for a horse with large patches of white on its body of another color, or vice versa, is pinto. To make matters even more confusing, pintos also have subcategories of piebald (black and white only), skewbald, tobiano, overo, and tovero.

- *Roan:* any color of horse with an even number of white hairs dispersed throughout its coat. If a chestnut color, it is called a strawberry roan. If grey, it is called a blue roan. When is a blue roan a grey and vice versa? You can start a lively debate down at your local tack shop with that one.

- *Sorrel:* bright, copper-colored chestnut, with mane and tail the same copper color, and no black points.
- *White:* pure white, from tip to tail, without any other color of hair. Many white horses, particularly Lipizzans, are born black or dark brown, and fade to white over time and technically are grey. A true white horse is born white, and has pink skin. Some have blue or light-colored eyes; however, that doesn't mean they are albinos. A true albino would have no pigment and therefore would have pink eyes like an albino rabbit. Also, those pink eyes aren't actually pink. Albinos have no pigment at all, and the pink color comes from reflected blood from tiny blood vessels in the eyeball. It is alleged that there is no such thing a truly albino horse.

Markings

Besides coat color, the white markings on a horse's face and legs also have names. If you're looking at some horses, you don't want to say, "I want that one with the white thingie on its face." Don't make the other horse people roll their eyes!

Face Markings

- *Apron:* a band of white, or blaze, that drapes down over the sides of the face and over the muzzle in an apron shape.
- *Bald:* similar to apron, except that it extends over the eyes. It's a very wide blaze that extends all the way to the muzzle, and to or past the eyes, which are sometimes blue.
- *Blaze:* a white stripe starting above or between the eyes, and running down the middle of the nose, of varying length and width. Narrow blazes are called stripes or strips.
- *Blaze and Snip:* blaze down the face, extending down between the nostrils, where it's sometimes wider.
- *Snip:* a white marking of varying size on the muzzle between the nostrils.
- *Star:* a white spot of varying size on the forehead between the eyes.
- *Star and Snip:* a star between the eyes, and another between the nostrils.

- *Star and Stripe:* a wide star above or between the eyes, narrowing into a blaze down the nose. If extending down between the nostrils, it's star, stripe, and snip.

- *Stardust:* this term is of my own making, because it's what my Penn has. Under his big bright star is a sprinkling of white hair down his nose, all the way to a cute little snip between his nostrils. That sprinkling is a shower of stardust.

- *Strip or Stripe:* a narrow white mark of varying length anywhere along the horse's nose, from just above the eyes, down to the nostrils.

Leg Markings

When a horse has black "points" on the legs, this means that the leg is black, usually from the knees and hocks down. A horse with black points usually has them on all four legs. A horse with black points can also have a white marking on one, some, or all of those legs. The white leg markings include:

- *Ermine Spots:* dark spots on top of a white sock, usually down near the coronet band of the hoof.

- *Heel:* a small white mark on the bulbs of a horse's foot—in the back, above the hoof—that does not go all the way around.

- *Sock:* white mark extending from the top of the hoof to anywhere below the knee or hock. The sock may be referred to by where it stops on the leg, such as a coronet or cannon.

- *Stocking:* white mark extending from the top of the hoof to at least the bottom of the hock or knee, and may extend above.

Anatomy

When talking horses, you need to know what their parts are called. Their "knees" are on their front legs; however, anatomically speaking, the equine equivalent of a human knee is its stifle, the hind leg joint nearest the belly. The middle joint on the back leg, the hock, is the equivalent of a human heel and the back fetlock is the equivalent of the ball of a human foot.

A horse's knee is the equivalent of the human wrist, and the front fetlocks are the equivalent of the top knuckles on a human hand. Their hooves on all four legs evolved into one long toe over millions of years, and are the equivalent of a human middle finger, the hoof being the fingernail. However, an elbow on a horse is still an elbow on a human. A visualization of a horse and its anatomy can be seen with figure 2.

The overall structural appearance of the horse is called its "conformation" (not "confirmation," unless your horse is Catholic). There are conformation ideals in general for horses and for each breed. A swaybacked horse is sway-backed in every breed, but a Thoroughbred's long, straight nose would be considered undesirable in an Arabian, which is prized for a beautifully curved, delicate dish-shaped head.

Some conformation issues can make a horse more susceptible to soreness, injury, or lameness, and may require some correction, like hock or fetlock pads, or custom saddle fitting. Others are just cosmetic. A horse that's cow-hocked—where its hocks are close together—might have trouble as a jumper, but would be just fine for walking around and being your buddy. As long as the horse is functionally sound and not in pain, who cares if it has a few warts. Don't we all?

The Elements of Choosing a Breed

With all these breeds to consider, you might be wondering if your own ele-mental default temperament comes into play when choosing a horse. To some extent, yes. But it's a weak yes with several caveats. Forget the breed, and focus on the individual temperament and personality of the horse.

If you're a slow and steady earth type, you might love those big coldbloods, but heavy horses are huge and are more expensive to feed and shoe, harder to haul, and not really bred for riding, although many are ridden. However, in keeping with your earthy temperament, you'll probably want a horse with the calm, obedient nature of a coldblood, but in a smaller and less-expensive-to-maintain package. Look for a horse with coldblood *energy*, unless you're planning to cut down logs and haul them down a mountainside in your spare time. Look for an older, experienced, bombproof horse.

If you're an air type, with high expectations and little patience for slow learners, that doesn't mean you need a sleek jumping horse. You need a bright, intelligent horse that likes learning. Arabians or Morgans come to mind, but most any horse can have its curiosity piqued and enjoy learning all sorts of things. Air types might enjoy miniature horses quite a bit as companions too,

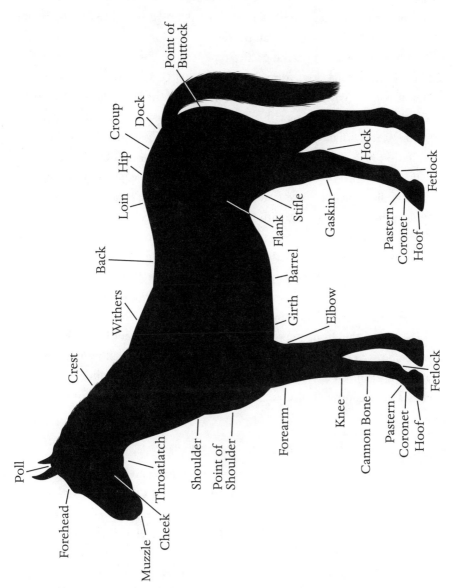

Figure 2: Horse Anatomy

because they love to play and learn, and can be taught tricks. They're cute little devils, and air types are often attracted to things outside the mainstream. Seek out a horse that is smart, alert, and willing. A horse that loves to learn, and does so quickly, will satisfy your air needs.

If you're more of an on-the-go fire type, you might want a peppier horse, just like if choosing a dog, you might prefer a large sporting breed to a quiet lapdog. If you know you want to go trail riding and charge up hills and through brush, you might be happier with a scrappy Appaloosa than a fancy-pants dressage horse. You'll likely enjoy a healthy, athletic horse that still has plenty of miles left on him. Any of the American warmbloods would be well-suited for that. If you want to get out and have fun with your horse, get a little rowdy, or get a little dirty, pick a horse that is sound enough, well-trained enough, and still young enough to do that with you safely.

If you're an emotional water type, you probably mostly just want a horse to love on and spend time with. You are truly seeking a heart-to-heart companion. This sort of temperament is more about age than breed. Even spicy Thoroughbreds and Arabians can become quiet, lazy lovebugs as they age. That hothead that zipped around the racetrack or over fences in its prime will likely be pretty chill in its twenties. Once again, the element in real live horses is more about personality than breed, and age tends to mellow most horses. Look for a calm, quiet, friendly horse that's more interested in carrots, neck scratches, and getting showered with love than taking off over the hill at full gallop.

Elemental Horses Aren't Real Horses, and Vice Versa

While it's fun to draw lines between Elemental Horses and real ones, and many horse breeds are iconic types that perfectly represent Elemental Horses, don't get too attached to conflating the two. Elemental Horses are defined by the job they do, and although there are breeds known to excel at those same jobs in the real world, Elemental Horses do their jobs on a purely metaphysical plane.

Elemental Horses are pure archetypes—not real horses. Much like angels and people have some similarities, we imagine angels in human form because that's the easiest way for us to understand them. However, angels and people aren't the same thing at all, and neither are Elemental Horses and real horses.

Elemental Horses aren't physical creatures that live under physical rules. For one thing, Elemental Horses don't age. However you created them in your mind, that's how they stay. Real horses age, just like humans, and have aches and pains, soreness and stiffness, just like us, and over time are more interested in relaxing and taking it easy than intense physical activity. Age slows us all down, and mellows us all out, no matter how many legs we have.

Elemental Horses are inspirational, spiritual, mental archetypes as opposed to real, living, breathing creatures with unique personalities that change with time and experience. Elemental Horses perform a particular task in a particular way, every time. Real horses are far more eclectic than the specialized Elemental Horses. They also poop way more.

Let your Elemental Horses do what they do, on the abstract, spiritual, metaphysical level, and here on the physical plane, evaluate each real horse you meet as an individual to decide if that horse's temperament and yours seem compatible.

You'll Still Need It All

While Elemental Horses and real horses are two different entities, the elements are present in a real horse: earth is its power; air is its speed; fire is its courage; water is its gait; and spirit is its soul. The Elemental Horses can also assist you while working with a real horse, because you must be strong and calm like earth, use your head and be prepared to think fast like air, ready to dive into whatever adventure you want and face challenges that pop up in a moment like fire, and have an abundance of patience and empathy while teaching your horse like water. You must settle into spirit to connect with spirit in your horse.

— IV —
YOUR HORSE, PARTNER & FRIEND

Chapter 10

BONDING AND GROUNDWORK

This is the chapter all you Horsey Girls have been waiting for: moving on to working with real, live horses—one of your very own! You've taken all you learned in the last section, and now, you're ready to bring your horse home! And surprise, there's still more to learn.

We'll cover the getting-to-know-you phase all the way through some basic horsemanship tips and ideas for simple groundwork. While the focus is on the soft, natural horsemanship approach, we'll also touch upon leadership and obedience, both of which are necessary to keep you and your horse safe. All of this begins with learning how to communicate with a horse, and sometimes, *like* a horse.

We'll also explore the inestimable value of just spending time with a horse, which is much more than a big, strong animal that carries you or follows you around. Horses are spiritual creatures that communicate much more subtly than most people realize, and have much deeper and richer emotional worlds than you ever imagined.

Learning to connect with your horse on a spiritual level, and understanding it as a unique, intuitive creature, will create a much fuller relationship than if you merely focused upon getting it to do what you want it to do. Many horsemanship experts are singularly focused on getting a horse to *obey*. Sure, they are concerned with nutrition, safety, and health, but more in the way you'd take care of a car to keep it functioning so it will do what you want. If we were interested in things that always did what we want, and what to do to keep them that way, we'd be reading a book about cars, not horses.

Since we're after more than just obedience, we'll wrap up this chapter with learning how to communicate and bond with your horse on a more mystical

level, and ways to draw and direct the energy you want from the universe to
your horse.

Getting to Know You

We've finally arrived at the big moment. You've done your search, you've
found "The One," and there it is, standing in its paddock, looking at you
looking back at it. Are you surging with excitement? Of course you are! And
maybe some trepidation? Yeah, probably. Actually, so is your horse. It's in a
new environment, its old herd is nowhere to be found, and it has no idea who
you are. Your new horse may be wound up, prancing around, head up high,
tail flagging in the air, snorting, or bolting away from you. That's okay and
totally normal. Your horse may also be one of those "been there, done that"
old boys, who looks around, shrugs, and seems to be saying, "Yeah, whatever,
cool. When's dinner?" That's also normal, as is everything in between. Watch
your new horse for a while and observe what it's "telling" you about its new
environment.

The very first thing you need to do, long before saddling up or trying new
things in the round pen, is to establish a bond. Just like a new relationship with
a person, it can't be forced. Come on too strong, and the other person may run
away; so might your new horse.

Your bond is not merely about just becoming great pals. You will need
to establish yourself as the leader so that your horse can relax and follow in
complete trust. If you're a poor leader, your horse will step up and fill that role.
Right now, your horse doesn't know whether you are the leader or it is, and
it's going to test that out. Your horse needs to know, because there must be a
leader to keep the herd safe. You need to show your new pal, firmly but kindly,
that you are its leader so it can relax.

Let's Get Acquainted

When you bring your new horse home, don't ask for too much too fast: just let
it be. Let your horse decide that the paddock is safe, nothing is there that will
eat it, and its new neighbors are very interesting—there may be a lot of squealing and striking as noses touch and exchange breath, which is totally normal.
If your horse is all wound up, let it burn off some rocket fuel on its own. Once
your horse comes down out of orbit, throw in some hay, offer a carrot, and

don't ask anything of it for now. Put on your Paleolithic ancestor hat for a while and simply enjoy watching your new equine friend.

If your horse prances over your way, talk to it, offer a hand to sniff, give it a pat or a scratch if it seems open to it, but don't be offended if your horse dances away the first couple times. If you just met someone, even if you were interested romantically, you'd probably pull away if that person just said "hi" and then leaned in to plant a wet kiss on your mouth when you weren't ready. Your new horse feels the same way: *Whoa, there, pardner, too much, too fast! Let's get acquainted first!*

Some people would saddle right up and start riding right off the bat because that's what *they* need, but it's not what the horse needs. And besides, at this point in our Horse journey together, we know that we aren't "some people." We are Horse people. Just because a horse tolerates all the inconsiderate, thick-headed nonsense humans throw at it doesn't mean it's optimal for the horse.

Consider the situation from your horse's point of view: It was just living in one world that it knew well, then stepped inside a small, constrained, rattling monster can that we call a trailer, got jostled around for a long while, backed out of that monster can, looked around, and—uh-oh—every single thing it knew vanished. Suddenly, your horse found itself in a completely new world where nothing was familiar and its herd was nowhere to be seen. Out in the wild, being without its herd means death, so let your horse be a little freaked out if it needs to be. It won't last long, and eventually your horse will get to know its new stablemates and adapt to a new herd. Your horse is biologically driven to do so.

If out in a pasture with other horses who've established their pecking order, you can expect some nips, kicks, rearing, and squealing because a stranger has entered their orderly world and needs to find its place in the pecking order of the group. Keep an eye on it to make sure that it doesn't escalate from the usual jostling around and bickering into a full-on fight that may end up with someone calling their vet. Also, be prepared for possible fights before you turn your horse out with unfamiliar pasture mates: Plan in advance how you will deal with a situation that escalates out of control, and have another experienced horse person with you until you see how it goes.

When your horse seems calm and relaxed, whether that's ten minutes later or the next day, it's time to get in there and get to know each other. We'll begin with the important stuff: carrots.

Your horse will learn very quickly that you're the one who brings the hay, and are the Keeper of the Carrots. This will make it very fond of you very quickly. My husband frequently accuses me of bribery, and says Penn only follows me around like a puppy dog for that reason. Well, one person's bribery is another person's positive reinforcement. It's just logical: If you want a horse (or cat or dog or person) to like you, teach them to associate you with something they like and not something they don't. If they exhibit positive behavior, reward it: so simple.

And really, aren't we all bribed every day? Do you choose to hang out with people who "smack" you with words and insult you, or instead pick people who "bribe" you with laughter and friendship? And who would keep working without the "bribe" of a paycheck every two weeks? Put me at the head of the "not me" line.

Pack your pocket with carrot bits—horse treats will work too, but they're way more expensive—sling the halter and lead rope over your shoulder, head to the center of the paddock, hold out your hand, and introduce yourself. Call your horse's name and make a little clucking sound. If your horse walks right up to you, perfect, give it a piece of carrot. If it runs away, that's okay, let it. Don't reinforce its idea that you might be a predator by chasing it. Chasing or following your horse when it walks away is exactly the *opposite* of what you should do.

Breathe slowly and calmly, and envision your horse stopping and turning to face you. When your horse stops, it'll probably look at you. Keep that hand held up. If your friend just stands there staring, take a couple steps backward. That may pique its curiosity and entice it to follow. Talk to your horse in a soft, soothing voice. Unless it's had a horrible experience with humans, your horse will probably start walking toward you. Stay where you are, keep doing what you're doing, and wait. Patience pays off. Those tentative, trembling, velvety lips touching your palm will send tingles of joy through your body. Give your horse that treat.

Back up a few more steps with your hand extended. Your horse will probably follow. Offer another treat. Horses learn very quickly, and you won't have to do this very many times before your equine friend will be coming right up to you.

What Is Your Horse Saying?

Really look at your new horse, take it all in like a beautiful painting. Observe its body language and look at its face. Are your horse's eyes clear and bright, looking at you curiously? Is your pal sniffing you and checking you out? Head low and relaxed? Ears pricked in your direction? These are all signs of a calm and comfortable horse.

Besides the familiar whinnies, neighs, and snorts, horses communicate with their eyes, ears, head, feet, and tail. In particular, there are two very subtle behaviors to watch for. One is licking the lips and making a soft chewing motion, which means, "I get it. I understand." The other is heaving a big, long sigh, either just air or like the sound you make when you exhale through your mouth and let your lips flutter together. That means your horse is comfortable with whatever is going on, and maybe even slightly bored.

Horses's eyes are the windows to their minds. They communicate so much with their eyes, which reflect their internal reality every moment. When the eyes are wide open and ringed with white, it means the horse is alarmed by something and is evaluating how likely it is that it may be eaten by whatever is frightening it, and whether or not it needs to dash away to safety. If you see just the brown of your horse's eyes, it's not feeling threatened. When you become sensitive to it, you'll see when a horse's eyes are "soft" and it's feeling receptive to you, and when they're hard and your horse would really prefer to be left alone.

If your horse is looking away from you, head down, ears sort of floppy, eyes dull, it's not connecting to you, and may be bored or just not that into you at the moment. Your horse may also not be feeling well. If that's a strange behavior for this horse, check for signs of injury, illness, or pain. If you can't find any and it's still behaving this way, call the vet.

When a horse looks full on at you, ears pointed toward you, it's probably looking right into your eyes. If it seems calm, engaged, and inquisitive, as if saying, "Well, hello there," you have your horse's undivided attention and it's ready for whatever you're planning to do next. As you get to know your horse, you'll know exactly how it's feeling just by looking into its eyes.

One of the most adorable facial expressions horses exhibit is a slightly pursed upper lip, pushed out a bit in front of the lower lip. It looks like a goofy little smile, and almost like the beginning of a kiss. When horses do that, they're very happy to see you, and feeling good and calm about being with you. They're saying, "I really like you, little two-legged!"

When a horse holds its head up high in the air, llama style, like it's looking right down its nose at something in the distance, something has alarmed it and it's watching carefully to decide whether fight or flight is the appropriate course of action. Moving the feet around nervously means the same thing: *I'm prepared to run.* Time to bring the energy down. Keep hold of the lead rope gently, but firmly, talk to your horse reassuringly, pat it on the neck, keep soft eye contact, and breathe slowly, calmly, and deeply. Imagine calm. You might even heave a big horsey sigh with your lips to communicate that this situation is no big deal, totally boring. Nothing to see here, my friend.

If that's not working, and your horse's energy is spiraling up rather than settling down—snorting, whites of its eyes showing, circling around you or ignoring you—you'll have to be more forceful. You may have to move into "because I'm the leader and you're not" mode. However, be sure you know how to back up those words with action. You might have to jerk the halter, walk your horse in circles, and speak to it in a much more forceful tone. If your horse is clearly getting out of control, particularly if you are feeling afraid, put it back in its paddock and seek guidance from an experienced horse person.

If a horse gives you the "mare nose," even if it's a gelding, it's trying to establish dominance. With ears back and eyes flashing, the horse pulls up its nostrils at the corners as if sneering, and snakes its head around at you. This is how lead mares in a herd boss the underlings. Even horses that haven't lived out in pasture or in the wild will exhibit—and understand—this behavior.

If you get the "mare nose," your horse is communicating disrespect, and intends to herd you like a horse that's lower on the pecking order. A more subtle expression of this "I'm the boss, you're not" behavior is bumping you with its nose or stepping into your personal space. I learned the hard way what happens when you ignore this behavior. Disrespectful behavior, even if subtle, needs correction. That horse needs to learn to respect your space, which we'll talk about later in this chapter.

When a horse flattens its ears back against its neck, and its eyes emit fiery anger, your horse is letting you know that it's about to resist whatever it is you think you're going to do next. It may even lunge at you in an attempt to drive you away, mouth open, and try to bite. This horse has chosen "fight" rather than "flight," and is straight-up challenging you for dominance. It has absolutely zero respect for you. This horse is stronger than you and it knows it. This makes it dangerous. Don't handle the horse until you get guidance from an experienced horse person; stand back, watch, and learn. Don't be surprised if more "traditional" discipline is applied. Yes, there are situations that may call for that. Hopefully, they are the exception and not the rule.

Watch that tail. Swishing the tail vigorously, not just swishing flies, is a sign of disgruntlement, like when a cat or dog growls. It's a warning that something worse is on its way if you keep doing what you're doing. If a horse spins and turns its butt to you, tucks its tail tight, turns its head ever so slightly, watching you out of the corner of one eye, ears back and pointed in your direction, beware. This posture means, "I'm locked and loaded, and ready to launch you into orbit." This is also dangerous behavior for which you'll need expert intervention.

These are some of the most common communications from horses. Reward the positive communications, and have a plan for consistently and firmly discouraging the negative ones, which you'll learn as you watch more experienced horse people school your horse. Begin with good communication and nurture that bond, establish yourself as the leader, and hopefully, those disrespectful behaviors will be few, if at all.

Leading Your Horse

Before you can lead your horse, you need to put the halter on. If you've never done this before, you need to have someone show you how. If you're thinking, "Why not just leave it on all the time?" it's because it increases the probability that the halter will hang up on something and your horse will get hurt. A halter that is left on all the time will also rub hair off your horse's face.

The halter should be loose enough that your hand can easily slide under it at any point. The horse should be able to graze without the noseband becoming tight when it chews. If your horse flings its head up in the air when you attempt to put the halter on or touch its face, it's called being "head-shy." You'll have to desensitize your horse and teach it that human hands don't always hurt and that more often, they hold treats. To start desensitizing your horse, offer a treat and slowly reach toward its face. Withdraw the treat if your horse throws its head up. Only reward the desired behavior.

Is your horse calm, has its halter on, and all systems seem ready to go? Let's take a walk.

When leading, the horse is typically to your right (the horse's left), because it's what most horses are accustomed to and because most people are right-handed. However, if you're a leftie, you might want to train your horse to walk to your left. Your horse may seem a little confused at first if it's never been walked from its right side, which some call the "off side." Some believe that horses naturally dislike being handled from their off side, but I think that's just hogwash. It's a learned behavior and if people always approach, lead, saddle, or mount a horse only from the left side, that's what they're familiar with. Practice doing things from both sides of your horse and it won't have an "off side" for long. That said, you'll still have to put a halter on from the horse's left side. I haven't seen a halter yet with buckles or ties on the right side.

When you lead your horse, it must learn to walk where you want. I want Penn's head just in front of my arm so I can see him out of the corner of my eye, but he would prefer to be a length in front of me. We still need to have a few rounds of "who's the boss" from time to time.

Practice walking in a circle, turning around and going the other way, saying "whoa" and gently pulling back to stop, and then making the clucking sound with your tongue to start walking again. Say "back" and tug gently on the lead rope while walking backward, then stop and go forward again.

Mix it up, do the unexpected. This prompts your horse to really pay attention to you and reinforces that you are the leader and it is the follower. Walk randomly and stop and say "whoa" in unexpected places. Walk quickly and then suddenly walk very slowly, pick up the pace again, and slow down again. For all these minilessons, you want to keep your horse in that sweet spot next to you and not pulling ahead of you. You want to work toward doing all these things with the rope loose and communicating with your voice and body language.

Praise your horse when it responds correctly, and give it a treat when the lesson's all done, even if it wasn't quite perfect. If your horse has been cooperative and done its best, this is called "rewarding the try," which means whenever your horse takes a baby step in the right direction and is clearly trying to do what you want, no matter how clumsy the result is, reward it. In psychology, its called "shaping": rewarding any increment of the desired behavior.

Grooming Is Bonding

Part of your daily routine with your horse is grooming. If you view this as a chore that you must do quickly so you can saddle up and get going, you're completely missing out on a bonding opportunity. Horses groom each other to bond, often standing side by side in opposite directions and simultaneously nibbling gently on each other's necks, withers, backs, or docks of their tails. When you groom your horse, it interprets this the same way. It doesn't know you're cleaning it up; your horse thinks you're bonding with it. Clear your mind and just enjoy the process of brushing your horse, noting the changing swirls and directions in its hair, cleaning its feet, combing its mane and tail. Sink into the experience of just grooming and being in each other's presence.

In Robert M. Pirsig's classic novel *Zen and the Art of Motorcycle Maintenance*, which is neither actually about Zen Buddhism nor motorcycles, he delves into the "quality" of experiencing the process, not the product. Some people groan and declare this book "a long, stupid story about a stupid motorcycle trip and fixing stupid motorcycles," and they're totally missing the point. The book is brilliant. Pirsig slows you down in the actual reading process and, as the reader, you experience the "quality" of simply paying attention to what you're reading. That's what raking sand to meditate is all about, and brushing a horse can be your sand raking. You'll start discovering that you feel calm and clear after spending time grooming your horse. You are immersed in what you're doing, and that's Zen. I call my grooming time "Zen with Penn."

Grooming a horse isn't like grooming a wiggly dog or cat. The horse stands there, still and relaxed, head dropped, and has its own Zen moment while you groom it. People frequently comment that Penn is falling asleep when I groom him. He's not falling asleep at all, but he *is* deeply relaxed. I've done massage therapy for twenty years, so I know what relaxation feels like under my hands, and that's exactly what's happening with Penn. I don't know if horses go into the golden slumber state that humans do during a massage, where you're neither awake nor sleeping and your thoughts drift along without your control. I like to think Penn goes into golden slumber under my hands, feeling so completely safe that he can let go of all his stress, thoughts, and fears. It sure looks like he does.

A Native American Approach to Bonding and Horsemanship

When I read GaWaNi Pony Boy's *Horse, Follow Closely,* I was thrilled to discover that I'd been taking a Native American approach to bonding with Penn intuitively. Pony Boy's book focuses on building a relationship with a horse as a means for better horsemanship, and it begins with simply spending time together.

Pony Boy recommends spending an entire day with your horse loose in its paddock or the pasture, or on a lead rope hand-grazing, with no agenda at all. Just watch and observe how your horse moves, eats, and swishes at flies. Talk to it, and just *be* together. Let your horse wander where it will, see where it takes you, and notice what your horse is attracted to and what it ignores. In essence, spend time with your horse as it would spend time with another horse. Interact and communicate as another horse. Let all that Horse energy just sink in while you're at it.

Pony Boy emphasizes that just spending time with your horse as you get acquainted isn't a one-shot deal; it's relationship maintenance. Spending quality "just being" time whenever you can is the heart of bonding with your horse. You don't always have to arrive at the barn with a lesson plan, intent upon accomplishing something. Sure, there are days when you have specific goals for your horse, but for bonding purposes, let the bulk of your time revolve around *be*-ing rather than *do*-ing.

Pony Boy explains the relationship of *intancun* (leader) and *waunca* (follower) and emphasizes that it's imperative for your horse to accept you as the leader of its two-person herd. This is the foundation of everything else that follows.

I've tried several of Pony Boy's methods of subtle communication and direction, and was astounded to see Penn respond to them, such as turning him loose in the arena and focusing my attention on one spot on the ground until he came to stand in that spot, which he did. I also discovered that I must discard my preconception that this method is preposterous, and really believe in the goal, or Penn will ignore me. He isn't the only one who's learning.

Groundwork

When you're feeling really good about leading your horse around and your bonding is coming along nicely, there's lots more you can do than just walk around and chat, even though that's very satisfying. You can bump up your groundwork a bit by trying some of these exercises:

- *Pick up those feet:* Lead your horse over logs or low obstacles. Besides being a good groundwork lesson, it's great for loosening up your horse's legs. Sometimes I place jumping poles on the lowest rung on two standards and walk Penn back and forth, and around and over, several times. He's old and stiff, and this makes him gently flex his knees and hocks, elbows and stifles. However, as a former jumping horse, he sometimes gets bored with this. One day, we approached a pole after having gone over several times, and he took a little bunny hop, cleared the pole, and then looked back at me as if to say, "See, Mama? *That* is how we go over poles. We jump them." Cracked me the hell up!

- *Go climb a hill:* Walking up and down hills is a great toning and strengthening exercise for horses, particularly old, stiff ones, and offers plenty of leading practice. When facing downhill, cue your horse to back up, uphill. This is excellent for strengthening their back and hindquarters.

- *Throw it in reverse:* You can try a variation for the cue to back up. Most horses are familiar with someone pulling or tugging on the lead rope and saying "back." Sarah introduced me to a different method because sometimes you may be standing in front of your horse and need it to back up, like on a narrow trail. She tells the horse to "back" while snaking the lead rope gently back and forth under its chin. Done more vigorously, it's a cue to "get out of my space" if your horse is habitually exhibiting bossy behavior and inching too close to you or bumping you with its nose.

- *Move it away:* Another method of using a softly swinging rope is to cue a horse to step part of its body away from you by gently swinging the loose end of the rope in a slow circular motion toward the hip or shoulder, depending which part you want the horse to move. Don't let the rope touch the horse, just loop it slowly in the air. Most horses don't really care for this motion, and will willingly move away. This is good practice for situations when you're out walking or riding and you want your horse to move only one part of its body in a certain direction rather than back up.

- *Keep those joints mobile:* Put a few jumping poles on the ground, about a pace apart, and lead your horse back and forth over them. You can also use little pole supports or even empty buckets to alternately lift one side and then the other of each pole, and walk through again. Go through the middle, go through the low sides, go through the high sides. Stepping over the poles helps keep your horse's joints mobile, and you can take the opportunity to crunch your abdominal muscles when you lift your legs to step over the poles too.

- *Go in circles:* The longe line is one of your most valuable groundwork tools. It's a very long lead rope, used to guide your horse around you while you stand in the middle of the circle. Horses can walk, trot, and canter on the longe line, and burn off some extra energy if they're a little peppier than you'd like. It's also a way to give your horse some exercise if you spend most of your time walking around. Your horse may already know how to longe, and if so, great. If not, you have another groundwork lesson cut out for you. If you've never longed a horse before, you may need some guidance.

    With the horse on the longe line and yourself about ten feet away, the goal is to get the horse moving around you. You cue a horse to move forward by making that classic clucking sound, and leaning toward its flank and focusing your eyes and energy there. If your horse needs a stronger message, you can use a longe whip or long training stick as an extension of your arm to point and direct energy—not to whip it! Point the whip at your horse's flank and direct your energy down your arm and the whip toward the flank, while clucking. Your long-term goal is to not need the whip at all.

    In the beginning, just walk. Before advancing to trotting or cantering, work on stopping and turning. Leaning forward and directing your energy toward the hip means move forward, and leaning upright or slightly back and directing energy toward the shoulder means stop. It takes time to teach and learn this, so be patient and keep practicing. I'm *still* working on this! Back in the day, we used a longe whip for, well, whipping. I'm learning new methods right along with Penn.

When you're feeling good about longeing and your horse is reading your cues, you can try this in a round pen without the rope. Direct your horse with energy, verbal cues, and body language only. It may take awhile, so infuse yourself with some Water Horse patience, and praise every try until your horse understands. Have a pocket full of treats handy.

• *Use novel teaching tools:* Flags, plastic bags tied to sticks, and dog training clickers are just some of the novel things you can use when teaching new groundwork skills, or even tricks. You want to keep things interesting because horses get bored too. Pony Boy recommends that these items only be used for teaching so your horse knows it's time to "go to school." His novel item of choice is a special bandana, which he waves to communicate with a horse.

I tried a cat's stick toy for this purpose, because in a horse's eyes, that's pretty novel. It's about two feet long with glittery ribbons, feathers, and a little bell on the end. When I first showed it to Penn, he was a little concerned. He snuffled it with his nostrils flaring, and his eyes big, wide, and worried, but a couple treats later, he decided the stick toy wouldn't eat him and we proceeded.

I was preloaded with peppermint horse treats in my pocket—peppermint essential oil wakes up the mind and keeps it bright and clear, which is great for learning. I only give Penn peppermint when we're doing groundwork lessons. He *really* loves it, so it's a little extra motivation to pay attention and try harder.

The first time I used the stick toy, I wanted Penn to move his hindquarters, which is the precursor to turning around to go the other way on the longe line. At a standstill, I pointed the stick toy at his hip and jiggled it a bit. When his hip moved ever so slightly, I immediately praised him and gave him his first peppermint treat. He looked like he had exclamation points in his eyes. The old boy really loves his peppermint!

I asked him with the stick toy to move his other hip, and he did, and immediately got another treat. I could almost hear the *ding ding ding* going off in his head: moving my butt gets me peppermint. He started swinging those hips right around as soon as I pointed the stick. However, when I proceeded to cue him to move his front end away by pointing the stick toward his shoulder, he just kept swinging his hips enthusiastically, ears pricked eagerly toward me, eyes shining, anticipating that peppermint. I had to stop the lesson at that point because I was laughing too much. Big old goofy horse! What an overachiever!

Establishing Leadership

Of all the groundwork you do, the most important lesson is establishing leadership. *Leader*-ship. The state of being a leader. Not a tyrannical dictator, mind you. A firm, calm, no-nonsense benevolent leader: someone to be respected, not feared.

When you're on your horse's back, it's obvious who the leader is: you. If it's not, you need some riding lessons. However, on the ground, it's a different story. The same horse that obeys while you're riding it might feel it has the upper hand on the ground (read: Penn). Some horses will eventually accept that you are the leader and they are the followers, while others like to revisit that arrangement every day to see if you really mean it. One of the ways Penn tests my leadership is to encroach into my personal space. This subtle but bossy behavior is meant to move lesser-stature horses along or out of the way.

Penn loves to sidle right up next to me, nudging his nose into me. At first I thought he wanted attention and that he'd love to crawl right into my lap and have me cradle him like a big baby. I thought he just wanted to be near me because he loved me. Turns out, not so much.

Sarah enlightened me to what Penn was actually doing: expressing dominance. He wasn't being affectionate. He was attempting to show me that he was the leader, and I was not. As she put it so aptly one day, "He's flicking a cigarette at you." Unfortunately, I was reinforcing this behavior by stepping away when he stepped toward me, a hardwired reflex I'd learned years ago to avoid getting stepped on. However, Penn didn't read it that way. In his mind, he was telling me what to do and I was obeying: *get out of my way*. Allowing this behavior, even when it seems subtle and innocuous, set a bad precedent.

Sarah explained that we have a bubble of personal space around us, and so does the horse. A horse must learn that they may not enter your bubble unless invited; however, you—the leader—may enter its bubble at any time. You're the boss, he's not.

Sarah told me that I couldn't let this pushy behavior slide. When Penn pushes, I must push back, every time, no matter how small the transgression. He gives me plenty of opportunity to practice this because he's a bossybutt by nature, and had a history of just dragging people around on the lead rope rather than walking obediently. He still tests me on this particular point with greater frequency than I'd like. Sometimes I suspect he's merely cooperating, rather than actually obeying. It's more of a "Okay, Mom, I'll let you be the leader today," not "Yes, Ma'am!" You really do want that "Yes, Ma'am" response from your horse. Respect is a safety issue. I learned that the hard way.

One lovely sunny day, Sarah and I turned Penn loose while we went out walking in the pasture. However, the ranch's little cattle herd was out grazing, and cows just blow Penn's mind. Those are the ugliest horses he's ever seen, they speak a weird language, and he wants no part of them whatsoever. But it's a big pasture, so I figured he could easily avoid the cows.

We got maybe one hundred feet away when I heard galloping hooves behind me, coming closer. I turned just in time to swing the lead rope toward Penn's panicked face to make him swerve around me, but the force of it knocked me to the ground hard. I wasn't hurt, but this near miss was an eye-opener. I could easily have been trampled.

"The cows freak him out and he thought we were leaving him there, and he panicked and ran back to me," I told Sarah.

Sarah wasn't buying it. No more excuses.

"He has no respect for your bubble," she said. "He has to respect it, even when he's scared."

After that, Penn got a little "quality time" with Auntie Sarah in the round pen while I observed the "get out of my space" lesson along with him.

Sarah snaked the rope under his chin while striding toward him forcefully, commanding him, "Get out of my space!" And, boy did he! Penn backed right up, and looked quite surprised—and obedient. Clearly, Sarah was the boss. A more couple times, and she told me to give it a try.

I went in the ring, took hold of the rope, snaked it, and said, "Get out of my space," but it sounded like I was saying "Please." Penn just looked mildly annoyed, and begrudgingly took a couple steps back.

"No, not like that," said Sarah, returning to Penn, commanding very loudly, "Get out of my space!" while snaking the rope harshly and walking straight at him, right into his bubble. He got out of her space. His head was up in the air, his eyes wide, snorting, and he was giving her his undivided attention. Sarah meant business, and Penn knew it. He backed away quickly and kept his distance, and stayed there until she invited him to come forward.

No cigarettes were flicked at Sarah. Penn learned his lesson and so did I.

Leaving Old Ways for New

Right about now, you may be wondering how I could have been around horses for so much of my life and have a horse that still challenges me, sometimes being openly disobedient and bossy. It's because back when I was riding and showing, groundwork was unheard of. Nobody did that. There were Western riders who had halter classes at horse shows, but most of us hunter-jumper types just laughed those classes off as an activity for people who couldn't ride.

In the show-jumping world of my youth, even when just practicing, we got our horses out of their stalls, led them straight to the crossties, saddled and bridled them, walked straight to the arena, and got on. If our horses were lagging or not behaving properly, or moving around when we mounted, we just yanked the reins, and the pain of the bit being jerked in their mouths usually knocked them back into line. If it didn't, there was always a riding crop handy in our other hand, and fists if we needed them.

Not once in my entire time of riding instruction did we ever receive one moment of groundwork instruction. We got on, did the lesson, got off, and put our horses back, without any regard for their internal world or feelings, sort of like a dirt bike. We had a plan, the "bike" was expected to carry out that plan—or get spanked and spurred if it balked—and then the "bike" was put away until the next time.

Back in those days, I was quite proficient at bullying a horse into submission. This was the only way I was taught to handle a horse, and I'd learned that lesson well. It was the only tool in my box. I had no qualms about immediately slapping a horse and yelling at it for "misbehaving," and giving it a couple vicious jerks on the rope or reins, with never a thought about *why* the horse was "misbehaving." Was the saddle not fitting well? Bridle pinching? Spooked by a lawnmower? Not my problem, horse. Do as I say, or else.

Smacking, yelling, bullying a horse into submission with stud chains and whips if necessary, and completely ignoring the horse's needs or feelings or making any attempt to understand its behavior is the "or else" method. I want more for my horse, and myself. I know the "or else" strategy well, and could easily have used it with Penn, but I didn't *want* to. I was fascinated with this brand-new world of natural horsemanship, of moving energy to communicate and learning to understand a horse rather than merely control it. However, I'd overcompensated and become far too polite with Penn. He expected me to be a leader, as he has also grown up in an "or else" world, and if I didn't assert myself as the leader, he would. Both of us are still learning how to interact in a new way, and it's all about leadership and groundwork.

Empty Your Cup

When I returned to horses midlife, I was already a skilled rider and knew my way around horses. Theoretically, I didn't need anyone's help. However, I was so impressed watching Sarah work her magic with her own horses that I put my ego on the shelf, threw out most of what I knew (okay, picking a hoof is still picking a hoof), and viewed horses with fresh eyes. I learned tons of new things I had missed during my first horse education, which I'd never have learned had I brushed Sarah off, and said, "I already know it all."

A friend of mine, Rich, is the first true "horse whisperer" I've ever met. He goes out to his field and mentally communicates to his horses to come to the fence. He hops on, and rides around without a bridle or saddle, barely moving a muscle or making a sound. Those horses know exactly what he wants them to do, and respond immediately. The first time I saw him ride like this—long before I met Penn—using only his mind and body to communicate with the horses, I could not believe my eyes. I've seen horses being ridden in saddles and bridles that didn't respond like that, let alone with nothing on. It was like his mind and the horse's were one.

Rich is also a karate master, so moving energy and communicating with it is right in his wheelhouse, whether with people or horses. He treats horses with respect and understanding, like the elegant, sensitive, smart beings they are, and the horses return it. Rich once told me that an experienced person can be at a disadvantage because their ego may block new information. An accomplished karate student once came to Rich for instruction, but was resistant to doing anything differently. The student thought he already knew it all and Rich couldn't teach him anything.

"If your cup is already full, then I'm unable to fill it with anything else," Rich told me. "If you want to learn something new, you'll have to empty your cup."

Brilliant.

Horsemanship is just like that. If I'd clung to my old, familiar ways, I'd have missed out on so much. If your experience cup is already empty, great! You have plenty of room for new content. If you have years of horse experience under your belt, you'll have the hardest time "dumping that cup." Try setting your ego aside and making room for new information. If you don't like it, you can always go back to how you were doing it before, but you probably won't want to.

Escalating, Desensitization, and Ending with a Win

Sometimes what seems like a simple lesson to you turns into a panic attack for your horse. Say your intention for the day's lesson is to walk your horse over a plastic tarp you've laid down in the arena. Your horse may take one look at it, start snorting, and slam on the brakes: "Oh *hell* no!" You circle your horse around, go back toward the tarp and once again, it's giving you the big "Nope!" Now, because you're pushing the issue, your horse's head is up high, and it's snorting louder. You think to yourself, "Okay, this is just silly. It's just a tarp. It's harmless. Once it steps on it will see it's no big deal." To *you*, anyway.

Your horse sees a rattling blue thing that's going to swallow it alive, and now it's trembling, nervously dancing around, head up, eyes wild, pulling on the lead rope, communicating to you that if flight isn't possible, fight is an option. When a horse gets more and more wound up, less and less cooperative, and starts exhibiting flight behaviors, it's called "escalating." When your horse is escalating, it's time to abort the mission. It's not going to learn anything in that mindset, and you're not going to win this battle—not now.

Do you just give up and never cross the tarp? No, because that horse's fear of the tarp will remain. One day out on the trail, a tarp may be flapping, it might have to walk past one, or someone may come walking by dragging one, and your horse will still panic. You don't give up, but you don't exactly give in either. You need to desensitize your horse to that tarp, in the tiniest of steps.

On another day, set your tarp out, and lead your horse toward it. If it stops and gets worried, let your horse look at it and snort to its heart's content, as long as it stays there. Praise your horse and pat it comfortingly for staying still despite being frightened. Give your horse a treat. When it drops its head or heaves a sigh and relaxes, give it another treat, and call it a day *right then*. You've succeeded at the smallest increment of the desired behavior. Sarah calls this "ending with a win," and says when you end a lesson on a win, that's what your horse will remember about that lesson.

When your horse tolerates an incremental baby step, take another. Each day, get a little closer. Put the tarp in your horse's paddock with a weight on it to keep it from blowing around and gradually move it closer to your horse's feed bin. Drop some hay or your horse's favorite treats right on it. Always end on a win, praise your horse lavishly, and give it a treat. The ultimate goal would be to gently brush the tarp over your horse's body, without a meltdown. Whenever your horse escalates, back off. Always try to end on a win.

Early on in our groundwork lessons, Sarah was going to teach me how to longe Penn without a rope in the round pen. When she picked up the longe whip to use as an extension of her arm to direct energy, she got more than she asked for. Penn went straight into escalation mode. He started galloping around the pen frantically, out of control.

Sarah suspected the whip was the problem, so she set it down, slowed him, and reattached the lead rope. The lesson turned into letting Penn sniff the whip at a standstill, gently trailing it all over his neck and back, under his belly, over his legs, and back again. He stood still, head up to the sky, eyes ringed with white, snorting like a bull, trembling from nose to tail like a frail leaf in the wind.

"This horse has been beaten," I commented. "A lot."

"Yup," she replied, and continued praising him and trailing the whip over him. That ended up being his whole lesson that day: just standing and allowing the whip to be gently dragged over him as he trembled.

Eventually, he adapted to longeing in the round pen, with and without the longe line, with and without the whip, walking and trotting willingly. After practicing for a while, I decided one day to try it in the arena so we could advance to cantering. The moment I asked him to canter, he charged into a frantic, out-of-control gallop again.

It took weeks and weeks of patience and practice before Penn realized that I wasn't asking him to gallop and, moreover, I was not there to chase him like a predator. Then one day, just like any other, I asked him to canter and he just rolled into a nice, rocking slow canter. I let him go around only once, stopped him in the middle of his win, and praised him like he'd just won a gold medal. He was licking his lips and grinding his teeth. He got it. We both walked away proudly feeling the win.

Horses Have Triggers Too

Oh, if only Penn could talk and tell me what mistreatment he'd endured to be that afraid. It rips at your heart to see a big, powerful animal as terrified as a tiny rabbit. Just like people, horses can have triggers and phobias, and freak out when the thing they fear—like a longe whip—is near. Sometimes it's something as simple as a crackling plastic bag or kid with a balloon, and your horse will react like a mountain lion is about to devour it. Your horse can't tell you why it feels this way, so the best you can do is desensitize it, little by little.

I think that at some point in his young life, Penn was a handful. He can be a handful now, and I can only imagine what he was like as a young, strong, rambunctious colt beginning training, with an innately bossy nature and testosterone coursing through his veins. Dealing with him would have been like trying to control a tornado with a leash. That's probably why he's a gelding.

I suspect that someone in Penn's past started longeing him at a gallop to burn off some steam before riding him, and whipped him to get him moving and keep him moving. That would explain why a longe whip and being cued to canter turns to panic in Penn's mind.

Longeing before riding is a common practice, and while there's nothing wrong with getting some energy out on the longe line before riding, it shouldn't get out of control. In fact, anything you do with a horse that whirls out of control is to be avoided.

When a horse gallops in a panic, they're in prey mode, and by default, in their mind, you're the predator. Some people don't really care that their horse sees them that way when longeing, as long as it results in them being able to pre-exhaust their horse, and get on and "drive that car." For me, I care, and it's not the relationship I want with my horse.

We Won't Cross That Bridge When We Get to It

Longe whips weren't the only things that sent Penn into a panic at first. He was fine in the arena, but walking him out to the pasture was a challenge. He'd start snorting, dancing circles around me, and pulling on the lead rope. I'd just let him dance around, remaining grounded and centered, breathing calmly, talking to him, and often heaving a big sigh as if completely bored with all this fuss. This is also a way of de-escalating: make it boring.

Penn was also particularly afraid of a bridge that led to an open field near the ranch. He'd tense up as soon as we approached it, so I knew it was time for some desensitization.

I broke the situation down into bite-sized pieces. We'd approach the bridge and then just walk away. When that was accomplished without a reaction, we'd take one step on the bridge, and walk away. Each day, we advanced a little more: two steps, both front legs on the bridge, and finally all four. Penn was learning that stepping onto the bridge meant getting treats, and that this big "monster" wasn't such a big deal after all.

We worked our way up to halfway across, and finally, all the way over and into the field, where Penn discovered he could graze on all that lush green grass. After that, he started crossing the bridge like a champ.

I was feeling mighty proud of myself with that accomplishment, because leading Penn into the field to go on walks was a goal I'd set for myself. What I didn't realize, however, was that this goal opened up a new phase in our relationship: just walking out to graze, letting time, stress and anxiety just roll by. This was the game-changer for me. This was where the real healing started, where I learned to let go of my anxiety, and where the various issues I was struggling with started to tumble into place. That bridge is so symbolic. On the other side of it was peace and serenity, for me *and* my horse.

Never Punish Fear

In Tim Hayes's delightfully insightful book *Riding Home: The Power of Horses to Heal*, he enlightens us about how horses constantly view the world: as prey animals. They are always vigilant for anything that might be a predator. Hayes says a horse really only has one job in life: to not get eaten. That's why a horse will spook at an unfamiliar flag flapping in the breeze, an umbrella, or a weird-looking log. The horse doesn't know what it is, and therefore it might eat it until proven otherwise. Just like its Paleolithic ancestors, the horse who snorts and runs away lives to graze another day!

Hayes's book gave me renewed sensitivity for my big old chicken horse and deepened our bond. Penn isn't being dumb or disobedient; he's frightened to his core, whether I think it's silly or not. He lived his life in an arena, and he's never seen a log-splitter left out in the field or had jackrabbits burst forth from the underbrush at his feet. I do my best to calm him, and tell him, "Penn, you have your very own personal alpha predator! I won't let anything hurt you!" Penn often remains skeptical, but now I understand what's going on in his head and can even predict it.

One morning, someone left a large slab of Formica leaning on the fence next to the hitching post where I groom Penn. I saw it before going to get him, and met up with Sarah while leading him there.

"Watch, he's going to spook as soon as we round the corner," I told her, "Wait for it…wait for it…3…2…1…" and bam—he saw that "predator," jumped straight up in the air and landed with his legs sort of splayed like a dog, his eyes white with fear, snorting like a rhinoceros. How can you not chuckle at this! I patted him and slowly led him close so he could get a better look, and with flared nostrils huffing and a full body tremble going on, he slowly reached out his neck and touched his nose to the Formica like it was a bundle of dynamite that might explode at any second. Then he pulled his head back and thought about it, reached out to touch it again, sniffed it, heaved a big sigh, and bellied up to the hitching post waiting for sweet attention to be lavished upon him. Crisis over. This humorous little incident perfectly illustrated Hayes's point. Horses will decide what might eat them and what won't—not humans.

Some unenlightened horse owners call this behavior "spooky" and react in annoyance, jerking on the halter to get their horse's attention, and scolding it for "misbehaving." Remember being frightened as a child? How might you have felt if you got spanked for being afraid? It's no different for a horse. If you want a trusting, loving bond with a horse, punishing it when it's afraid to make the behavior stop is one of the surest ways to prevent that from ever happening.

When Horses Disobey

Although we strive for softness, kindness, understanding, and patience in our horsemanship, and move away from relying on punishment to force obedience, there are times when a horse needs an old-school smack with the lead rope or your hand. If a horse tries to bite you, run you down, strike, or kick at you, that's not merely misbehavior, that's straight-up disrespect, and it's also extremely dangerous. That sort of openly aggressive behavior must be met with sharp, immediate discipline.

A horse that's disrespectful has discovered that it's stronger than you, can take the leader role, and that aggressive behavior makes humans go away. You must correct that behavior, just like you would with a dog that bites. It can't go without consequences. A horse that has no respect for humans and is actively aggressive or vicious is a danger to people and ultimately to itself. At some point, if no one can handle that horse, it may "go to auction."

Which brings us to Obie.

Penn wasn't the only horse benefiting from my doting attention in our early days. There was a scrappy, dirty, unkempt little black Arabian gelding across from Penn's paddock. He got enough food and water, and his paddock was cleaned every day, but he was such a ragamuffin. His mane and tail hung in long, dirty, matted dreads. He seemed to be curious about people, but would dart away if you approached. Nobody ever interacted with him. They walked right past him like he was invisible, because he was just... weird.

Something was just not quite *right* with this horse. His odd, unsociable behavior, head high in the air and looking angrily down at everyone with fiery eyes, just turned people off. There were plenty of other horses at the barn who weren't so freaky. Why waste time on this one?

He wore a halter all the time because catching him was so difficult. He'd run the other way when anyone went into his paddock. In addition to being skittish, he was extremely head-shy. The moment you reached for his halter, his head went up to the sky. He had no life at all other than to walk around that dusty paddock and swish away flies.

I'm a sucker for hard-luck cases. I want to save all the cats, and all the horses too. I started visiting with Obie at the fence. I didn't like his actual name (Pearl), so I gave him one: Oberon, like the king of the fairies in Shakespeare's *Midsummer Night's Dream* (Obie for short), because he was small and dainty, but had such huge energy. His big, dark, stormy eyes, pleading and also mistrusting, seemed to say, "I hate you, please love me."

Obie quickly learned that I always had carrots, so he started coming right up to the fence. One day, I reached in and scratched his back. He trembled, like having one foot on the accelerator and one on the brake, enjoying that sensation while simultaneously wanting to flee. Pleasure won the day, and he stayed. He even tipped his nose up and stuck his upper lip way out, which horses do when you scratch "The Spot," just like dogs when you scratch them and their hind leg beats against the ground in ecstasy. Obie quickly started going right up to the fence for scratching and treats when he saw me coming. He wasn't stupid, just feral.

With his owner's permission, I ventured inside Obie's paddock, but as usual, he bolted away. I told him, "Okay, I'm done," turned, walked away, and left. I glanced back, and he was watching me go, looking thoroughly confused. This wasn't the dance he knew: *People chase me and I run away. That's what we do. What the heck is this?*

I did this every time he started to pull away. It didn't take him long to stop running off. I did the same thing with touching him—if he moved away, so did I. I didn't even give him three chances. As soon as he pulled away, I left. Pretty soon, I was petting him and scratching his neck without a flinch. I was very encouraged. Obie was a quick learner, and despite his antisocial behavior, he seemed starved for attention.

The next challenge was to snap a lead rope to his halter, using the same strategy: if he'd jerk head away, I'd leave. Then came haltering. I used Penn's big halter right over Obie's, taking it off and putting it on again, with treats flowing freely. Before long, I was haltering him without a fuss, and started grooming him and combing out his mane and forelock. Before long, I was leading him all around the paddock without any fuss.

I kept my little Obie rehabilitation project secret, and one day suggested to Sarah that maybe we could do groundwork with Obie too, just for fun. She chuckled, "Nobody can even get a halter on him!" I asked her to come watch what I could do with him. I thought her jaw would fall off when she saw me go into the paddock, walk right up to Obie, and snap the lead rope on without any fuss. I led him around like a little lamb, and was quite pleased with my own horse whisperer talents. Sarah said maybe we *could* take Obie out of his paddock sometime and try some things in the round pen.

Then one day, it all blew up.

There was an elderly, rickety, extremely unfriendly llama named Maxine at the ranch that lived in the pasture. Maxine was so homely that she'd become sort of a ranch mascot. No one could get near her, let touch alone her. Obie was weird, but Maxine was weirder. She wanted nothing to do with any other creature, whether on two legs or four. The horses that were turned out in the pasture from time to time just ignored her, and that suited her just fine. All she wanted was to lie there in the sunshine and be left alone.

One day, someone turned Obie out with Maxine, and he decided that he didn't like this bizarre-looking horse one bit. He lunged at her, knocked her to the ground, and then laid down on top of her while biting her viciously. Sarah later told me this is a wild stallion strategy to defeat an opponent: knock them down or bite their legs until they fall, and then crush them. I suspect that Obie interpreted Maxine's natural llama posture as a threat: neck straight up, head parallel to the ground, chin up high, staring right at you with huge, dramatic eyes. Maxine was mirroring Obie's own bizarre "get away from me" behavior, and he responded by challenging it.

Sarah was nearby when all of this went down, realized what Obie was doing, grabbed a long dressage whip, and ran out to stop him. She couldn't just let him kill Maxine. She hit Obie over and over, but he just ignored her. He finally got off of Maxine, and Sarah stood between them with the whip, but he wouldn't give up. He was determined to get back and finish the job on that llama.

Sarah knew that Obie would eventually outlast her, so she switched strategies on the spot to get him away. She crouched, growled, and mimicked predator behaviors when Obie faced her and stood up quietly when he turned away. And, it *worked*.

Suddenly, Obie tired of the whole scene, sort of like a bully trying to save face. He walked off and started grazing like nothing had happened, and it was a chance to lead poor Maxine into a stall. The vet said she miraculously didn't have any broken bones and advised rest and a "wait and see" approach. A couple days later, Maxine seemed a little better, and was returned to her pasture.

Later that afternoon, she laid down in her favorite spot in the sunshine, and died.

Dealing with Difficult or Dangerous Horses

The harsh fate of poor, old Maxine isn't merely a bizarre and sad story. It illustrates that even a horse you think you know well can blow up. Horses can have hidden triggers, which you may discover in a moment's flash, and you need more than one way to deal with it. If all Sarah knew was the "or else" method—fight until somebody loses—she would have lost that battle. You can't outlast a horse. They're ultimately always stronger than people, but you can outthink them, as Sarah did. When she ran out into that pasture, she was thinking three steps ahead and had quickly run through all the scenarios and options in her mind, including the "behave like a predator" method.

This was also a reality check about my own limitations. I've never had to deal with an openly mean, aggressive horse, so I don't even have the old-school "or else" skillset for that. At this point in life, I don't really want to go there. I don't go into the paddock with Obie anymore. I still visit with him from the other side of the fence, but that's all. He'd proven himself to be unpredictable, with an aggressive side that could flare up unexpectedly, and it's not worth going in with him again. There's no dishonor in working within your limitations. Not getting hurt, or worse, is the most important horsemanship goal of all.

The story of Obie and Maxine isn't meant to frighten you, but to illustrate that no matter how gentle the horse seems, shit can happen. You can't just stand there floundering; you must be as prepared as possible for that rare, random stuff that pops up without warning. Anticipate potential problems and have some options in mind and lots of tools in your box.

Horses are not perfectly safe all the time, and it would be a huge disservice if I created the impression that nothing bad will ever happen, even when you're just leading them around. Chances are, everything will probably be just fine the vast majority of the time. Day after day of nothing but pure horsey wonderfulness—that's the norm. But, the potential for unexpected circumstances or behavior is always there.

This is why you must be a perpetual student of horsemanship. Be brave enough to ask for help or guidance. If you're puffed up with ego and think you already know it all and don't need to listen to anyone with a different perspective or method, well, keep it up and eventually some horse will prove you wrong.

Connecting the Physical and Metaphysical Dots

We've explored the basics of the physical and psychological approaches to bonding, groundwork, and horsemanship. Now we'll move into the spiritual and metaphysical approach. To our physical and psychological tools, skills, and insight, we'll blend in new ways to really appreciate and enrich your relationship with your horse.

Get a Feel for Your Horse

Your horse may look big, strong, and tough, but it's astonishingly sensitive, physically and psychologically. Gently touch a fingertip to a whisker or a hair sticking out from its ear, and see how the lightest touch will make your horse's lips tremble or its ear flick. Take a tiny stick and ever-so-gently touch or drag the tip on your horse's back and watch how quickly its skin shudders. That skin can sense a tiny fly landing there. Experiment with very softly running your palm all over your horse's body, in the direction of its hair, and note the calming effect this has. Your horse can feel every sensation, every movement, every touch. In the massage world, Reiki is the feel and movement of energy on and around the body, and the transmission of loving, healing energy. Horses respond to Reiki too. You don't need to be a Reiki master to try sensing energy yourself.

When both you and your horse are feeling relaxed and calm, and there's not a lot of noise and activity swirling around you, face your horse and place your hands up on the swells of its forehead, the heels of your hands resting on the hollows over its eyes. You horse's brain is right under your hands. Feel that, sense your horse's energy, and try to connect with it. Don't ask or say anything, just sense. Be still in your brain, like when you do a meditation, and invite your horse's energy to come to you. See if you pick up on a feeling. Send love through your touch.

Smooth your hands down over your horse's eyes. Cup them, and send love. Breathe and invite your horse's energy. Do you pick up on anything? Continue smoothing your hands down the sides of its face, then its nose, and cup its muzzle in your hands. Send love, and invite your horse's energy. Do you sense anything? As your horse relaxes, it may lean its muzzle into your hands ever so slightly and you'll feel something amazing: its lips will twitch all over, so very slightly, almost imperceptibly. Your horse is telling you something. Be open to feelings and images. What is it saying?

These are the beginnings of feeling energy flowing between you and your horse, and communicating nonverbally. You can make this gentle, healing, loving touch part of your daily grooming routine.

He Saw My Thoughts

Once while sitting in the arena, as Penn rolled, wandered around to visit and squeal with the horses in the adjacent paddocks, and checked the "bulletin board" (manure wheelbarrow) for messages, I was watching the flocks of swallows diving and swooping from their mud nests up in the rafters. It all lulled me into complete peacefulness, just floating images, no words at all.

Penn ambled over to me, ears and eyes fixed on me, which is his way of saying, "Let's go, Mom."

We'd been working on walking back to the gate without a lead rope, and I stood up to do this, noticing some jumping poles placed in a square shape at one end of the arena. As I started walking, Penn at my side, I "saw" us walking over those poles. I headed toward the poles instead of the gate, and he stayed right next to me, walking right over them. I turned to loop back over another, and he stayed right at my side. We did a cloverleaf, and he stuck right by me, walking over the poles in perfect unison, without a rope or one word spoken— just the image of what I wanted us to do in my head.

I was thrilled and astounded. We stopped and I praised him like he'd just performed his first piano recital. His ears pricked up and his eyes were bright and alert, and then there was the licking and chewing behavior, showing me that he got it.

When we think in pictures, we're thinking like a horse. We're thinking in the spatial, visual "language" of our right brain rather than the constant whirring of words in our left, just like a horse. We're on their wavelength; they "hear" us on that wavelength. Now we're speaking *their* language.

In Tim Hayes's book, *Riding Home: The Power of Horses to Heal*, he explains that horses "speak" in a spatial, nonverbal language. Although they understand certain words—Penn knows *exactly* what "treat" means—they aren't verbal creatures. We humans, being species-centric, ignore this and chatter on to them, but Hayes says they tune our babble out like birds chirping in the trees. Communicating with mental imagery is also a basic tenet of GaWaNi Pony Boy's horsemanship teachings: direct your horse with mental focus.

The experience walking over the poles that day reinforced what Hayes was saying. No, horses don't understand the words when we pour our hearts out to them, but they sense our energy and feelings, and somehow, receive mental images. I can't explain why. I can only tell you that I've experienced it. Remember the Pine Nut herd story I shared of Star "telling" Blondie that it was time for Cree to come back to the herd? No words were spoken then either, but the communication was sent, and received.

Charms, Chakras, and Other Mystical Tools

There are a variety of practices, charms, and symbols meant to attract all sorts of energies, such as protection, money, love, and luck. We want these things for ourselves, so why not attract them to our horses?

Brasses and Charms

Remember the harness brasses we discussed earlier? Get one for your horse too! Choose one that represents the energy you wish to draw toward your horse, and attach it to its bridle, saddle, or halter. There are also smaller bridle charms that serve the same purpose. One of those best-friend charms that are two halves of one whole would be perfect for you and your horse—put one on its halter and wear the other yourself as a pendant. Any human pendant would also work as a bridle charm, and can represent whatever energy you wish.

Whatever brass or charm you choose, before attaching it, hold it in your hands and speak your energetic intentions into it. For example, you might say "for strength and courage" as you attach a little tigereye pendant to your horse's bridle. It's not a decoration; it's a little magnet for particular energy or protection from the universe.

Tail Tips

Tail tips are easily transformed into miniature horsetails, which you can put in a special spot or altar to keep your horse's energy with you and send your own energy back to it. A tail tip from your horse is about the easiest and cheapest thing possible for creating a powerful symbol of love and protection. However, don't just whack off some hair and throw it on a shelf; put meaning and intention into making it.

To create your mystical tail tip, the next time you go out to the barn, come equipped with a rubber band and some sharp scissors. After grooming your horse, take a moment to receive and honor its energy. Gently comb the snags from your horse's tail until it's smooth. That beautiful tail begins at your horse's dock, which is the locus of a horse's root chakra, the grounding force, and where basic physical and emotional needs, or deficits, are held.

Put your hand on your horse's dock and run it down to the tip of the tailbone. Feel the surprisingly long length of spine running through that tail. It's not a fall of dead hair like a ponytail on your head. Part of your horse's body is inside that tail, and there's energy running through it. It's a powerful communication tool for a horse, not just a pretty decoration. Honor the root chakra energies as you run your fingers through its tail.

When you're feeling energy flowing between you and your horse, get your scissors and run one hand near the end of its tail, grasp the portion you want to cut (a few inches is plenty), bind it with the rubber band, and cut it just above with the scissors. Thank your horse for offering a piece of its beautiful tail. You can replace the rubber band later with a different tie if you wish, or cover it with a ribbon in the color representing the energy you want for your horse. Smooth an essential oil onto the hair that reinforces the energy you want, reaffirm your intention for this spiritual tool, dedicate it to your horse, and place it on your altar or in a special spot where it will serve as a daily reminder, focus point, or inspiration for the love between you, your horse, and Horse itself.

Mojo Bags

We discussed mojo bags for our own use earlier, but we can also make them for our horses. A mojo bag is a small pouch made of leather or fabric, into which items that you've infused with spiritual intention are carried. You can purchase a mojo bag online or make one yourself from a swatch of fabric, leather, or suede. They should be on the small side, the size of your palm or less. You'll also need a cord or leather lace to close the bag.

Penn's mojo bag is deep blue suede. Blue represents both water energies and the throat chakra, the locus of communication. In it I placed representations of all four elements: a tiny rock from a sacred place for earth, a slender feather for air, a pinch of dragon's blood incense for fire, and a seashell I found on a favorite beach for water.

I added a small tigereye stone, representing good luck, good health, and protection, and a small, plain pentacle, symbolizing protection of the entirety of the person—and horse—as well as further representation of the elements. There's also a strand of Penn's hair entwined with a strand of mine, because we are spiritually entwined. It sounds like a lot of things, but they're all very tiny, and fit perfectly.

I smoothed Lucky Mojo oil onto the pouch, and smudged the finished bag by swirling it in moldavite incense smoke—moldavite manifests positive change. As I circled the bag through the smoke in front of my altar, I said, with heartfelt intention, "Earth, his power... air, his speed... fire, his courage... water, his gait... spirit, his soul... All of these energies, all the energies of the Goddess and the universe, I ask your blessings for good luck, good health, and a long life for my horse." I tied his mojo bag to the back of my saddle, so all this energy is with us when I ride.

Make It Colorful

Color is one of my favorite ways to set my intentions, and it's easy to do for your horse. All you need is ribbon! Attach small ribbons of particular colors to your horse's tack, mane, forelock, or tail. For example, if you want to move quickly and boldly while riding that day, use ribbons in the color of fire: orange or red. Maybe you just want your horse to be calm and peaceful, so you invite water energy with a blue or purple ribbon. Whatever energy you need to enhance that day, there's a corresponding color, and ribbons come in every color there is.

You can also select a halter and lead rope in the color that represents your intention for your horse when you go out walking or into the round pen to do groundwork. In addition to attracting a certain elemental energy, color is also a visual reinforcement to keep you on track when you are striving for a certain goal. It keeps *you* focused.

I bought Penn a halter and lead rope in throat chakra blue, representing clear communication for groundwork lessons. The blue lead rope additionally symbolizes the two-way communication necessary for each of us to understand what the other is saying. To be clear, Penn doesn't give a shit what color his halter and lead rope are. The color is *my* visual cue to keep my communication clear, and listen to his.

In addition to colors being associated with the elements or chakras, they also have classic meanings for setting spiritual or mystical intention. They differ slightly between different traditions, but this is how I use them when setting my intention of what I need from the universe:

- *White:* purity, innocence, the full moon, feminine energy, lunar energy, the Goddess, crown chakra, spirit
- *Purple:* psychic ability, intuition, healing, third eye chakra, spirit
- *Blue:* creativity, emotion, communication, serenity, calm, throat chakra, water
- *Green:* money, wealth, luck, heart chakra, earth
- *Yellow:* morning, youth, happiness, new growth, new energy, the sun, taking action, solar plexus chakra, air
- *Orange:* boldness, celebration, adventure, fun, pleasure, joy, fearlessness, sacral chakra, fire
- *Red:* passion, romantic love, sexuality, assertiveness, self-confidence, bloodlines, root chakra, fire
- *Pink:* motherly and self love, healing, tenderness, gentleness, empathy, softness, femininity, heart chakra, water
- *Grey:* neutrality, muting, lowering intense energy, invisibility to blend in
- *Brown:* grounding, calming, safety, stability, earth
- *Black:* indomitable spirit, hexes, repelling, banishing, the new moon, determination, domination, power, protection, complete invisibility

Stones and Crystals

Besides color, I love using stones and crystals to set intention and attract certain energy. I can put a healing stone or crystal in my pocket on my way to the barn to reinforce my intention for the day, or bring one on a pendant to attach to Penn's tack. I hung a clear quartz crystal on one of his bridles, because it magnifies energy and intention, and symbolizes the crown chakra.

Do the stones actually attract attention and affect what happens? That's debatable. What's not debatable is that they remind you of your intention and help keep you on track. If it works, does it really matter why?

Chakras

Horses have chakras, just like humans. There is a locus for each, in essentially the same places, with the same whorls of energy, in the same colors, which is illustrated in figures 3 and 4. Just as in a human, when the chakras are aligned and spinning freely, all is well. When one is blocked, dull, or stuck, it expresses this in certain feelings or behaviors. Each chakra has a color, and each has a specific significance. For humans, the chakras are:

- *Root:* red, at the base of the torso: grounding, survival, security, bloodline
- *Sacral:* orange, above the pelvic line: sexual energy, passion, pleasure, creation
- *Solar Plexus:* yellow, at the bellybutton: courage, energy, strength
- *Heart:* green, between the breasts: love, compassion, empathy, kindness
- *Throat:* blue, mid-throat: clear, honest communication
- *Third Eye:* purple, middle of the forehead: intelligence, psychic abilities, intuition
- *Crown:* clear crystal, floating just above the head: divinity, deity, cosmic connection, enlightenment

While some view the crown chakra as lavender, I prefer the alternate representation of crystal clear, because I imagine the divine light of the universe passing through it and illuminating all the others in the bright colors of the rainbow, just as a prism does when hung in a sunny window, making rainbows dance around the room.

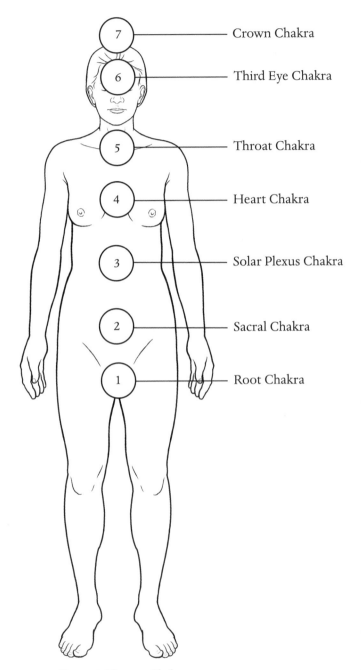

Figure 3: Human Chakras

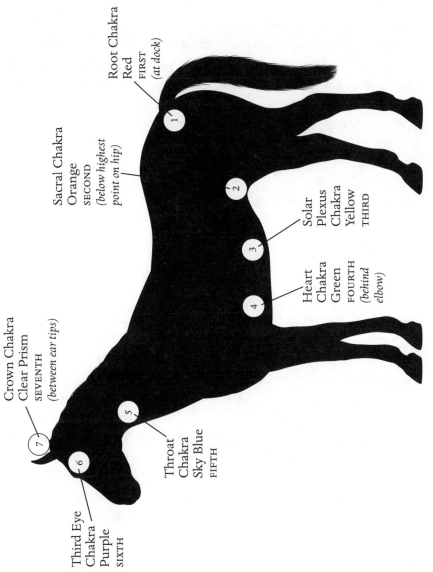

Figure 4: Horse Chakras

I learned a shorthand method for attuning with my own chakras at an Ec-static Living tantra retreat and reshaped it for my own meditative purposes, forming a mental chant of mantras.[32] I return to this anytime I need to calm myself, to reconnect body and mind, or to help me fall asleep. Beginning with the root chakra, I envision each one as bright orbs of color and energy at their respective locations, in and above my body. I inhale a long, slow breath into that chakra and gently exhale, as I say the following in my mind:

"I connect." (root)

"I create." (sacral)

"I take action." (solar plexus)

"I love." (heart)

"I communicate." (throat)

"I know." (third eye)

"I am." (crown)

After envisioning and connecting with all my chakras, I pull up "below" energy through my root chakra and up through the others with one breath, then pull "above" energy through my crown chakra and down through the others with one breath, imagining it illuminating each one.

Practice this until you really connect with the color and energy of those chakras, and notice that you feel calm and whole as you do it. Then, you can transfer this to attune with your horse's chakras, using the exact same mantras and steps. Do this in a quiet place, without typical barn hustle, bustle, noise, and chaos. All by yourselves works best.

Start by feeling your horse's chakras in each spot. It feels like a ball or dome of energy, or a pull. It feels like it's *right there*. When you feel confident about where they are, begin by placing your hands above or beside the root chakra, and start the same mantra chant: "I connect." Breathe up into your own chakra, and straight into your horse's, and exhale in reverse, back into the ground. Do this for each of the remaining chakras in the same way, and end by pulling energy from the earth through all the chakras, and then pulling energy from the universe through as well. Then place one hand on your horse's chest

32. Carter, "Chakra Wisdom Meditation."

and one on its hip, eyes closed, breathing slowly and peacefully. Rest there and connect to your horse's energy.

When you're all done, before removing your hands from your horse, tell it gently and respectfully, out loud, "Namaste," which means, "The divine in me honors the divine in you." If your horse is really relaxed and tuned in to you, you might finish by touching your third eye chakra to your horse's or place your palms flat together like in prayer, and touch your fingertips to your third eye and then your horse's. Again, say, "Namaste."

How does your horse look afterward? Penn always seems calm, still, and quiet. I'm betting yours will too, particularly after it learns to recognize this peaceful, special moment you two share.

Attuning with the chakras is a lot like Reiki. If you chase after it, it eludes you. The less you try, the easier it is. Relaxing and letting your mind go calm and clear is the key. You must be still, calm, and quiet to hear a butterfly whisper.

Namaste.

Chapter 11

HORSES AS HEALERS

Do humans heal horses or do horses heal humans? Both, actually. It's symbiotic. The bonding process is the fertile ground where love, insight, and change happen, whether it's a horse that hasn't had a very positive experience with people, or a person who's experienced the same. Together you bond, together you heal.

As you spend time with your horse, and see it blossoming and enjoying your company, you discover that you are innately doing the same, without even trying. Your time together becomes an ongoing exchange of serenity and support.

You start to realize that when you spend time with your horse, you just *feel* better. You further find that as you focus on your horse, your mind quietly starts working out its tangled issues on its own, like a computer program running in the background. New ideas or angles on your struggles start to emerge, as if floating up from the bottom of a pond to the surface.

Without even trying, healing happens.

Horses to the Rescue

Tim Hayes's book *Riding Home: The Power of Horses to Heal*, is a thoughtful, articulate exploration of the ways horses have become four-legged therapists for those grappling with all sorts of emotional and psychological challenges. From PTSD, to autism, depression, juvenile delinquency, or convicted criminals, Hayes says therapists are noting quantum leaps in improvement in their clients just from being near horses, or sitting on their backs and being quietly led around by a therapy assistant. Horses can break through barriers with distressed or challenged people where two-legged therapists, drugs, and institutionalization cannot.

Hayes explains that horses are completely pure. They are always genuine, they never lie, and they live completely in the present moment. They additionally do not judge, or speak in words, and can reflect the truth of a human's inner emotional state back to them. Horses are acutely aware of human body language and emotions, and will react accordingly. As the horses start reacting differently, the humans do too, and so begins the therapy process.

"Horses cause all of us to become better people, better parents, better partners, and better friends," says Hayes. "And this amazing ability of horses to heal by teaching us about ourselves is accessible to anyone."

Horses are once again the powerhouses for moving humanity, but this time for emotional, psychological, and spiritual transformation. In our very stressed, very isolating modern world, recent interest in horses is surging. In the frenetic perpetual whirl of commitments, confrontations, and tension in which most of us live, running from one thing to the next without taking a breath in between, we live our lives focused on the next thing we need to do rather than the thing we're actually doing.

If we do find ourselves momentarily unoccupied with someone or something demanding our attention, we immediately whip out our cellphones and stare into those addictive little screens with furrowed brows, frantically tapping away with our thumbs, absorbing a thousand percent more shock, grief, anger, and conflict via social media than humanity has ever before been exposed to. We are constantly bathed in cortisol because our sympathetic nervous systems are churning on full throttle, 24/7, and then wonder why we have all sorts of stress-related conditions and illnesses. We've completely lost our ability to feel grounded and present, and discover that we can regain it in the presence of horses.

Whew. Suddenly, we can exhale.

Life has become so unsettling that we crave the quiet, grounded power and strength of our oldest spiritual ally: horses. Horses are a port in our psychological storm. With horses, we're safe.

Whatever It Is, Horses Can Help

While many equine-assisted therapy programs focus on a particular physical, psychological, or social issue, we don't need to have one of those issues to feel stressed, unhappy, or unfulfilled. We want to change the trajectory of our lives—but how? We're aware of what we don't want, but not what we *do*. Just as horses did with transportation, working the land, and helping to build kingdoms, horses can be our partners in navigating and reshaping our internal world.

Horses can help. Notes Hayes, "Horses have supported and contributed to the survival of humans more than any other animal. And today, when war, addictions, shattered families, and technological advancements all conspire to depersonalize twenty-first-century humans, the horse yet again comes to our rescue."

Most pointedly, he adds, "The power of the horse will not be found by sitting on its back. It will be felt on the ground from its heart."[33]

Mirror, Mirror

In both Linda Kohanov's book *The Tao of Equus* and Tim Hayes's *Riding Home*, they emphasize how horses are genetically wired to mirror a person's emotional state, even when the person is trying mightily to conceal it, and will behave accordingly. Horses know when we're being deceptive, and they see right through us. If they detect internal and external incongruence, they're unlikely to cooperate, let alone obey. They're intrinsically gifted at reading human behavior and emotion and have done so for eons.

Incongruent behavior and emotion is unsettling to horses. Horses read a human's behavior and harmonize with it. If you're frightened, so is the horse. If you're calm, so is the horse. This is why horses act alarmed around people who are afraid of horses. Horses recognize fear instantly, and start searching the surroundings for predators. Then the person gets more nervous, so the horse gets more nervous, and round and round we go.

Beyond mirroring our feelings, horses have an uncanny ability to present our own issues to us. Remember that day Penn nearly trampled me in the pasture? It sparked an epiphany. I told Sarah afterward that Penn does to me what I allow far too many people to do to me. When they're being rude,

---

33. Hayes, *Riding Home: The Power of Horses to Heal*, 246.

disrespectful, insult me, or yell at me, rather than shut that down on the spot, I often just swallow my anger, and say nothing.

It's not that I'm afraid, or submissive even. It's that I've conflated being assertive with being mean. The more I care about someone, the more likely I am to shove my pain down and say nothing. I can't bear the thought of being mean to someone I care about. It's an erroneous connection I've made in my own mind. By being silent, I'm reinforcing bad behavior and allowing myself to be walked on. I'm essentially "Debra the doormat."

"I guess it's up to me to do start doing something about it," I told Sarah.

"Ya think?" she chuckled.

The experience accentuated that whether it was my horse or other people, if I didn't respect myself enough to assert my psychological boundaries, why would anyone else? I needed to learn to confront rude, hurtful comments appropriately and, more importantly, immediately, rather than mulling it over and realizing the next day that my feelings were hurt. By the time I'd recognize my feelings were hurt, it would be too late and I'd just let it slide, once again, reinforcing bad behavior and allowing it to continue. This was and continues to be one of the most difficult and frustrating stumbling blocks for me. Penn's pushy behavior, particularly that day in the pasture, snapped this into focus. It wasn't going to stop unless I put it to a stop. If he started being disrespectful, I didn't have the luxury of waiting until the next day to deal with it. It had to be dealt with immediately. My life might depend on that. What I needed to do with Penn, I needed to do with people.

Outside my personal life, I can put up a tough public front, but inside, I'm a mushball. It might fool people, but it won't fool a horse. Penn knew that when push came to shove—literally—he could invade my space any damn time he chose. He didn't view me as the leader; he viewed me as playing the role of a leader, and he was merely playing along most of the time because it served his purposes: carrots.

Penn held up a mirror that day, and forced me to look at the sack of psychological pus I'd been hauling around my whole life. Being an emotional doormat is something I learned growing up in an alcoholic and severely dysfunctional family. My old circumstances were infecting my current ones. When faced with loud, angry, rude, out-of-control people, my first impulse was to shut down and avoid the conflict. I may have managed to walk away from that confrontational situation and seem perfectly calm, but my heart was banging away against my ribcage like it wanted to break free. I'd learned in my childhood to keep my exterior completely calm and neutral, regardless of how my emotions were churning. That's a basic survival tool in an alcoholic family. Unfortunately, I'd continued using that tool long after childhood. Much longer.

Penn showed me that it was time to turn and face my own psychological dragons. Nobody was going to correct that dysfunctional behavior but me. That's some pretty heavy psychotherapy for an animal that doesn't even have a high school diploma, let alone a psychology degree.

Spending Time Together Is Where Healing Begins

Sometimes the flashes of insight don't happen as a result of a dramatic incident, like when Penn knocked me down. Sometimes insight slowly materializes when you're just spending time with your horse, seemingly doing nothing at all.

My most therapeutic time with Penn isn't trotting around in the arena on his back, or trying to work on a goal in the round pen, but having the entire back field to ourselves, the blue sky above us, gentle breeze tickling the lush, long wild grasses. We mosey up to the top of the hill, where we can see other horses grazing peacefully in the distance. Way up on "our" hill we're clear of the constant thrum of activity and loud, frenetic squawking of riding lessons in the arena. We're completely alone, together, with the whole world to ourselves.

Down the hill, the creek sparkles and burbles along its way, and an amazing array of birds flits about or soars in the sky, looking for their next meal: warbling red-winged blackbirds, robins, and small birds chirping and hopping about. It's so quiet there, you can hear bees buzzing on the little yellow and purple wildflowers that dot the hillside in the spring, and the drone of dragonfly wings as they hover nearby to consider you and what you're doing in their realm. All of these sights and sounds prompt me to relax. However, the loudest sound of all, the one that cues me to let it all go, is the sound of Penn tearing up mouthfuls of grass and chomping on it rhythmically, over and over.

Something about watching him graze is hypnotic. Whatever worries I had when I arrived at the barn drift away when we're out in the field, just grazing and doing nothing. The verbal chatter in my brain goes quiet, and I'm still and calm inside my own head. Sometimes I stretch my hands to the earth and feel my feet planted there; breathe in the sweet, fresh air; stretch the top of my head to the sky and feel the fire of the sun; and enjoy the sparkling, bobbling water rolling past in the creek. Together, we're one with nature, the elements, and with life. Penn and I are simultaneously the center of the universe itself, and a mere, miniscule fleck in the expanse of eternity. It is truly divine. I feel whole, I feel calm, I feel connected to the earth, the sky, the elements, and the universe, and my horse is the catalyst.

This is the miracle of having a plain old companion horse. Out on your own together is where healing happens, not slamming your boots into its side in an arena. You don't have to be riding or doing groundwork to gain new insight about yourself or your life or to start imagining change. In fact, you don't have to be doing anything at all, other than just being in the moment. People spend years in yoga, meditation, and other spiritual practices trying to achieve a state of calm, peaceful presence in the moment, and mastering the art of being here now. You can get there a lot faster by just spending quiet time with a horse. Once you stop trying so hard, you discover you're already doing it.

This Moment, Right Here, Right Now

Being in the moment. Be here now.

"What does that even mean?" you may be thinking. Maybe what you're thinking about right now, in this moment, is about everything that's worrying you, swirling in your head like leaves in a windstorm, and that's certainly not a comforting place to be at all. It's a location problem: you're not "here," you're in your head.

To get out of your head, toss out any thoughts that your horse would not be able to think about right then and there. Only allow in what your horse can see or sense. Make your brain mirror your horse's. There are no words or thoughts in that space. Your horse doesn't know who's running for president. It doesn't know about the mass shooting of the day. Your horse doesn't know that your boss is an asshole or that your aunt is dying of cancer or that the polar ice caps are melting. It doesn't know *any* of that, ever.

As you're standing there watching your horse graze, it is blissfully oblivious to all the things that cause humans stress and worry; prompt us to get into ridiculous, rancid squabbles on social media; and keep us awake in the middle of the night, staring at the ceiling and fretting. Your horse only knows that exact moment: the ground firm beneath its feet, breathing in and out, the taste of sweet fresh grass, the soothing touch of your hand on its neck, the sun warming its back. It feels content. Your horse is in that exact moment only, being here now.

When you're out grazing or leading your horse, only allow yourself to observe the same things it can: what you see, taste, hear, touch, and smell. Get out of your head and experience living from the neck down for a while. Just breathe. Feel your heartbeat slow down and your neck and shoulders relax. Just experience those sensations, right in that moment. Breathe into and out of your navel, just like you would during a meditation.

When you do this, you're giving yourself the gift of taking a break from your worries while you're with your horse. You really can let go of them for that little slice in time. I promise you, all of your concerns and problems will be right where you left them when you get back home. Maybe put a little "worry box" beside your front door, and as you head out to see your horse, "place" all those worries in that box. You can take them all back out when you return. Or not. You may decide, after getting all of that clatter out of your head, your perpetual anxiety isn't really doing anything other than frying your nervous system. Maybe you'll leave those things in your worry box forever. After learning to be calm and in the moment with your horse, and not mentally chewing so hard on your problems, you may discover that some solutions come drifting into focus.

Pia's Story

Spending time talking with Pia, a forty-two-year-old college outreach coordinator, you'd never suspect that this relaxed, gentle, soft-spoken woman had ever struggled with psychological issues.

"I was very much manic-depressive and not in good shape," she says, in a petal-soft German accent. "I was very nervous and didn't know what to do. I was unhappy, stressed out, and anxious."

One of our mutual friends, Rich (my horse whisperer pal), was listening to Pia talk about her feelings one day, and suggested she come spend some time with his horses. She did and found that being around horses calmed her. She took a liking to one of Rich's horses and discovered that she could calm down and focus—something she'd struggled with for a long while.

"With him, I felt centered again. I could breathe, and my anxiety went away."

Although Pia was benefiting immensely from her new relationship with this horse, something was standing in her way: that horse belonged to Rich.

"I needed to have a connection with an animal that is mine, my personal Pia Life-Saving Horse."

She set out to find that horse, and spotted one on Craigslist stabled right near her home. Because she had little horse experience, she asked Rich to go with her to see it. He agreed, but had one condition: the horse must be bombproof.

The horse was a fifteen-year-old gelding named Jango, who'd been retired from his cattle-cutting days. To test his bombproof-ness, Rich handled and rode the horse, doing everything wrong on purpose, just to see how Jango would react.

"He didn't even care," says Pia. She decided to test-ride Jango right there in the rolling hills, even though she was still a beginner, and immediately felt a connection. "I felt like he was going along and doing his thing. I felt safe—that this animal would keep me safe."

Rich was so impressed with Jango, he told Pia that if she didn't buy him, he would. It was one of those "orchestrated by the universe" relationships because Jango was the first, and last, horse Pia looked at. She bought him on the spot.

"When I met him, right away, we clicked. That look in his eye...I thought, 'You are kind of like me.' He has some spunk, but calmness and wisdom. And, my horse is wise. I want to be wise, and I want to learn from *him*."

Her new relationship with Jango started moving the pieces of her life. Rich continued giving her guidance, Pia took riding lessons, and was soon handling and riding Jango on her own. She began to cherish time with her horse, and discovered that it wasn't the riding she looked forward to—it was just being with him.

"I'll say I'm just going to go to see him for twenty minutes and it's always a two-hour visit."

Pia didn't really like the busy stable where Jango was boarded, so she moved him to a small, private ranch, continuing her riding lessons. Even though her skills were steadily improving, Pia discovered that she didn't have an urge to ride—only to be near Jango. A typical day means that Pia and Jango have "a nice long grooming session which he and I really enjoy." If she does ride, they usually just walk around in a round pen or arena.

"We do a lot of stopping and standing. He likes to stop and stand, and I just like to sit on him, even in the pasture grazing, on or off the lead. I sit on him sometimes, sometimes I just stand and watch him being calm and happy."

One of the first changes Pia noticed in herself after getting Jango was that she was learning how to slow down.

"Both me and my whole family, everything was always *go go go*, the calendar full of things and we still put more in. We grew up believing that you have to always be doing something, otherwise you're lazy. A horse is kind of lazy in a good way.

"Horses are huge, and they have an amazing big body on skinny legs, and they know how to move without collapsing or hurting themselves. They're slow-walking creatures, and I am a fast-paced person. I don't take the time to slow down and really look after what I need for myself, and to make sure I'm healthy. Seeing how he has to be so careful so he doesn't hurt himself makes me aware of how I should become more careful and considerate with my own body."

Pia says she was always in such a rush to get from one activity to the next, she'd actually bump into things and hurt herself. Before getting Jango, Pia was chronically tense and had back problems. After getting outside with her Jango, even though it didn't really feel like exercise, Pia started feeling better physically.

"I feel more mobile, walking with him, bending over, brushing him—I'm just moving more than I did before."

In slowing her life down, even with her full-time career, Pia admitted to herself that she liked doing some traditionally "housewifey" things, like cooking, cleaning, and gardening, that she never allowed herself the time to do. She decided to start doing those things, regardless of what others thought about it.

"I felt the societal pressure that I needed to have a successful career, and to focus all my energy on achieving this goal. Now, I take time for the things I like. It makes me happy."

Besides living her life at a more reasonable pace, Pia also learned to recognize when she's tired rather than just push through it as she had always done. She learned the value of "no."

"Now I can say no. No, I'm not going out for dinner. I have too much on my plate."

Discovering that she could put her own physical and mental health before the requests of others shed light on the dynamics of some of her friendships, and to experience people differently—more like a horse would.

For example, she brought someone to see Jango, and the person wanted to ride him. Pia explained that Jango liked a loose rein and a soft touch, but this person thought she knew more about horses than Pia did, and ignored her. She rode Jango with the reins tight, jerking on his mouth, and Jango reacted.

"My horse said, 'that's not okay,' and even though he is an extremely gentle horse that rarely complains, this time, he voiced his concerns in strong behavior."

For the first time ever, Pia saw Jango buck, and that made her think, "Why am I letting people do what's not healthy? I should buck!"

And she did. She began to "buck off" her unhealthy relationships.

"My horse helps me to distinguish between good energy and bad energy from people," she says.

She started distancing herself from those who gave off bad energy, and to recognize her own pattern of excusing certain behavior, like people judging or criticizing her, or saying she "wasn't a good friend" if she didn't want to participate in their plans. This criticism of her newfound assertiveness bothered her because she'd jump to help her friends when they were sick or needed something, but once they didn't need help anymore, she didn't hear from them again—until the next time they needed something.

"I'm a non-dominating person. I'm always trying to please everyone instead of saying and feeling what I really think, and with Jango, I'm slowly getting over that."

Pia further realized that she was attending lots of parties filled with people that she didn't really consider friends. With a new appreciation of her own wants and needs rather than putting everyone else's first, Pia started weeding out some "friends" from her life that didn't really act like true friends.

"Horses showed me it's important to select which people you spend time with."

How Did It Happen?

When asked exactly how or when her own emotional transformation occurred, Pia pauses, and struggles to articulate what happens out there during quiet time with Jango.

"Things that didn't make sense to me, a lot of emotions...he helps me sort that out. It's like meditation. Something is going on in my mind, I sit, and he is grazing, and at the end of our time, I realize, 'Wow, I got a lot of this emotion cleared.'"

She says her thoughts drift from her own problems and feelings to what Jango might like.

"While grazing, its a very primal thought, like 'where can he find the best grass.' Some days, it's all about him; some days, it's about my own thoughts. Either way, I'm happy."

If she's struggling with painful feelings, Pia says, "I have to hug and cuddle him a lot, and sometimes, I don't think consciously about it anymore. Whatever my problem or feeling was, it goes away and I have a clear mind afterward. Subconsciously, I process it."

She says she doesn't really speak to Jango to work her feelings out. It's a quiet, internal communication.

"I don't really talk. There are moments I talk, but not to tell him all my problems like I do with my dog. That's a different relationship. The dog looks at me like, 'I want to make you happy.' And I think, 'You are cuddly and sweet, but you're not helping me right now.' Jango says to me, 'Calm down, think about your problems the way I do about my own: not at all.'

"It's more constructive for me to learn not to get worked up, but rather, relax and take life step by step. I don't need to do anything with my horse. He's just there for me no matter what. I feel in general, that a dog or cat wants something. The horse is happy to see me, but if he doesn't see me for a day or two, he's still fine."

Even so, however, Pia says Jango is clearly pleased to see her coming.

"I call, 'Jango Mango Tango,' and he looks up, runs to me, and whinnies."

Their bond is unique to them; he is hers, and she is his.

"The other horses see me, but they don't react the same way toward me and I don't react the same to them. There is this special bond between Jango and me. It's like a marriage, but there's not a divorce option."

Confronting Fear and Anxiety

Before bringing Jango into her life, Pia hadn't been around horses since she was a teenager in Germany, growing up near a large piece of property with lots of horses that came and went. She rode them with a friend who knew how to ride, even though Pia says she didn't know anything about horses.

The girls would pick a horse, saddle it up, and, "jump on and walk peacefully through the countryside." However, she remembers them as "old, sick, mean horses," and sometimes she'd get bucked off. Getting thrown scared her, but overall, she still liked riding. What she didn't know at the time was the real reason their owner didn't care if she rode them.

"They were all headed for slaughter," she says, and felt horrible for those horses once she discovered their fate.

The memory of being bucked off gave her some anxiety when she first started spending time with Rich's horses, but he helped her work through that fear, and showed her that horses react to human behavior.

"Horses are scared of *us*. If we move fast, the horse moves fast away from us. But if you slow down and stand there, they are just happy."

She advises others who are fearful about horses to "spend time at a facility that offers horse therapy lessons. Meet horses that are already calm and gentle, and already have wonderful personalities and won't hurt you. They won't have negative behavior, and you can spend some time with them and see how it feels."

A New Direction

With a new recognition that she feels unfulfilled in her current career, Pia says she's interested in taking her education and experience in a different direction: a degree in equine-assisted therapy.

"I'm an educator by degree. I've worked with disabled people, and I have a mental health condition myself. Combining all of these facets with horses would be a perfect fit."

She believes the calming energy of therapy horses is the key for helping people with disabilities.

"It's stressful with disabled people, just to get through the day. But with horses, it's like time stands still. You see patients interacting with the horse, and see things in that person you hadn't noticed before."

Something Has Changed

After spending time with Jango and re-evaluating her life, Pia sees things she never noticed before. She recently went back to her childhood home in Germany and was stunned to discover that in all those years, despite riding horses at a nearby ranch as a youngster, she never noticed there was another horse boarding facility right by her childhood home. Being around her high-octane family again, she also noticed that she had changed—and they noticed too.

"I'm calm, so calm that everybody who knew me for years, even my own family, they notice I'm different."

When she felt stress building up during that visit, she knew what to do: find some horses.

"I took a walk to that place with horses. I was there for thirty years and never noticed it. Now I see horses, and I see that I need them when I'm overwhelmed."

As for those who are hesitating about getting a horse, Pia believes their apprehension comes from the perception that having a horse means riding a horse.

"You don't have to ride obsessively, you don't have to ride to be happy—neither the horse or you. It's a misconception. People see work and responsibilities, and feel pressure to ride, or that they need such a high level of skill to ride."

She says none of that is important. The only thing that matters is the relationship with the horse.

"It just changes everything in your life, if you let it. If you let it, a horse can change it all."

Horses Know Who Needs Help

Therapy horses are carefully selected for smooth, even temperaments and remaining calm regardless of human behavior. If a patient had a seizure near a horse, for example, you wouldn't want to use an easily startled horse near that person. Some horses are just born with an unflappable, unexcitable nature, and some aren't.

Take Penn, for example. His previous sheltered, limited life as a show horse, where he only experienced a small slice of the world, makes him fearful of anything unfamiliar. One day someone opened a patio umbrella near his paddock to paint the fence, and Penn reacted like a cougar was poised to eat him alive, tearing around and snorting, and searching for an escape (it materialized in the form of Mama, with halter in hand).

A different day, a throng of people was milling around at the barn, yacking and chatting. Among them was a young girl in a wheelchair. I was grooming Penn a ways off when she spotted him and started rolling in his direction. "Uh-oh," I thought "A human with built-in wheels will surely send Penn to the moon." Before I could cut this interaction off, there she was, right under his nose.

"Hi Penn," she said, holding up her hand to his nose, looking up at him joyfully. I prepared myself to grab that lead rope before he went rocketing backward, but he didn't.

Penn looked back at her, touched his nose to her hand, and slowly, gently dropped his head, placing his nose right in her lap, allowing her to pet his face and stroke his neck. He was as still and kind as an old golden retriever.

Knock.

Me.

Down.

With a feather.

My big old chicken horse knew when to freak out and when to be soft and patient. There it was—that mirror phenomenon again. Penn read the girl's gentle energy and returned it. He detected her helplessness and innocence, and accepted her affection and returned it. I learned Penn was quite capable of regulating his bossiness, and entirely more intuitive and empathetic than I'd thought. He reinforced this to me another day while I was practicing a technique I'd learned from GaWaNi Pony Boy.

On that day, I turned Penn loose in the arena and sat on the mounting block. He did his usual routine, rolling, shaking, and visiting. Meanwhile, I just sat there and stared at the ground about ten feet in front of me, avoiding eye contact. The purpose of this Pony Boy exercise was to stare in one spot and mentally direct your horse to go stand there. To be honest, I didn't really believe it would work, but I was trying it anyway.

Soon, I heard the *trudge trudge trudge* of Penn's hooves in the dirt, slowly approaching, stopping to watch me, and getting no reaction. He walked right up next to me. I just kept staring at the spot. Then, slowly, he walked around in front of me and stood *right where I was looking*. Holy crap! Still staring at the spot and joyfully absorbing this small miracle taking place, Penn did something I never expected: he walked behind me, and ever so gently, he placed his muzzle right against the back of my neck and just stood there, his warm, slow breath tickling my hair.

Get out that knock-me-down feather again.

Penn read my behavior as extremely odd. It concerned him, and he was clearly trying to comfort me. That's not his M.O.

Although Penn is a wonderful friend and clearly enjoys my company, he's not cuddly. If I hug his head or neck, he'll tolerate it for about two beats and then pull away. For whatever reason, he's uncomfortable with a human wrapping their arms around his head or neck. As much as I'd like to cuddle, I want him to respect my boundaries, so I have to respect his. However, that day in the arena, I stood up and stroked his neck, and told him what a good, kind boy he was, and ran one arm under his jaw and patted his check. Then, he leaned his head into my arm and let me hold it for a long while, as if telling me, "I know something's wrong, and I'm here for you."

What a golden moment. Penn revealed that he's far more perceptive than I'd given him credit for, and quite capable of *deciding* to step in and offer comfort when he chooses, when he observes that it's needed. Not only does he *know*, he *cares*.

Twelve Steps and Beyond

Tom, a former firefighter and fire chief, was in his sixties when he decided to have a gastric bypass to help tackle his lifelong struggle with weight. While the operation solved one problem, it created another: alcoholism. Because his body could no longer metabolize alcohol efficiently, far more of it made it into his bloodstream than would have without the bypass. It didn't take long before the alcoholism was out of control, and Tom sought professional help initially because "the concerns of family and friends were starting to be validated. Ultimately, it was literally to save my life."

Tom entered the traditional Alcoholics Anonymous Twelve Step program, but it wasn't enough to get him back on track. The years that followed were a parade of detox and rehabilitation programs, as well as moving into residential sober living programs. He fell off the wagon several times, but always climbed back on.

In the course of his treatment, Tom discovered equine-assisted therapy, which he said was "sprinkled into my travels." During this equine-assisted treatment, Tom discovered an affinity with his newfound, four-legged therapists. He didn't have any experience with horses, and says that the only thing he actually *knew* about horses was that he loved them. Finally, something really clicked for him in his search for healing, and with the horses themselves.

"I loved my first equine therapy session, my last, and every one in between. I started reading, watching, and asking questions."

Before long, others thought Tom was a natural with horses, but he didn't really see it that way, even to this day.

"More than a few people would say that I have a way with horses," he says, adding that while this may or may not be true, he consciously decided that he was going to learn to understand horses and develop relationships with them.

"I decided very early on that I would not be afraid of the horses, or timid with them, even to the point of saying to myself every so often that being killed in a horse mishap wouldn't be so bad."

Amongst the first things he did was simply to watch the horses in the program to try and improve his understanding of their behavior and emotions.

"I remembered that the original horse whisperer spent hours and hours simply watching. Horses are very perceptive, almost spiritual."

Tom also realized while he was watching the horses, they were also watching him and interpreting his own body language, almost as if reading his mind.

"I was leading a horse down an alley of traffic cones. I briefly looked left, almost imperceptibly. Dead stop."

Another time, there were about twelve therapy participants in an equine session. They were instructed to sit in chairs evenly spaced close to the rails for about ten minutes, and watch four horses and a mule wander around. Then, the participants were instructed to turn their chairs around, facing outward, and wait ten more minutes.

"The shrink says, 'Okay turn around.' WTF? I could not believe it. Not only were all the animals looking out through the gaps in the railing, they were evenly spaced with at least one human between them."

The therapist explained to the group that the first ten minutes "served to make the humans part of the herd. Naturally, when the four-leggeds saw what was happening, they wanted to see what those idiot new folks were looking at."

In that equine-assisted therapy program, Tom was given a partner to help him down his path to healing and sobriety.

"The big Belgian cross I was assigned to was perfect for me. In my first couple of days at the program, I jumped on Kojak and went to fetch the newspaper—bareback. Just a lead rope. I never rode bareback before. Just Kojak and me, while everybody else was still sleeping."

The flood of mixed feelings that followed delighted him.

"Somebody needs to invent a word that captures the joy and terror of something like that, that feeling of happy terror, wondering which bones you *will* break—not *if*."

Tom discovered that Kojak was always constant, present, and ready to spend time with him—unlike many of the people in his life.

"No matter what else was going on, I knew there was always a happy, calm, steady refuge for me with Kojak. Yes, there were a couple of times he could smell alcohol on my breath, but he never mentioned it."

At this point, Tom had suffered several relapses with alcohol, describing it as "lather-rinse-repeat, over and over again." In the equine-assisted therapy program, however, this time, something was different. Something in his recovery process finally broke free.

"The puzzle pieces were all on the table, and most of them in position. I don't know who placed them there or who to thank, except for Kojak. There is no doubt that I would not have stayed sober without him."

In the course of his "forward three steps, back two" battle to stay sober, finally Tom was moving forward. However, at this point, he'd become estranged from his friends, wife, children, and grandchildren, and he says the grief from that separation in the past would have been enough to make him reach for the bottle again.

"I would not have been able to keep going without K-man."

Now two years sober, Tom hasn't forgotten the role his equine therapist played in that accomplishment.

"It's said that every man should have one great dog and one great horse in his lifetime. I am on my second hand counting my great dogs, and I got a slice of a great horse."

Retrain Your Brain

What are *you* struggling with? PTSD? Grief? Anxiety? Midlife crisis? Just lost? Create a simple, positive statement for yourself that is directly counter to that feeling, such as, "Today, I will breathe when I feel stressed." Or, "Today, I will take note of every beautiful thing I see." Or, "Right now, in this moment, I am completely safe." Stick it in your "pocket," and whip it out whenever the negative thoughts start nipping away at your serenity and self-esteem, and say it, *out loud*.

I learned this cognitive therapy tool while seeing a therapist to deal with a flying phobia. Just thinking about flying would make panicky tears well up. On some level, bubbling somewhere beneath my chronic terror, I knew my fear of flying was limiting my life. There were so many places I wanted to go, and it was starting to sink in that my life would go by and I'd never see any of them unless I got on an airplane. Pushing the issue was the fact that I was about to fly across the country to visit my boyfriend (and future husband), who did the visiting up until that point because I wouldn't get on an airplane. It was time.

Whenever I thought about the upcoming flight and the panic started boiling, I said *out loud*, "Debra, you will have a safe and relaxing flight." My therapist explained that your brain hears and processes a statement differently if you say it out loud as opposed to only thinking it, and that your brain immediately pays attention to hearing your own name out loud, even if it's coming out of your own mouth.

As the day of the flight approached, I probably said that statement to myself thirty or forty times. When it came time to go to the airport, my positive statement was on an endless loop, and oh yeah, I still had to take Xanax to keep my feet moving one in front of the other up to the ticket window, through security, and onto the plane. However, without that cognitive therapy, an entire bottle of Xanax wouldn't even have gotten me to the airport.

We're going to borrow this cognitive therapy tool and take it to the barn. While walking and talking with your horse whenever you feel those negative thoughts simmering, say that positive statement out loud, beginning with your name: "Susan, you are completely safe and serene, and nothing will harm you here." This redirects your attention to that calming statement and the present peaceful moment, and your brain will start associating that calming, positive statement with being near your horse. This is another angle for finding that elusive "present moment."

You can even do this with your Elemental Horses. Instead of a verbal statement, call the image of whatever Elemental Horse you need into your mind, as vividly, clearly, and in as much detail as possible, and imagine it as a rubber stamp. Stamp its image right over your negative thoughts: canceled! Using an imagery strategy, rather than a verbal one, is a "right brain" tool, and it's much faster than words. You can see an image much more quickly than you can say a sentence.

When you're over in your left brain, thinking in words rather than pictures, and saying your positive statement out loud, the committee in your head has time to start objecting to that statement or contradict it or come up with an alternate plan. Committees suck, even the ones in your head. If you pop an image into your right brain, the cognitive correction is already in motion. Boom, canceled. There's no verbal activity in your right brain, so the committee—which lives in the left brain—isn't alerted to start resisting or tinkering with your idea. You see your Elemental Horse and you're restructuring your negative thoughts before your left brain has a chance to sabotage the whole plan.

Horses Keep You Healthy

In addition to assisting us psychologically and emotionally, horses heal us physically too. They make you stronger, healthier, and fitter. No, they don't trot you around the round pen like we do to them, but they do inspire you to make changes in how you view your own health and body.

You need physical strength to ride, and even to go out and about walking. You may discover when you first start riding or caring for a horse that you're really tired and sore. If you've never ridden, or it's been a long while since you rode, boy oh boy, will the insides of your thighs burn after that first time in the saddle. You use muscles while riding that you might not otherwise. You'll know which ones they are because they'll be screaming.

If your arms are out of shape, you'll find that all that brushing and grooming, lifting and carrying saddles, hauling fifty-pound sacks of feed, moving bales of hay, and mucking a stall or paddock might make them a little ouchy at first. But, before long, you won't notice it anymore. What you will notice is that you're suddenly feeling stronger without really trying. You might even shed a few pounds. I lost ten pounds within three months of getting Penn, just walking around, without making any other alteration in my diet or exercise.

As you start feeling stronger and healthier, you really start looking forward to your horse time, and feel cheated and disappointed if you can't have it. It starts to become the most important part of your day. Because it becomes so important, you quickly discover that some of your old habits are incompatible with your new passion.

I've been a party animal most of my life. I used to love sitting around with friends late into the evening, knocking back some wine, laughing too loud, and solving the world's problems. If I felt groggy and swimmy-headed the next morning, it didn't used to matter. A couple of Advils and a nap, and I'd be good to go by afternoon. However, after I got Penn, over-imbibing the night before meant I couldn't ride the next day, and didn't enjoy my time with Penn because I was achy and exhausted. Horses and hangovers don't mix.

I'd be out with friends and think, "If I keep drinking, I won't be able to ride in the morning." I'd ask myself if it was worth it. The answer was always no. No wine tastes as good as riding a horse feels. Similar to how I'd lost ten pounds without trying, my alcohol intake dropped to nearly nothing. I never missed it. Drinking less resulted in sleeping better, which in turn boosted my energy. My brain felt bright and clear every morning, and I began to cherish that feeling. Sometimes, I can't wait to go to bed so I can hurry up and get to morning and go spend time with Penn.

Better Than a Gym

When I started walking Penn up the hill in the pasture, by the time we'd get to the top, I'd be panting like an overheated hound dog, and he wouldn't be phased in the least. With Penn as my pace car, I was getting some serious cardio workouts. Rather than aimlessly pounding away on a Stairmaster,

I dropped my gym membership and Penn became my personal trainer. The choice between mindless plodding away at the gym or getting out in the fresh air with my horse was a no-brainer.

I also realized early on that I needed to improve my flexibility. Getting on a tall horse wearing a saddle and thick saddle pads felt like trying to do the splits. I wanted to be able to clear that saddle without dragging my boot over Penn's rump. To loosen and strengthen my hips, I'd stand while holding on to the back of a chair and swing my legs straight up sideways, and step up and down on a step or curb to strengthen my thighs and knees. Now I can clear that saddle in both directions, and Penn doesn't have to roll his eyes at my clumsiness anymore.

While we're out grazing, sometimes I do squats to improve thigh, knee, and lower back strength, bent knee lifts to increase core strength—also important in the saddle—and some Tae Bo punches to improve arm strength, which are, ironically, done in the "Horse Position": feet farther apart than your shoulders, toes out, and knees bent to a forty-five-degree angle, forcing your inner thighs to really work while you're punching. Penn wasn't a fan of martial arts happening at the end of his lead rope at first, but eventually he got used to it.

When I turn Penn out in the arena, I do a little yoga, because flexibility helps prevent injuries on the ground and in the saddle. While I do my little routine, Penn stares at me and wonders what sort of nonsense I'm up to. In the saddle, I do some twists using the pommel and cantle for added leverage, and stretch my hands toward my toes, lock them out in front of me to loosen my back, and then lock them behind me to release my sternum and chest.

Riding itself strengthens your legs, butt, back, core, and arms. Even in a Western saddle, I do a little posting—moving up and down in the saddle in time with the horse's trot—and that's a thigh-burner. At least I don't have to do it like we did back in my jumping days—without stirrups, and round and round the arena until there were tears in our eyes because it burned so bad. We all had thighs of steel, even when we were twelve.

The human body evolved to move. It feels *good* to move, and as you discover this, you also discover that spending a lot of time sitting *hurts*. It's not starting an exercise program that causes pain—it's the sitting.

When you move around and improve your muscle tone and strength, as well as get your heart and lungs working a little harder, you feel better overall.

Sometimes physical activity is a shortcut to feeling better mentally. Getting outside with your horse and moving your body can kick-start the process of feeling better emotionally, particularly when you're drinking less, getting more sleep, becoming more aware of how you feel physically, and realizing what promotes that and what doesn't. Horses make you healthy, mentally *and* physically. They really do.[34]

Loosen Up

Horses aren't only psychological therapists—they're physical therapists too. Horseback riding loosens the spine and strengthens your back at the same time. The next time you're riding—particularly bareback—concentrate on releasing all the tension in your lower back and waist. Walk slowly, feeling the movement of your horse's back muscles under your seat bones, and let those muscles move your body. The long muscles running on either side of the horse's spine aren't for holding up its belly. They're for back and forth movement while walking. Sink into your seat and let yourself sway with the horse's gait. This is such a relief if you have lower back pain. You can feel the vertebrae being released by the movement of the horse. You're experiencing the flowing, smooth gait of Water Horse, as well as fresh energy flowing through your spine.

Since I returned to riding, I haven't had lower back pain once. It seems counterintuitive, but it's true: riding a horse is great for your lower back. You start using your core muscles rather than your back muscles to keep your body straight and balanced, and your lower back finally gets a break.

Of course, not all back conditions, such as a herniated disk or severe osteoporosis, are improved by horseback riding and may even be aggravated by it. I just had plain old garden-variety lower back pain from simple overuse and lack of core strength. If you have back issues, check with your doctor before riding and get the all-clear first.

What a Horse Really Wants

Sarah asked me one day, "What do you think a horse really wants?"

I immediately ticked off all the things horses need and appreciate: a safe place to live, room to run, plenty to eat, fresh water, love and care, and an abundance of carrots.

---

34. Conrad,"The Top 15 Benefits of Horseback Riding."

"Nope," she countered. "They just want to get through their day."

This simple concept was so profound: unlike humans, horses don't have an agenda. A horse has no need to accomplish anything or learn a lesson, nor a desire to gallop over an eventing course or drag heavy loads around, prance along in a parade, chase after cows, or any of the other crazy things humans ask horses to do. A horse may do all of these things willingly, but it's not anything it actually *wants*.

Getting through their day means staying safe from predators, grazing as long as they like, finding fresh water, the company of friends, grooming and being groomed. Grazing, gazing, and grooming, that's it. Those are the simple needs of a horse, not expensive bridles and blankets, or weekends at horse shows chasing ribbons and trophies that humans covet and horses don't give two shits about.

Just getting through their day is all about being in the present moment; horses just want to be here now. They know how to do this innately. We humans have become so far removed from our natural selves that we now have to learn how to calm down our monkey brains.

When we go out walking and wandering with our horses, being with each other and in the moment, we're experiencing "just getting through our day." Our horses are teaching us possibly the most important lesson of all: how to actually experience the moments of our lives, as they're happening. We have to *learn* to do what comes naturally to a horse. Luckily, they're excellent teachers.

Chapter 12

SAYING GOODBYE

Just after bringing Penn into my life, Sarah said to me one day, "You realize you're taking him for *the rest of his life*, right?" It pinched, because although I'd assumed so in some general sense, I hadn't really thought about that in its inevitable finiteness. Penn is an old boy already and although he's in great shape, I know he won't live forever. However long that may be, it won't be long enough.

It's difficult to fathom the depth of emotion that wells up when you say goodbye for the last time, and your horse passes over that Rainbow Bridge. I've seen horses dying, one that even passed right under my hands, and I've seen the broken hearts of their loving owners. It's agony. The depth of our grief is a measure of the breadth of our love.

The final goodbye can come for any horse owner, sometimes quite unexpectedly, at any time, and the best we can do is support each other because someday, it will be our turn to need that support. It's far better to be aware of this part of your horse's journey than it is to be caught emotionally unprepared. It's a fantasy to believe that all horses will just live out their days and then fall asleep one morning in the sunshine and drift happily away to Horsey Heaven.

You can never predict how long a horse will live. Old age is only one factor in a horse's longevity. Horses almost never die from simple old age, or on their own. They don't just go to sleep and not wake up; that's a rarity. Almost always, there's human intervention involved. Euthanasia becomes a better option than allowing a horse to continue suffering. It can be anything from a broken leg to a septic infection to colic, and these things can happen to a horse regardless of age. You never know when you'll have no other choice than to make "that call" to your vet.

How Old Can Horses Get?

Horses live, on the average, about twenty-five to thirty years. A rare few make it as far as forty. The official calculation is that horse years are the equivalent of six and a half in human years, which makes no sense to me, because that would mean all those thirty-year-old horses out there are one hundred eighty years old in human years. What makes sense to me is that one year to a horse is three to a human, making a thirty-year-old horse equal to a ninety-year-old human. Horses that see their fortieth birthday would be one hundred twenty years old in human years. There are only a few humans that have reached that mark, and about as few horses.

Penn is now twenty-two; however, the vet suspects he may be closer to twenty-five or twenty-six, based upon the appearance of his teeth. When Penn's innocent owner purchased him, he was "nineteen, but his papers were lost," so when I took him, I wasn't really sure of his age. Remember that classic old horse trader scam? I'll be lucky to have ten more years with my beloved companion, and I can't take any of them for granted.

After riding or walking with Penn, or just grooming and bonding at the hitching post, when I return him to his paddock, I stroke his neck, and tell him how much I love and appreciate him. He always points his ears forward and his eyes sparkle. He *knows* he's loved. Your horse should know this every day because the future is more of a wish than a guarantee.

Despite his age, Penn is bright and alert and reasonably healthy, but the hair on his face is slowly greying like an old dog's. Time marches on, oblivious to life and death, or our feelings about it. Someday, I'll be the one needing comfort from my stable sisters.

Hard Choices

Why am I bringing up depressing topics again? Because just as it wouldn't be honest to allow you to believe that all horses are completely safe all the time, it also wouldn't be honest not to forewarn you that a horse's life may be cut short without warning. It's part of the gig. An untreatable injury or colic can happen quickly and you may *have* to do the unimaginable: choose to end your horse's life, imminently.

Colic is the scourge of the horse world, along with accidents and laminitis, which is untreatable inflammation in the foot, causing the rotation of the coffin bone within the hoof.[35] Also called "foundering," the horse can no longer support its own weight and must be put down. While laminitis is a common worry for horse owners, colic is the word that strikes fear in every owner's heart.

In one recent summer, two otherwise healthy mares were stricken with colic and were put down at the barn where Penn lives. Injuries are another unpredictable twist on the road. That same year, a beautiful three-year-old filly was kicked so severely by another horse that part of her hock bone was torn off. The veterinarian said there was no hope for recovery, and she had to be euthanized. She was a purebred Trakehner, worth about $30,000. Gone, with the prick of a needle.

To see such big, strong animals suddenly wracked with agony, struggling to stay alive, whether from illness or injury, causes such cognitive dissonance. We think our horses are our huge heroes and can do anything, but some things are too difficult to defeat, even for a horse, or a hero.

A horse's hard-wired herd instinct compels it to fight to the very last breath to survive, unlike other animals—dogs for example—that may curl into a ball, whimpering. Horses know instinctively that showing pain, weakness, or helplessness increases the probability of being caught by a predator. This is what fuels a horse's stoic nature. A horse will push through pain and discomfort to obey us, because it's hardwired to know that giving in to pain and letting it show could be fatal. When it comes to severe colic, however, eventually the pain overwhelms the horse, and it goes down. There can come a point with colic when all the options dissipate except one.

Euthanizing an animal is devastating. However, relatively speaking, it's not as cruel as what would happen to them in the wild. Out in nature, a severely sick or weakened animal's end would be far more brutal. Sometimes euthanizing our beloved animals is the kindest, most humane thing we can do, and preferable to extending their suffering because we can't bear to say goodbye.

---

35. Walker, "The Big Four: The Most Common Causes of Equine Fatalities."

When we deny an animal a quick and humane death because of our own feelings, we're making decisions based upon what we want rather than what the animal needs.

I learned this with my own beloved cat, Angelo, who was in the final stages of polycystic kidney disease. I couldn't bear to put him down, but I couldn't stand to see him suffer either. I asked the vet how to decide when to euthanize an animal.

"When an animal spends more of its life suffering than enjoying it, it's time," he replied softly.

It was time.

End-of-life decisions taught me a lot about the definition of compassion. A decision must be made, and it must be made right *now*. Particularly when it comes to horses. There's no cuddling them, putting them to bed, and hoping for the best the next day. With severe injuries and colic, your moments together are finite, and ticking away rapidly. One day everything is fine, and the next, you're calling the vet for the last time.

When It's Time

Besides the agony of deciding to end your horse's life, what happens next? You can't just bury it in the backyard, unless your backyard is a hundred acres. Cremation is expensive, and that's if you can even find a place that will cremate a horse. The usual step is to call the rendering plant, which sends out a high-walled truck to remove the body and take it to a rendering plant. I've seen the truck come for horse carcasses, and the really eerie part is that the other horses somehow know what the rendering truck is. When it arrives, they all get agitated. They *know*. I don't know how, but I've seen it with my own eyes. When the rendering plant truck comes rumbling up, the horses get uncomfortable.

If only we all had enough property and space to dig a huge hole with a backhoe and place our horses back into the earth, to let them return to the ground in a natural way. I've also liked the idea of having an open prairie where I could place my horse's body under a tree and let the weather and scavengers do what they do to recycle the biological shell naturally. That would be my first choice. But, I have neither the property, nor the equipment, nor the wide-open spaces.

I would like to think that when the time comes, I could have Penn cremated and turn the treasure-chest sized box into a coffee table or something, but I fear that his last ride may be on the high-walled truck as the other horses whinny and worry. The cost of cremation or taxidermy can run in the thousands, and in either case, you also have to pay to have the carcass transported, just as you will have to pay for the rendering plant to come pick it up. How much exactly depends upon where you live and the proximity to the places that perform those services.[36]

I was talking about this with Sarah one day, determined that I would have Penn cremated when the time came. She discouraged me from that, and said, "Why spend all that money on Penn when he's gone? He's not there anymore. Why not spend that money on a new horse that needs you?"

Fair enough. I guess none of us knows what we'll do until the time comes.

Crossing the Rainbow Bridge

Many people, Pagans and non-Pagans alike, believe in the Rainbow Bridge, over which our beloved animals cross when leaving this world for good to go to the afterlife. The origins of the Rainbow Bridge story aren't certain, but most originate from a familiar story of unknown authorship:

"Just this side of heaven is a place called Rainbow Bridge. When an animal dies that has been especially close to someone here, that pet goes to Rainbow Bridge. There are meadows and hills for all of our special friends so they can run and play together. There is plenty of food, water and sunshine, and our friends are warm and comfortable.

"All the animals who had been ill and old are restored to health and vigor. Those who were hurt or maimed are made whole and strong again, just as we remember them in our dreams of days and times gone by. The animals are happy and content, except for one small thing; they each miss someone very special to them, who had to be left behind.

"They all run and play together, but the day comes when one suddenly stops and looks into the distance. His bright eyes are intent. His eager body quivers. Suddenly he begins to run from the group, flying over the green grass, his legs carrying him faster and faster.

---

36. Equine Rescue Network, "Rendering Horses Versus Slaughtering Horses."

"You have been spotted, and when you and your special friend finally meet, you cling together in joyous reunion, never to be parted again. The happy kisses rain upon your face; your hands again caress the beloved head, and you look once more into the trusting eyes of your pet, so long gone from your life but never absent from your heart.

"Then you cross Rainbow Bridge together ..."

—AUTHOR UNKNOWN

If you can read that without crying, you're a tougher bird than me.

When horses die, many horse owners crop off the ends of their tails of their beloved partners, just below the tailbone, binding it together to keep as is, or to be woven into a bracelet or band in loving memory of that horse. That's how you can spot the horses that were truly loved as they gallop over that Rainbow Bridge—their tails are cropped. It's my wish that someday, all the horses that cross the Rainbow Bridge will have cropped tails.

Honoring Your Horse

After losing your horse, you're left with a tail swatch, an aching hole in your heart, and an empty halter hanging on the wall. Grief for a horse is real, and it's agony. Processing grief for a beloved animal is just as necessary as processing grief over a human. While sadness and grief linger, you can soothe your aching soul by creating an altar just for your horse, an album of photos you keep on the coffee table, or have a favorite photo of it framed for your wall or dresser. On an altar for your horse, you can place its photo next to a rose quartz crystal representing your love for it, but also healing self-love for yourself during this difficult time. Whatever symbol feels loving and soothing, place it there. Maybe even that mojo bag or tail tip you created before. Put images or representations of all of the Elemental Horses around the altar for your horse, because it lives with them now, and has become part of their herd.

You can also hold a memorial service at your home or at the barn complete with photos and poetry, songs if you like, and a gathering of people who knew your horse. Don't feel ashamed about being torn to pieces over losing your horse. It's heart-crushing. They had been your beloved soul mate, best friend, and healer. Love is real, and so is grief.

I conducted a service for a friend's horse that died abruptly from colic. I wrote some heartfelt words about the horse and in front of a poster board display of some beautiful photos of her horse, we shared fond memories. I also read the Rainbow Bridge story, choking on tears. I was unable to read, let alone recite, the goodbye poems I'd found, but if you find you need to plan a memorial, here they are:

- *Don't Cry for the Horses* by Brenda Riley-Seymore
- *When It's Time to Say Goodbye* by Caddie Dufurrena
- *Beyond the Rainbow* by Cate Guyan

Feel the Grief and Do It Anyway

Grief is a splinter. It has to work its way out, and until it does, it hurts like hell. You have to experience grief, but you can't allow yourself to get trapped there. You've learned to "feel the fear and do it anyway" with your horse, and now you must "feel the grief and do it anyway."

The best way to honor the life of your wonderful horse is to take all the lessons you've learned—the love, kindness, compassion, and wisdom it taught you—and pour them into another horse so that it can be loved and have a kind and loving life. Take the love for your horse and in its memory, pay it forward. Don't let all that your horse taught you go to waste.

Remember all those horses we talked about that are desperate for a second chance at life, a last-minute rescue before facing a gruesome death? They're still out there. It's a conveyor belt of death that never stops. Transform your grief into love and compassion, and funnel it toward another horse that desperately needs you, and who has lessons of its own for you—beginning with helping you work through your grief. You'll get through this tough time, you and your new equine companion, just walking and talking, side by side.

CONCLUSION

Horses are the miraculous culmination of eons of evolution that shaped them into creatures capable of surviving each and every challenge presented to them along the evolutionary way. Their unique talents and qualities altered the course of human culture and existence. They are capable of manifesting that tectonic change on the macro and micro level, from cultural to individual.

That horse standing next to you carries the DNA of those horses that frolicked on the walls of Paleolithic caves and outfoxed all those predators, including humans, to become the magnificent, miraculous creature it is today. Take a moment to consider what evolution has created, right before your eyes, and feel honored to be in your horse's presence. At the end of that lead rope stands time and survival itself.

Horses should be like other prey animals and flee from us, but they don't. They're certainly swift and powerful enough to escape, or overpower us; however, they *choose* to remain at our side, perform whatever we ask of them, and bond with us on a spiritual level. Their physical actions are huge, but their communication is quiet and subtle, and easily overlooked by those who don't, or won't, take the time to understand and appreciate the inner world of our four-legged spiritual partner.

Welcoming Horse into my life and working with horses in a new, natural, and compassionate way that honors them as sensitive, spiritual creatures brought all the disparate veins of my life to the place where they all connect: the heart. Horse. My heart. My center. My life is different because of horses, and Horse. When I reconnected with horses, I reconnected with myself.

Many spirit animals attract energy, insight, and healing into your life, but they're presented as gifts. Horse also has gifts, but requires that *you* put them to use. You can't just go along for the ride. You must participate in your own change and healing. In other words, Horse doesn't merely heal you—it empowers you.

Essential Reading

These four books will enhance your understanding of the amazing spiritual connections between horses and humans:

- *Zen Mind, Zen Horse: The Science and Spirituality of Working with Horses* by Allan J. Hamilton: Hamilton approaches horsemanship from an Eastern perspective, applying *chi*, which is energy that flows all around us. His book focuses on groundwork rather than riding.

- *Horse, Follow Closely: Native American Horsemanship* by GaWaNi Pony Boy: Pony Boy shows how Native Americans bond with their horses before doing anything else. He offers a variety of methods, and his insight into horses and becoming more sensitive to the natural world is spiritual and inspirational.

- *Riding Home: The Power of Horses to Heal* by Tim Hayes: This book reveals how sensitive horses are to human energy and body language, and how they pay far more attention to that than words. One of my very favorite concepts is that "a horse is honest all the time." They don't lie, cheat, or deceive, and don't pretend or put on facades. They are what they are, all the time, and will teach us know-it-all humans about the true meaning of genuineness.

- *The Tao of Equus: A Woman's Journey of Healing and Transformation Through the Way of the Horse* by Linda Kohanov: This book revolves around Kohanov's experiences after her horse was injured on the trail and could never be ridden again. By just spending time with that horse, Kohanov discovers a whole realm of equine spirituality, as well as a new career: equine-assisted therapy. She gained insight and wisdom from her horse because she *didn't* ride it—further proof that the real magic happens on the ground.

EPILOGUE

I've battled anxiety my entire life and eventually discovered that fighting it wasn't the solution, letting go of it was. I didn't learn that in therapy, in support groups, or with self-help books. I learned it from a horse. I'd thought Penn was a rescue horse, but it turned out, I was a rescue human. It wasn't him that needed saving, it was me.

My horse accepts me exactly as I am. He doesn't know that my hair is silver or that I need to lose twenty pounds or that my clothes look lame. He only sees *me*. He's happy whenever he sees me coming, just as I am, without criticism or judgment. He is a fount of unconditional love and acceptance.

Out grazing with Penn, one present moment after the other slides by, and I don't realize it until I notice the angle of the sunlight changing and the shadows lengthening. Two hours will feel like fifteen minutes; time disappears. In the unhurried presence of my horse, the ever-churning hamster wheel in my head rolls to a stop. I stop obsessively gnawing on my problems, and when the mental static and clatter dissipates, I can finally hear whispers of *"Do this instead."*

When I first got Penn, I was more than two decades into a soul-crushing job as a small town community newspaper editor, where I accepted verbal abuse, insults, and belittling as normal, and stifled my anger or hurt. Growing up in an alcoholic household, I was a master at stifling my feelings, which made me exquisitely prepared for this environment. Out of necessity, I learned to verbally punch back, but that wasn't my true nature.

I stayed with that job for twenty-six years despite meager wages because it was abundantly stable. Stability is crack to an adult child of an alcoholic. When you grow up in constant chaos and dysfunction, anything that resembles stability or normalcy is irresistible. The trouble is, when you grow up in an alcoholic family, you have no template for understanding what stable and normal are, or what they look like. That's how I ended up in my first marriage—the package looked different, but the contents were the same: alcoholism and emotional abuse.

By the time I was nearer to sixty than fifty, my kids were grown and on their own, I'd upgraded to Husband 2.0, and with all the dust settled, I could still see the one thing in my life that was an ongoing source of dissatisfaction: my dead-end job. I started looking for a new one, and discovered that ageism is a thing. Nobody wanted an old person when fresh, young applicants were a dime a dozen. All the lines I cast came back empty. I'd stayed in place far too long. My ship, as they say, had sailed.

I realized far too late that I'd chosen the wrong career path, so I convinced myself that I was only working to support Penn. That made it okay, most of the time. But out there on our grassy hill, my churning discontent would occasionally whisper, *"You deserve better. You are better than you're able to be in this job. You must move on."*

It was absolutely true, but I couldn't see any options. I was too old to get a new job and too young to retire. Even so, the universe was poking me to move on. I could feel it. But to where? Just quit? That option made my anxiety start simmering again. I was entirely uncomfortable with the idea of letting my husband support me like some helpless 1950s housewife. I needed my own income. I had a horse to support.

My old pal, anxiety, was always ready to strap me into the safety seat and keep me firmly in place, in a car with no wheels.

The funny thing about the universe, however, is if you keep ignoring it, sometimes it just shrugs and gives up on you, taking opportunity with it. Other times, it grabs you by your belt and the back of your collar and heaves you out the door. I got the heave-ho.

When a new publisher bought the newspaper, it became immediately evident that we didn't click. There's no hope of winning a war when your opponent owns the battlefield. The only way to win in that situation was to leave. I'd finally arrived at the same place with my job that I did in my first marriage—the only thing more terrifying than the thought of leaving was the thought of staying.

Just before my fifty-ninth birthday, I walked out of that office for the last time and never looked back. I focused on my massage practice and indulged in spending a lot more time with Penn, wandering the hillsides. Although I felt adrift, I was starting to enjoy this peaceful life of massage and horses.

Months rolled by, and one sunny afternoon out on our grassy hillside, I realized that I hadn't had any anxiety in weeks. Perpetual worry wasn't simmering on the back burner in my head 24/7 for the first time in my life. I liked it. A lot. However, I still felt like I needed to accomplish something. I just didn't feel "done" yet.

One morning, as I watched Penn graze, wondering where my life was drifting to, I flashed back to that lunchtime conversation with my friend Lyndsay, and her insistence that Penn appeared in my life because I was supposed to write a book about horses. Suddenly, it was clear: not a book about horses per se, but about their healing energy and spirituality; love, trust, lifelong learning and stretching past your comfort zone; finding your genuine self, feeling the fear and doing it anyway; and learning to *be*! I thought about how I was a million miles beyond the psychological minefield where I used to dwell, and it was all because of this big old red horse munching away at my side! I thought to myself, "*Write about that, for Goddess's sake! Write about the power of Horse, because you've lived it!*"

I thought about all the people who are hurting or lost, and feel alone in a crowd, searching for something but not knowing what it is, juxtaposed with the overabundance of unwanted, "useless" horses languishing in pastures or being marched to their death in droves, and I knew I needed to connect those dots. There's hope for the people *and* the horses. In rescuing horses, we rescue ourselves. By welcoming and embracing Horse, we reclaim our lives.

The Proof

Following the realization that I needed to write a book, a kaleidoscope of ideas tumbled in my mind, from the elements to bonding with horses, to embracing change. I started organizing it in my head, but didn't start writing. I didn't want to write a book and then discover no one wanted to publish it. It would be too heartbreaking. However, I did pitch the concept at an author's pitch event in 2018 at PantheaCon, an annual Pagan convention held in San Jose, California each February (the last convention was held in 2020). Honestly, it was a wimpy pitch because I was still in the process of sorting my post-journalism self out, didn't present a solid idea, and it went nowhere. Why would anyone believe in me when I still didn't quite believe in myself?

A couple months later, I was telling a friend and fellow author about my book pitch earlier that year and how it didn't go so well, and he adamantly told me not to give up. He encouraged me to go back to PantheaCon in the spring and try one more time.

"Don't give up," he insisted. "Try again."

I had nothing to lose, so why not.

When I'd pitched before, I didn't prepare anything. I just had a loose little conversation and a handshake, and that's about it. This time, I arrived completely prepared, and gave my earnest five-minute pitch to one of Llewellyn Publications' representatives, Heather. She listened and said she'd get back to me.

I thought, *"Yeah, right. Just like all those jobs I applied for. Oh well, at least I tried."*

But Heather *did* get back to me.

A month or so later, she contacted me and said Llewellyn was giving me a chance. I nearly went into orbit. She asked me if I could be finished by their upcoming deadline, June 1—about two months away at that point. Could I be done by then?

"Sure, I can!" I replied, bubbling over with positivity and enthusiasm, despite not having written one word yet.

Writing an entire book from scratch in two months is insanity. Nobody writes a book in two months. But I was certain I could. Why? Because of Horse.

This entire book was carried by one Elemental Horse after another. I employed every mental image and strategy, mantra, altar, color, stone, and then some to draw Horse into this process. I didn't just *write* about these Horse concepts and practices. I actually *did* them while creating this book. I called upon Horse to do for me what it has done for humans throughout history: carry me forward to do the impossible. The first draft of this book was completed right on time, in two months.

Horse did not fail me. And will not fail you. This book you hold in your hands is physical evidence. Horse exists; this book is proof.

GLOSSARY

Bald: a very wide blaze extending to or past the eyes

Barrel: the ribcage

Billet: a strap on a saddle that secures a cinch or girth

Bit: metal piece inside the horse's mouth, attached to the headstall and reins on a bridle

Blaze: a white stripe down the middle of the face of varying length and width; more narrow blazes are called stripes or strips

Bridle: headgear used for riding, usually holding a metal bit

Broodmare: mare used for breeding

Buck: kicking out of back legs or propelling upward from all four legs

Canter: three-beat gate between trot and gallop, with at least one foot on the ground within one stride; also called a "lope" in Western-style riding

Cantle: raised area on the back of a saddle, forming the seat

Cast: legs stuck against a stall wall or fence, preventing a horse from getting up

Coldblood: heavy, large draft breeds such as Clydesdales and Shires, typically used for pulling

Colic: severe abdominal distress that can be fatal without immediate veterinary care

Colicking: the process of going through colic

Colt: unaltered male horse up to four years of age

Cowkick: kicking forward or sideways with the back legs

Crest: top line of the neck; top of the curved neck

Cribbing: when a horse grasps a pole, fence, or stall door with its mouth and sucks in air

Croup: area of the spine in the highest part of the hindquarters at the lumbosacral joint

Dock: where the tail begins on the spine

Docking: the amputation of part of the tailbone, particularly amongst carriage and draft horses

Donkey: a separate species in the same evolutionary family as the horse, also called an ass

Dressage: highly skilled discipline requiring communication between horse and rider with the goal of mastering predetermined ballet-like movements, often exhibited in competitions and at the Olympics

Elbow: joint on front leg above the knee, just below the shoulder

Escalating: when a horse becomes increasingly excited and fearful

Eventing: equestrian competition involving three disciplines within one event: dressage, cross-country jumping, and show jumping

Farrier: one who trims hooves and/or shoes horses, with expertise in hoof care

Feathers: long hair on the lower legs, often found on draft horses

Fetlock: joint above the pastern

Filly: female horse up to four years of age

Foal: horse of either sex from birth to one year of age

Forelock: the part of the mane beginning at the poll—a spot between the ears—and falling forward over the face

Founder: chronic painful inflammation inside the hoof

Frog: a spongy, V-shaped area on the bottom and back of the hoof

Gallop: a four-beat gate at top speed, with all four feet off the ground in one stride

Gelding: castrated male horse

Girth/Cinch: strap that secures a saddle around a horse's belly; girth in English riding, cinch in Western riding

Grade horse: unregistered or mixed breed, or of unknown breeding

Groundwork: a variety of non-riding activities and lessons done while leading or in a round pen

Hackamore/Bosal: bridle without a bit

Halter: headgear used for non-riding needs, such as leading or tying

Hand: four-inch increment used for measuring a horse's height from the bottom of a front hoof to the top of the withers

Headstall: the leather portion of a bridle, excluding bit and reins

Hock: middle, backward-bending joint of the hind leg

Hotblood: breeds associated with more high-strung temperaments, such as Arabians and Thoroughbreds

Hunter: jumping horse judged subjectively on appearance, manners, and style in addition to actual jumping performance

Jack: male donkey

Jenny: female donkey

Jumper: jumping horse judged objectively on performance and speed

Knee: middle, forward-bending joint of the front leg

Lead Rope: a rope of about eight feet in length, clipped to the halter for leading a horse around

Longe: moving a horse around you in a circle at the end of a long rope

Lope: Western riding term for "canter"

Mare: female horse at least four years of age

Miniature horse: under thirty-four inches (not measured in hands) at withers, with the proportions of a full-sized horse; often called a "mini"

Mule: offspring of a male donkey and a female horse

Muzzle: nostrils and lips

Off side: the right side of a horse's body

Pace: two-beat gait between walk and canter/lope, with legs on the same side moving in the same direction

Pastern: area between the fetlock and hoof

Pleasure horse: a horse used for non-competitive riding

Poll: bony protrusion at the back of the skull, located between or just behind the ears

Pommel: raised area on the front of a saddle

Pony: less than 14.2 hands, with different proportions than a full-sized horse

Post: moving your body up and down in the saddle with your thighs in time with a horse's trot

Rear: standing up on hind legs

Sheath: pocket of skin that protects the penis when not extended

Snaffle: bit with a joint in the middle

Snip: white marking on the muzzle between the nostrils

Sock: white mark extending from the top of the hoof to anywhere below the knee or hock

Stallion: unaltered male horse at least four years of age

Star: white spot of varying size on the forehead between the eyes

Stifle: joint above the hock on the back leg just below the flank

Stocking: white mark extending from the top of the hoof to at least the bottom of the hock or knee

Strike: kicking forward with the front legs out of fear or aggression

Stud: unaltered male horse used for breeding

Stud chain: a chain at the end of a lead rope, wound through the halter over the nose or under the chin

Thrush: a common, but smelly infection of the frog and surrounding sole of a horse's hoof

Trot: two-beat gait between walk and canter/lope, with legs on the same side moving in opposing directions

Warmblood: middle-weight breeds selectively bred by crossing coldbloods with hotbloods, such as Hanoverians and Morgans

Withers: area of the spine between the top of the shoulder blades, usually the tallest point of the back

BIBLIOGRAPHY

Books

Cook, MacKenzie. *Epona: Hidden Goddess of the Celts*. London: Avalonia, 2016. Kindle.

Davies, Sioned, and Nerys Ann Jones. *The Horse in Celtic Culture: Medieval Welsh Perspectives*. Cardiff: University of Wales Press, 1997.

Freeman, Philip. *Celtic Mythology: Tales of Gods, Goddesses, and Heroes*. New York: Oxford University Press, 2017.

Hamilton, Allan J. *Zen Mind, Zen Horse: The Science and Spirituality of Working with Horses*. North Adams: Storey Publishing, 2011.

Hausman, Gerald, and Loretta Hausman. *The Mythology of Horses: Horse Legend and Lore Throughout the Ages*. New York: Three Rivers Press, 2003.

Hayes, Tim. *Riding Home: The Power of Horses to Heal*. New York: St. Martin's Press, 2015.

Hourly History. *Celtic Mythology: A Concise Guide to the Gods, Sagas and Beliefs*. CreateSpace Independent Publishing Platform, 2016.

Howey, M. Oldfield. *The Horse in Magic and Myth*. London: William Rider & Son, Ltd., 1923. Unabridged reprint. Mineola: Dover Publications, Inc., 2002.

Kohanov, Linda. *The Tao of Equus: A Woman's Journey of Healing and Transformation Through the Way of the Horse*. Novato: New World Library, 2001.

Marshall, Joseph M. III. *The Lakota Way: Stories and Lessons for the Living*. New York: Viking Compass, 2001.

Monaghan, Patricia. *Encyclopedia of Goddesses and Heroines*. Novato, CA: New World Library, 2014.

National Museum of the American Indian. *A Song for the Horse Nation: Horses in Native American Cultures*. George P. Horse Capture and Emil Her Many Horses, eds. Golden, CO: Fulcrum Publishing, 2006.

Patent, Dorothy Hinshaw. *The Horse and the Plains Indians: A Powerful Partnership*. New York: Clarion Books, 2012.

Pony Boy, GaWaNi. *Horse, Follow Closely: Native American Horsemanship*. Irvine, CA: BowTie Press, 1998.

Telyndru, Jhenah. *Pagan Portals—Rhiannon: Divine Queen of the Celtic Britons*. New Alresford, Hants, England: Moon Books, 2018.

Williams, Wendy. *The Horse: The Epic History of Our Noble Companion*. New York: Scientific American/Farrar, Straus and Giroux, 2015.

Online

American Nomad Outfitters. "Tibetan Wind Horse Prayer Flags—What to Know Before You Hang Them Up." Last modified April 30, 2019. https://americannomadoutfitters.com/index.php/2019/04/30/tibetan-wind-horse-prayer-flags-what-to-know-before-you-hang-them-up/.

American Wild Horse Campaign. "BLM to Proceed with Barbaric Sterilization of Wild Mares, Despite Repeated Public Outcry and Legal Opposition." Accessed December 26, 2019. https://americanwildhorsecampaign.org/media/blm-proceed-barbaric-sterilization-wild-mares-despite-repeated-public-outcry-and-legal.

American Wild Horse Campaign. "Myths & Facts About the BLM Wild Horse and Burro Program." Accessed May 15, 2019. https://americanwildhorsecampaign.org/myth-vs-fact.

Andrews, Evan. "Who Was Lady Godiva?" History. Last modified August 22, 2018. https://www.history.com/news/who-was-lady-godiva.

Baggaley, Kate. "Impalas Are the Wimps of the Animal Kingdom and Other Species Know It." Popular Science. Last modified March 27, 2018. https://www.popsci.com/zebra-impala-alarm-calls.

Barnwell, Ross. "Reckless: America's Greatest War Horse Has Statue Unveiled." War History Online. Last modified February 13, 2019. https://

www.warhistoryonline.com/instant-articles/sgt-reckless-statue-dedicated
.html.

Beam, Christopher. "They Shoot Horses, Don't They? No, They Put a Bolt Through Their Brain." Slate. Last modified February 25, 2009. https://slate .com/news-and-politics/2009/02/how-do-horse-slaughterhouses-work .html.

Budanovic, Nikola. "A Horse Named Comanche Survived the Battle of Little Bighorn Despite Being Shot Seven Times." The Vintage News. Last modified October 25, 2017. https://www.thevintagenews .com/2017/10/25/a-horse-named-comanche-survived-the-battle-of-little-bighorn-despite-being-shot-seven-times/.

Carter, Lokita. "Chakra Wisdom Meditation." I Am Not My Body. Accessed August 18, 2019. https://lokitacarter.com/portfolio-item/chakra _wisdom/.

The Celtic Religion. "Origins of the Universe." Accessed July 8, 2019. https:// celticreligion11094.weebly.com/origins-of-the-universe.html.

Char4u.com. "Understanding the Horse in Chinese Culture." Accessed May 31, 2019. https://www.char4u.com/content/understanding-the-horse-in -chinese-culture/.

Cleaver, Emily. "Against All Odds, England's Massive Chalk Horse Has Survived 3,000 Years." Smithsonian Magazine. Last modified July 6, 2017. https://www.smithsonianmag.com/history/3000-year-old-uffington-horse -looms-over-english-countryside-180963968/.

Coe, Charles. "Lady Godiva: The Naked Truth." Harvard Magazine. Last modified August 2003. https://harvardmagazine.com/2003/07/lady -godiva-the-naked-tr.html.

Conrad, Sarah Evers. "The Top 15 Benefits of Horseback Riding." Certified Horsemanship Association. Last modified April 10, 2014. http:// www.cha-ahse.org/store/blog/The_Top_15_Benefits_of_Horseback _Riding.html.

Coutros, Peter. "When Did Horses Transform Mongolians' Way of Life?" Sapiens. Last modified January 24, 2018. https://www.sapiens.org/column /off-the-map/horse-domestication-mongolia/.

Cowie, Ashley. "A Celtic Creation: Sea-foam, the Placenta from the Birth of the Universe." Ancient Origins. Last modified February 22, 2018. https://www.ancient-origins.net/human-origins-folklore/celtic-creation-sea-foam-placenta-birth-universe-009635.

Darrow, Logan. "Horses of History: Kanthaka—Buddha's Royal Horse." The Mindful Horsewoman. Last modified January 26, 2016. http://themindfulhorsewoman.weebly.com/blog/horses-of-history-kanthaka.

The Druid Network. "Rigantona & the Realm of the Dead." Last modified December 2009. https://druidnetwork.org/what-is-druidry/deity-and-mythology/mythology/modern-mythology/rigantona-realm-dead/.

Equine Rescue Network. "Rendering Horses Versus Slaughtering Horses." Accessed August 18, 2019. http://equinerescuenetwork.com/?p=1659.

Ferguson, Philip M. "Clever Hans." Encyclopedia Britannica. Accessed July 15, 2019. https://www.britannica.com/topic/Clever-Hans.

Folk Wales. "The Magic of the Mari…" Last modified September 3, 2015. http://www.folkwales.org.uk/mari.html.

Freeman, Philip. "The Terrible Curse of Macha." Wonders and Marvels. Accessed July 8, 2019. http://www.wondersandmarvels.com/2017/03/terrible-curse-macha.html.

Handwerk, Brian. "Ancient Arboreal Mammal Discovered at Root of Carnivore Family Tree." National Geographic. Last modified January 9, 2014. https://news.nationalgeographic.com/news/2014/01/140109-dormaalocyon-latouri-fossil-carnivore-science/.

Harris, Elena. "Horse Spirit Animal." Spirit Animal. Accessed March 21, 2019. https://www.spiritanimal.info/horse-spirit-animal.

Haughton, Brian. "The White Horse of Uffington." Ancient History Encyclopedia. Last modified March 30, 2011. https://www.ancient.eu/article/229/the-white-horse-of-uffington/.

The Humane Society of the United States. "The Facts About Horse Slaughter." Accessed April 30, 2019. https://www.humanesociety.org/resources/facts-about-horse-slaughter.

Holloway, April. "The Mystery of the White Horse of Uffington." Ancient Origins. Last modified March 14, 2014. https://www.ancient-origins.net/ancient-places-europe/mystery-white-horse-uffington-001445.

Hood, Nathanael. "Top 10 Mythical Horses." Top Tenz. Last modified October 13, 2013. https://www.toptenz.net/top-10-mythical-horses.php.

Johnson, Ben. "The Kelpie." Historic UK. Accessed May 8, 2019. https://www.historic-uk.com/CultureUK/The-Kelpie/.

Justbod blog. "A Bold Example of Celtic Art: The Stanwick Horse Mask." Accessed July 8, 2019. https://justbod.blogspot.com/2018/09/a-bold-example-of-celtic-art-stanwick.html (site discontinued).

Keith, Steven. "Horses, Cows and Celestial Creatures at the Dawn of Civilizations." Ancient Origins. Last modified May 27, 2018. https://www.ancient-origins.net/history-ancient-traditions/horses-cows-and-celestial-creatures-dawn-civilizations-0010116.

Klimczak, Natalia. "Aine: A Radiant Celtic Goddess of Love, Summer, and Sovereignty." Ancient Origins. Last modified November 28, 2016. https://www.ancient-origins.net/myths-legends/aine-radiant-celtic-goddess-love-summer-and-sovereignty-007097.

Kneale, Alastair. "Magnificent Horse of the Celtic Gods—'Enbarr of the Flowing Mane.'" Transceltic. Last modified January 12, 2019. https://www.transceltic.com/pan-celtic/magnificent-horse-of-celtic-gods-enbarr-of-flowing-mane.

Kneale, Alastair. "Manannán Mac Lir, Son of the Sea, Celtic Sea God and Protector of Mannin." Transceltic. Last modified March 14, 2015. https://www.transceltic.com/manx/manann-n-mac-lir-son-of-sea-celtic-sea-god-and-protector-of-mannin.

Livius. "Alexander and Bucephalus." Last modified October 15, 2016. https://www.livius.org/sources/content/plutarch/plutarchs-alexander/alexander-and-bucephalus/.

Mark, Joshua J. "The Mesopotamian Pantheon." Ancient History Encyclopedia. Last modified February 25, 2011. https://www.ancient.eu/article/221/the-mesopotamian-pantheon/.

Mayo, Muriel. "What is the Role of the Horse 'Kanthaka' in Buddhist Mythology?" Quora. Last modified December 19, 2017. https://www.quora.com/What-is-the-role-of-the-horse-Kanthaka-in-Buddhist-mythology.

McCarthy, Susan. "Hollywood's Long History of Animal Cruelty." Salon. Last modified April 2, 2012. https://www.salon.com/2012/04/02/hollywoods _long_history_of_animal_cruelty/.

McCoy, Daniel. "Sol and Mani." Norse Mythology for Smart People. Accessed April 30, 2019. https://norse-mythology.org/sol-mani/.

Morris, Annie. "Lipica: The Original Home of the Lipizzaner." Dressage Today. Accessed July 31, 2019. https://dressagetoday.com/lifestyle/lipica-the -original-home-of-the-lipizzaner.

Mythology.net. "Sleipnir." Last modified November 4, 2016. https:// mythology.net/norse/norse-creatures/sleipnir/.

National Geographic. "Przewalski's Horse." Accessed April 15, 2019. https:// www.nationalgeographic.com/animals/mammals/p/przewalskis-horse/.

New World Encyclopedia. "Demeter." Accessed on January 20, 2020. https:// www.newworldencyclopedia.org/entry/Demeter.

Nikiforuk, Andrew. "The Big Shift Last Time: From Horse Dung to Car Smog." The Tyee. Last modified March 6, 2013. https://thetyee.ca /News/2013/03/06/Horse-Dung-Big-Shift/.

OpenBible. "100 Bible Verses About Horses: Job 39:19." Accessed May 31, 2019. https://www.openbible.info/topics/horses.

The Order of the Bards and Druids. "Epona." Accessed July 8, 2019. https:// www.druidry.org/library/gods-goddesses/epona.

Overbay, Dylan. "Camp Pendleton Unveils Staff Sgt Reckless Monument." Defense Visual Information Distribution Service. Last modified October 26, 2016. https://www.dvidshub.net/news/213028/camp-pendleton -unveils-staff-sgt-reckless-monument.

People for the Ethical Treatment of Animals (PETA). "Overbreeding and Slaughter." Accessed May 31, 2019. https://www.peta.org/issues /animals-in-entertainment/horse-racing-2/horse-racing-industry-cruelty /overbreeding-and-slaughter/.

Pickrell, John. "Timeline: Human Evolution." NewScientist. Last modified September 4, 2006. https://www.newscientist.com/article/dn9989 -timeline-human-evolution/.

Reuter, Coree. "Remembering Black Jack." The Chronicle of the Horse. Last modified November 23, 2013. https://www.chronofhorse.com/article/remembering-black-jack.

RoadsideAmerica.com. "Comanche, Little Bighorn Survivor." Accessed July 15, 2019. https://www.roadsideamerica.com/story/3312.

Rossabi, Morris. "All the Khan's Horses." Columbia University. Last modified October 1994. http://afe.easia.columbia.edu/mongols/conquests/khans_horses.pdf.

Sahsnotasvriunt, Týra Alrune. "'Holy Horse!'—Horses in the Germanic and Other Polytheistic Traditions." The Pagan Beanstalk. Last modified September 22, 2014. https://paganmeltingpot.wordpress.com/tag/horse-deities/.

Sedgwick, Icy. "Why Are Kelpies So Feared in Scottish Folklore?" Icy Sedgwick. Last modified March 29, 2018. http://www.icysedgwick.com/kelpies-folklore/.

Sgt. Reckless. "The Little Horse That Could…" Accessed July 8, 2019. https://www.sgtreckless.com/Reckless/About_Reckless.html.

Shaw, Judith. "Aine, Summer Goddess of Love, Light and Fertility." Feminism & Religion. Last modified July 31, 2013. https://feminismandreligion.com/2013/07/31/aine-summer-goddess-of-love-light-and-fertility-by-judith-shaw/.

Shields, Jesslyn. "If Those Aren't Human Hands in Ancient Cave Art—What Are They?" How Stuff Works. Last modified March 29, 2016. https://science.howstuffworks.com/environmental/earth/archaeology/non-human-hands-in-ancient-cave-art.htm.

Smithsonian's National Zoo & Conservation Biology Institute. "Przewalski's Horse." Accessed August 14, 2019. https://nationalzoo.si.edu/animals/przewalskis-horse.

Solas Bhríde Centre and Hermitages. "The Perpetual Flame." Accessed July 8, 2019. http://solasbhride.ie/the-perpetual-flame/.

Theoi Greek Mythlogy. "Despoine." Accessed May 31, 2019. https://www.theoi.com/Georgikos/Despoine.html.

Theoi Greek Mythology. "Areion." Accessed May 31, 2019. https://www.theoi.com/Ther/HipposAreion.html.

This Crooked Crown. "What Exactly Is Horsing?" Last modified October 17, 2013. https://thiscrookedcrown.tumblr.com/post/64348640143/what-exactly-is-horsing.

Tibetpedia. "Windhorse." Last modified May 27, 2016. http://tibetpedia.com/lifestyle/religious-life/windhorse/.

Traditional Native Healing. "Native American Counting Coup: A practice of the Great Plains." Accessed August 12, 2019. http://traditionalnativehealing.com/native-american-counting-coup-a-practice-of-the-great-plains.

Trimble, Marshall. "How Many Horses Have Been Injured During Filming of Hollywood Westerns?" True West Magazine. Last modified May 26, 2015. https://truewestmagazine.com/how-many-horses-have-been-injured-during-filming-of-hollywood-westerns/.

Turkish-trail. Steemit. "Creatures of Turkish Mythology—Tulpar." Accessed May 30, 2019. https://steemit.com/tr/@turkish-trail/creatures-of-turkish-mythology-1-tulpar.

Turner, Zeke. "Riding a Hobbyhorse: Yes, It's an Organized Sport." The Wall Street Journal. Last modified March 28, 2017. https://www.wsj.com/articles/best-in-sew-inside-the-growing-sport-of-hobbyhorse-riding-1490713811?mod=e2tw.

University of Exeter. "Archaeologists Find Earliest Known Domestic Horses: Harnessed and Milked." ScienceDaily. Last modified March 8, 2009. www.sciencedaily.com/releases/2009/03/090305141627.htm.

Valdar. "Riding the Seas: Kelpies, Hippocampus, and More Monstrous Horses." Ancient Origins. Accessed April 30, 2019. https://www.ancient-origins.net/myths-legends/riding-seas-kelpies-and-other-fascinating-water-horses-myth-and-legend-006170.

VisitScotland. "Why Is the Unicorn Scotland's National Animal?" Accessed July 30, 2019. https://www.visitscotland.com/about/uniquely-scottish/national-animal-unicorn/.

Walker, Bonnie Rae. "The Big Four: The Most Common Causes of Equine Fatalities." Dressage Different. Last modified November 18, 2013. https://dressagedifferent.com/2013/11/18/the-big-four-the-most-common-causes-of-equine-fatalities/.

Wasson, Donald L. "Bucephalus." Ancient History Encyclopedia. Last modified October 16, 2011. https://www.ancient.eu/Bucephalus/.

Wild Horse Education. "Reality of Wild Horse Slaughter—Caught in a Tangled Web, the Reality of Wild Horse Slaughter." Accessed May 15, 2019. https://wildhorseeducation.org/reality-of-wild-horse-slaughter/.

Wild Horse Education. "Discussion; Omnibus Budget and What Comes Next." Accessed May 15, 2019. https://wildhorseeducation. org/2018/03/23/discussion-omnibus-budget-and-what-comes-next/.

Yogananda, Paramahansa. "God Talks With Arjuna: The Bhagavad Gita." Pages 790-91. Google Books. Accessed April 30, 2019. https://books. google.com/books?id=dKYfdbxnukkC&pg=PA790&dq= Uchchaihshravas&hl=en&sa=X&ei= 9KefUeigMYji9gT154HYCQ&ved=0CDYQ6AEwAg#v=onepage&q= Uchchaihshravas&f=false.

Videos

Equus 'Story of the Horse,' episode 1 "Origins" and episode 2 "Chasing the Wind," PBS Nature. Accessed January 18, 2019.

Harry & Snowman, directed and written by Ron Davis, produced by Nancy Stanton, Knox Talcott, Clay Westervelt. Released September 30, 2016. Accessed June 30, 2018.

INDEX

To Write to the Author

If you wish to contact the author or would like more information about this book, please write to the author in care of Llewellyn Worldwide Ltd. and we will forward your request. Both the author and the publisher appreciate hearing from you and learning of your enjoyment of this book and how it has helped you. Llewellyn Worldwide Ltd. cannot guarantee that every letter written to the author can be answered, but all will be forwarded. Please write to:

Debra DeAngelo
℅ Llewellyn Worldwide
2143 Wooddale Drive
Woodbury, MN 55125-2989

Please enclose a self-addressed stamped envelope for reply,
or $1.00 to cover costs. If outside the U.S.A., enclose
an international postal reply coupon.

Many of Llewellyn's authors have websites with additional
information and resources. For more information,
please visit our website at http://www.llewellyn.com